Europower

The
Economist
Books

T I M E S B O O K S

R A N D O M   H O U S E

Europower

THE ESSENTIAL GUIDE TO EUROPE'S ECONOMIC TRANSFORMATION IN 1992

★ ★ ★ ★ ★

NICHOLAS COLCHESTER

AND

DAVID BUCHAN

Library of Congress Cataloging-in-Publication Data
Colchester, Nicholas.
Europower: the essential guide to Europe's economic transformation in 1992 / by
Nicholas Colchester and David Buchan.
p.   cm.
ISBN 0-8129-1873-8
1. Europe 1992.   2. European Economic Community countries —
Economic conditions.   I. Buchan, David.   II. Title.
HC241.2.C55428   1990
330.94′009′048 — dc20   90-34067

CONTENTS

PREFACE

After many months of striving to understand the complexities of the European Community's project 1992, we both thought that we had glimpsed the wood for the trees. The appetite among readers for surveys of the great market published in *The Economist* and the *Financial Times* suggested that there was a widespread appetite for such a glimpse. So we set to work, each tackling the aspects of Europe's great market that interested us most.

The result is not a guide-book: there are many other publications that deal with the minutiae of the European Community and its market. It is rather an evocation of what has powered the Community's relaunch, how it is changing the main areas of Europe's economic life, and what it may drive the Community on to.

For many, the European Community is a religion, for others it is a heresy. Both sorts of reader will be angered by the cavalier approach of this book. The former because it aims at demystification and pragmatism. The latter because it relishes the building of a liberal open Europe and explains how demons in Brussels are indispensable to such a Europe.

We both owe a debt to our editors, Rupert Pennant-Rea of *The Economist*, and Sir Geoffrey Owen of the *Financial Times*, who allowed us to be distracted from our real jobs; to Bob Taylor, a journalist steeped in Brussels lore, who vetted the proofs; to each other for an improbable lack of rancour; and to our wives and children, who understood.

Nicholas Colchester
David Buchan
January 1990.

1

THE QUIETER
REVOLUTION

Europe relaunched itself twice in the late 1980s. Eastern Europe pro-
pelled itself out of Stalinism, and thus made history of the most stirring
sort – people reaching *en masse* for freedom, the constant menace of
repression, the fall of rotten regimes, the crumbling of barriers and the
shining faces of the released. Cameramen were sated. Their images
imprinted themselves upon the world's consciousness.

Another relaunch was meanwhile occurring in Western Europe. It
was a cameraman's despair. The action took place in conference rooms to
the sipping of countless glasses of mineral water. The main danger was
of sleep. Without much initial passion to drive them, officials of twelve
governments talked life back into an old idea – that their economies
should form a truly common market. Such was their delight at managing this that another old idea took fire again, too – that their countries
should move away from national sovereignty towards a European political union.

Their timing was good: just as the Twelve realised that their efforts to
create a single market were working, they saw Eastern Europe turning
towards them. Relaunched under the codeword "1992", the European
Community had become the centrepiece of a new European order. Or
had it? Would Western Europe's painstaking demotion of the nation-
state really survive the ecstatic rediscoveries of national pride in the
East? This book tells of the quieter of the two relaunches – the tale of
1992 – and tries to discover whether the European Community's
relaunch has acquired enough momentum to transcend the breaking up
of the post-war order in Europe.

"It is hard to fall in love with a single market," said Jacques Delors,
president of the European Commission. And indeed the prospect of a
common standard for pressure vessels, so that they may be traded freely
between Aberdeen and Athens without exploding, does not set hearts

7

pounding. But that standard is just one of a myriad of barrier-flattening measures flowing from the European Community's 1992 project. Taken together they will create the largest single pool of freely-flowing goods, services, capital and people in the world. Only when you calculate what might be done with the economic fruits of this single market; only when the political ramifications of creating it are thought through, does palpitation set in.

Within the Community, the momentum of the 1992 relaunch is already such that it is pulling grander schemes behind it, notably a plan for the twelve EC states to band together in an Economic and Monetary Union (EMU). Outside, the world seems to be beating a path towards Brussels to seek new, or to improve old, relationships with the relaunched Community, or even to join it. The six members of the European Free Trade Association (EFTA) are now negotiating to see if they can strike a new deal with the Twelve to make an open economic zone of 350 million people. One of that six, Austria, has already asked for full membership of the EC. A populous neighbour, Turkey, has lodged a problematic application to join. The island "orphans" of Cyprus and Malta have served notice that they will soon want to become members, while virtually every country on the Mediterranean coast wants improved access to the Community.

Most dramatic of all has been the ending of forty years of enforced ostracism of the EC by the Eastern Europeans. Not even the most inventive propagandist for 1992 can pretend that the Community's single-market plan was the spark of democracy in Eastern Europe and the Soviet Union; the credit for that goes to Poland's Solidarity movement and, above all, to Mikhail Gorbachev. But, while 1992 had no hand in destabilising the sick communist order, it can now help stabilise the new orders that emerge there with offers of aid and trade into a vast market, and it can offer these countries a context in which they can plan their futures.

Fears of commercial exclusion have dominated the outside world's reaction to 1992. The US and Japan, in particular, have warned the Community not to turn itself into a "fortress Europe". The phrase has an unpleasant ring: it was coined by Goebbels when he urged a *"Festung Europa"* against Allied invasion during the Second World War. Western Europe's builders may yet put up protectionist ramparts. So far they have not. The Community passed the first big test of its free-trading intentions when it opened up an open market in banking services to outsiders. For the moment, foreign fear has ebbed, leaving a wary respect of the Community's increased potential. The Bush Administration is now taking the EC more seriously than any in Washington since the early 1960s. Part of its seriousness stems from a mounting desire for a Western Europe strong enough to cope with a winding down of the number of American troops stationed there. Japan's focus on 1992 is wholly economic. It is proceeding with strategic tact, hoping above all that its powerful industries – and above all its car industry – can establish themselves inside the great market as "good Europeans".

Though a compliment to project 1992, the interest of Eastern Europe is in one sense too much of a good thing. By increasing the number of possible candidates for EC membership, it has revived what is called the "wider-versus-deeper" argument within the EC. Should the Twelve continue to try to huddle still closer into economic/monetary, and increasingly political, union? Or should they forego rapprochement that might make it harder for others to join. This is no academic argument. It has the potential to break the Franco-German axis on which the Community has been centred during its first thirty years. West Germany, feeling nearer to reunification with East Germany than ever, is deeply distracted by what is happening on its eastern border. By the same token, France is keener than ever to keep West Germany in a Community over which its influence is well established.

France's pet plan for doing this, Economic and Monetary Union, also happens to threaten West Germany's autonomy in running an inflation-free monetary policy – one of its proudest post-war achievements. Add in Margaret Thatcher's protest that EMU would be "the biggest transfer of sovereignty we've ever had" and her ideological complaint that Brussels is trying with its European Social Charter to reimpose socialism on Britain, and one could be forgiven for believing that the original project to build a single market by the end of 1992 had slipped out of the limelight.

Far from it. The forging of the single market remains at the centre of all these events. Should it fail – and the odds must now be that it won't – European politicians can shelve their other ambitions for the Community. Should it succeed, much is possible. Eastern Europe, no matter how much Western aid and lending it receives, will have to lift itself up by trading. Poles, Hungarians, Czechs, Russians, let alone East Germans with their half-a-foot in the EC via West Germany – all stand to benefit from doing business in a huge market with the same gross national product as the United States. As for EMU, a functioning single market is the only basis on which it has a hope of surviving the political pressures that will in time be imposed upon it.

Like some marathon runner, the Community started slowly in its eight-year race to take the 280-odd barrier-breaking measures which it knew were needed to make the single market "single". It got into its stride only three years after the start, when an EC summit in February 1988 settled a distracting row about the EC's budget. Then came a burst of speed. The Twelve strode past some important milestones that would have finished them off earlier: they forged agreements to remove all exchange controls, to give banks "a single passport" to do business throughout the EC, to insist only upon essential technical rules for all industrial machinery, to give equal status to each other's higher-education diplomas, to phase out an absurd road haulage quota system that forces empty lorries to make wasted journeys across frontiers.

By the end of 1989, the twelve governments had reached final, or partial, agreement on 60 per cent of the 280 measures. So, in terms of numbers, their race was on schedule. But in terms of the willpower needed to stay the course most of the pain still lay ahead, and was making itself increasingly evident in late 1989 and early 1990.

Most of the pain arises out of the much-touted disappearance of all border checks between EC states. This over-ambitious goal stems from the Single European Act of 1986, which states that the single market is to be "an area without internal frontiers". But, if and when frontier checks vanish, how is the gun-toting, drug-smuggling international terrorist to be nabbed? How will nations remain their own masters in the increasingly pressing matter of immigration? Where, if not at borders, will checks be made to prevent animal and plant diseases crossing from one state to another? How will national systems of value-added tax (VAT) be kept leak-proof and fraud-free without border checks? Can VAT and excise rates be brought close enough to each other so that high tax-rate governments don't howl at the loss of revenue when their shoppers flock to lower-rated neighbours? And will governments really accept that in matters of foreign trade the only policy they have left is a Community one?

The Twelve have beavered away at these problems. But it is by no means certain that they will prevail. So difficult are the issues that any announced victories must be scrutinised with great scepticism. For instance, the governments have claimed a success in deciding that they can maintain, post-1992, the present system whereby goods leave a given EC state "zero-rated" for VAT and thus primed to bear tax in the importing country. They say they can henceforth do this without frontier controls. Perhaps: but the solution could well substitute red-tape for frontier checks and leave the promised market as divided as before.

So, the first 1992 illusion to watch for is the quick fix that substitutes a new way of dividing up the market for an old one. The second is the decision that gets nodded through the EC's Council of Ministers – the meeting of national ministers which is the Community's most important rule-setting forum – but which never gets written into the national law of the Twelve. By the end of 1989, the Commission was complaining that of the 88 single-market directives which should have been in force, only 14 had been written into every member's national law (though the vast majority were law for the majority of members). Chasing up the laggards among the Twelve – Italy and Greece, in particular – will be one of the main tasks from now on.

A third illusion could be built upon uneven enforcement of EC rules. Even if all twelve members were to have all 280 White Paper proposals on their statute books, the single market could unravel into a welter of recrimination if the rules were not evenly enforced. The Commission has not (thank goodness) got a hope of spotting all offenders here. Companies and individuals will have to fight for their rights if 1992 is to mean anything. Take the much publicised case in 1989 of a big contract for a Danish bridge. The Danish government was firmly slapped down for discriminating against companies from other EC states in awarding the contract. But the case was brought only because a powerful French contractor, Bouyges, was prepared to complain.

Then there are hidden truths to offset the illusions of 1992. A prime example – almost the leitmotiv of this book – is that project 1992, if it succeeds, will involve such a degree of mutual trust and influence between EC states that they will be half-way to political union without knowing it. For instance, it is agreed that a bank incorporated in one EC state can use that base to do cross-border banking in all other eleven states. This involves much trust by the eleven in the regulatory authorities of the bank's host state – and banking, remember, is a business of which economic crashes can be made. Goods allowed for sale in one EC state cannot be denied access to other states' markets. This idea of each state accepting the others' foibles, provided minimum EC-wide safety standards are met, is one of the keys to the single-market project's success so far. Another is the principle of taking decisions by majority voting, which also implies much mutual trust – the trust that the European majority is not going to ram something awful down a given nation's throat. It is an enduring illusion that such mutual concessions can be neatly labelled "economic": they are potently political.

The problem areas of 1992 are precisely the ones where the members do not trust each other. Britain wants to keep checking people coming from France at Dover because it does not sufficiently trust France or other EC states to do the job. In business, pharmaceuticals pose a particular problem. The idea was that "mutual recognition" should apply here, too, and that a drug licensed for sale in one EC state could be accepted automatically for sale in the other eleven. But drug-testing is so complex and the results of mistaken testing or prescription so potentially painful and emotion-laden that mutual recognition isn't yet achievable.

Yet it is in resolving the mind-numbing problems created by mutual mistrust over taxes, or medicines, or pressure vessels or entry visas that the basis of political union is best laid – much more powerfully than by the unworldly assertions of statesmen. If this seems far-fetched, consider how the Community has built itself by pragmatic steps whose effects have spilled over into other areas. Margaret Thatcher is loath to share Britain's political sovereignty; yet she was ready to sign the Single European Act in order to get the single market she wished for British businessmen. The success of the European Monetary System in giving its participants currency stability after 1979 was what laid the basis for the decision to lift all important EC exchange controls in 1990. This commitment to free capital movements has, in turn, incited measures to liberalise banking and insurance, and encouraged moves towards EMU. The latter is about as "political" as one can get.

Moreover, the single-market plan has prompted counter-balancing demands for more pervasive European social policies. The creation of a freer market in cross-frontier television has required Community agreement on what constitutes gratuitous sex and violence. Economic matters may make up the body of the Brussels octopus, but its tentacles reach unstoppably into the politics, social policies and cultures of the EC's members.

Economics is, *au fond*, the driving force behind politics in the modern world. There is much greater awareness today of the way that the political and military fortunes of states, empires, and coalitions have, through the centuries, undulated up and down according to their relative economic positions. The most striking late-20th century examples of this truth are Japan, with riches and no rockets, and the Soviet Union, with rockets and no riches. The latter finally conceded under Mikhail Gorbachev that its sick economy could no longer sustain an overblown military establishment. Even the still-mighty USA no longer seems so clearly number one, with Japan and the EC creeping up on it in terms of gross national product.

Without Sound and Fury; Signifying Plenty

Robert Schuman, a French founder of the EC, said in 1950 that "Europe will not be made all at once, or according to a single plan. It will be built through concrete achievements, which first achieve a *de facto* solidarity." That advice was honoured in the Treaty of Rome of 1957 which established the Community (more precisely, the Communities). It set a pragmatic first economic task and a timetable – the removal of tariffs and quotas between European countries within twelve years. Subsequent failed attempts to move the Community forward – most notably the ill-fated Werner report of 1970 which called for Economic and Monetary Union within a decade – showed how self-defeating it could be to tackle directly the strongest symbols of sovereignty. The brave oratory of one year became the hollow laughter of the next.

It was only in 1978–79 with the pragmatism of the European Monetary System, and in 1985 with the craving for and design of the Single Market that the Schuman approach was honoured. The result of the latter was densely complicated, but historic. Sir Winston Churchill once recommended "jaw-jaw" to "war-war". One suspects that the jargon-laden, untrumpeted slog of putting 1992 together would have changed his mind. Yet the more gloomy the epithets that are heaped upon the process, the more remarkable it becomes. Vested interests and national prerogatives are usually stripped away only by convulsions – by the sort of repression and release that made 1989 historic. The European Community has been relaunched by a dogged exercise of reason.

Time and again cynics could confidently predict that nationalism would not stand for this grey process: such voices are heard again, now that Germany is sliding towards unity and some in France are responding with cries of *"Europe!"*, and others with *"La France d'abord!"*. Yet somehow a consensus has prevailed that European national self-interest actually demands a surrender of independence. And the process has ground on. The Single-Market plan begat the Single European Act – a change in the EC's constitution profound enough to make project 1992 a success before that date became remotely known to the public at large. It is to this Act, and the parable of its creation, that the story of Europe's quieter relaunch now turns.

2

THE SINGLE
EUROPEAN ACT

A Triumph of Self-Delusion

In 1985, after a dozen years of stagnation and sliding morale, the European Community bewitched itself back into motion with the negotiation of the Single European Act. This Act was conceived in Milan in late June 1985 and delivered by the EC's heads of government (in France's case, its president) in Luxembourg in December 1985. It earned its anodyne name rather as an unwanted child might find itself called "Tom Jones", for it pleased none of its parents.

Ardent Europe, led by Italy and France, wanted an Act of "European Union". Reticent Europe, led by Denmark and Britain, did not want an Act at all. The name "Single Act" had nothing to do with notions of "one" Europe: it meant simply that a something-for-everyone bundle of amendments to the Treaty of Rome was wrapped up in one Act. The result was greeted with faint praise by all EC governments, by the European Commission and by the European Parliament. The media echoed the general disdain: *The Economist* called it a "smiling mouse".

Thus belittled, the Act was squeezed through suspicious national parliaments ("do not quibble with the orphan, please; you can have this or nothing") and then proceeded to give the European Community the most powerful kick it had felt in its thirty years.

Towards Supranationalism

The essence of the shock was that an ingrained habit of unanimity in the running of the European Community was swept away, except in defined areas of government policy, and was replaced with a form of majority voting. The habit had taken two forms. First, since the earliest days of the EC, it had been assumed that the only possible European substitute for the national rules governing business (which means many of the rules by which societies live) would be unanimously-elaborated Common Market ones. Second, since 1966, the Community's members had agreed, on General de Gaulle's insistence, that whatever the Treaty of Rome might say, any EC country could veto any fledgling piece of EC law-making which it judged threatening to an important national interest.

The Single Act, using the attractive-sounding idea of a frontier-free European market as its stalking horse, shook all this up. It got the EC governments to agree to limit unanimity in forging laws for the great European market to matters of tax, the movement of people, and conditions of employment. It also enshrined a new approach to creating such European laws. From now on, it said, each government would accept all other governments' commercial rules as valid on its own territory, provided that they met essential underlying standards agreed by majority vote in Brussels. This was the principle of "mutual recognition".

These two elements achieved the Single European Act's revolution. Since 1957, the European club of countries had in theory accepted a limited "tyranny of the majority", exercised over them through laws drafted and voted upon between its members in Brussels. Those laws took precedence over laws passed by their own parliaments. But they had actually allowed this system to apply few binding rules to them — and none that they might find politically hard to live with. Now they agreed to let that "supranationalism" work: they conceded that many laws made by their national parliaments could be rendered illegal or unworkable by a vote between ministers of other countries.

Sovereignty as an Extreme Sanction

There was more, too. The Act increased the power of the directly-elected European Parliament in Strasbourg to influence this supranational law-making. Where previously the Parliament had had the right only to comment on drafts of European law, without usable sanctions against the Commission and the national governments if it were ignored, it was now given enough scope to tamper with drafts of European law to make sure that its views would have clout. On average, three-quarters of the amendments that the Parliament wants are now accepted by the Commission and about two-fifths by the Council of Ministers.

The Single Act widened the scope of the Community set up by the Rome Treaty to include research and development, protection of the environment, a more ambitious regional policy, and health and safety at work. It reasserted Europe's goal of "Economic and Monetary Union" and laid down how the quest for this should be continued. It included, too, the flourishing – but until then informal – cooperation between European governments in some aspects of foreign policy. Lastly – or firstly, for it was the Act's opening paragraph – it recommitted the twelve EC members to the vague but impressive-sounding goal of "European Union".

These changes did not strip away the EC countries' sovereignty, in the absolute sense of the word. Protected by their own armed forces, they remained free to walk away from the EC, or to do to the Single European Act what General de Gaulle did to the Treaty of Rome in 1966: refuse to accept its supranationalism, and damn the consequences. But the price of continuing membership of the club – paid in surrendered powers of self-determination – was undoubtedly raised, and the cost of opting out was made more daunting.

The Fault Line Moves

The Single Act did not drop out of a blue sky. Like many of history's treaties or congresses, it came more as an earthquake than a thunderbolt: it was a sudden release of pressures that had been building up beneath the surface for some time. A European consensus was revealed and released, not sinisterly imposed; though the release certainly involved sleight of hand.

As with most earthquakes, the moment when the earth moved was a memorable one. It came in the afternoon of Saturday June 30th 1985, the second day of the European Council (or summit), in the medieval setting of the Castello Sforzesco in Milan. At one moment Margaret Thatcher was sitting in her customary position at the EC conference table – embattled but immovable, bearing the brunt of the argument because she does not make much use of the negotiating power of silence, presenting logical ways for the Community to pass its laws faster and to develop its cooperation in making foreign policy. The next moment, she was sliding uncontrollably and protesting towards just the sort of European Community that she, like General de Gaulle, could never willingly accept: one in which Britain's right of veto would be limited.

She faced a predicament that she has never known in her own cabinet: Bettino Craxi, the Italian prime minister, called for a vote. He made unprecedented use of Article 236 of the Rome Treaty to call a "conference of representatives of Governments of the member states ... for the purpose of determining by common accord the amendments to be made to this Treaty".

16

Mrs Thatcher protested that the tradition of the European Council was consensus. The prime ministers of Denmark, Poul Schlüter, and Greece, Andreas Papandreou, also complained that they were being taken by force. But the decision to call such a conference needed only a simple majority in the European Council, even though the decisions that it might lead to would ultimately require unanimity. Therein lies the insidious power of Article 236: it builds into the Treaty of Rome an old negotiating ploy whereby the unthinkable becomes, by definition, thinkable if its strongest opponent can be persuaded to talk about it with those who want it.

The ploy is fraught with danger because it may ultimately lead to a paralysing deadlock between members bound to decide something unanimously. Yet Mr Craxi judged it just right that day. His call for a conference was accepted seven-to-three. Years of preparation and many disparate influences had come together to make that June afternoon the right moment to launch a revision of the Treaty of Rome. Thus Italy pulled off an unrivalled example of the sort of coup with which all European governments like to end their six-month stints as president of the Community. The fireworks flew above the castle walls. The Italian prime minister was delighted, and can have had little idea at the time of the magnitude of what he was celebrating.

The Recipe for the Craxi Coup

The origins of the coup in Milan lay in the European frustrations and initiatives of the 1980s. There were six ingredients that left recognisable traces in the Single European Act.

● **The British Contribution** Curiously, the problem of Britain's contribution to the Community's budget was the first of them. From the late 1970s onwards Britain had complained that it was paying twice as much into the Community's budget as it was getting out of it, and that the extravagance of the EC's Common Agricultural Policy which benefited Britain relatively little, was the cause of this. The rest of the membership resisted Britain's penny-counting approach to their club's budget: members should take the rough with the smooth, they thought, especially if they join late. But Mrs Thatcher, waging total war against public spending at home, would not let the rest of Europe duck the matter and fob her off with *ad hoc* repayments. She wanted the European system rejigged to contain its waste and rid itself of its anomalies.

The Council decided, in May 1980, to reimburse Britain somewhat. More important, it told the Commission to develop other, non-farming programmes in the EC that might be better able to send Britain money. The Commission, under the presidency of Gaston Thorn, produced a report after a year's work. It argued that the Community could be swung away from agriculture only if it were rounded out with an energy policy, a regional policy, a technology policy, a proper common market and an established monetary system. These, in turn, would require changes to the Rome Treaty to give them legitimacy. The Thorn report suffered death by committee. But a principle remained: a fairer EC would be broader in its scope.

● **The Genscher-Colombo Vision** It was at the end of 1980, with Europe deeply gloomy at the onset of recession, that the foreign minister of West Germany, Hans-Dietrich Genscher, and his Italian counterpart, Emilio Colombo, tried to revive its spirits with ingredient number two. This was their proposal for a "European Act". It was not to be an amendment to the Rome Treaty, but an undertaking by the EC governments to cooperate in the making of foreign and security policy, in the fight against terrorism, in cultural matters and in laying down basic human rights.

● **The Stuttgart Declaration** The Genscher-Colombo proposal was an exercise in European idealism, and one might have expected it to suffer the fate normally reserved for such initiatives. Yet pulled this way and that for eighteen months it survived to form the basis of ingredient number three, a "solemn declaration on European Union" signed by the heads of government at their summit in Stuttgart in June 1983. This embraced the Genscher-Colombo vision but was weak on how it should be realised. It therefore achieved little directly, but it revived the hazy goal of European Union that had gathered dust since the oil crisis had overwhelmed it in the early 1970s. The preamble of the Single Act was based upon the Stuttgart declaration. So worried heads of government were later to be soothed by their officials with such words as: "nothing new in this part of the Act, prime minister, that you did not agree to in Stuttgart".

● **Now we are Twelve** Ingredient number four was the increasing size and unwieldiness of the Community. In 1983 the Commission suggested new rules for majority voting, designed to compensate for the arrival in the EC of Spain and Portugal, raising its membership to twelve. These suggestions were turned down by governments, but the Commission's thoughts were not lost for ever for they, too, were disinterred when the design of the Single Act got under way in the summer of 1985.

● **The Spinelli Initiative** A meeting in July 1980 of nine members of the European Parliament at a restaurant in Strasbourg called the "Crocodile" created the fifth ingredient. This was the Draft Treaty Establishing a European Union masterminded by an ardent Italian member of the European Parliament, Altiero Spinelli. The Spinelli initiative envisaged a radical revamp of the Community's constitution in a way that would give the European Parliament much more power. It sought to achieve this change by appealing directly to national parliaments, over the heads of government. It wanted a sufficient number of these parliaments to ratify the new treaty to oblige their governments to accept its validity. This was a naively long shot – given the vested interests of national parliaments – and it fell a long way short. The Italian parliament, one of the most laggardly when it comes to adapting national laws to European law, was the only national parliament to concur with the Spinelli draft. Yet this Italian enthusiasm was the forerunner of the Craxi initiative at Milan, and while the Spinelli initiative failed, it put the idea of revamping the Rome Treaty firmly on the agenda.

● **The Dooge Committee** Ingredient six, and probably the most important, was the Dooge Committee, established at the meeting of the heads of government at Fontainebleau in June 1984. This summit followed a year of deepening impatience over the British budget row and the agricultural impasse, in which there had been much talk of the European club breaking up into enthusiasts and laggards – "variable geometry" was the ponderous phrase. In the event the summit delivered a solution to the problem of Britain's contribution and set up the ad hoc Dooge Committee to suggest how the Community could work better. The committee's brief was couched in modest terms but, revealingly, was compared with that of the Spaak Committee, which in 1956 had brilliantly devised the Treaty of Rome.

The committee, led by James Dooge, a former Irish foreign minister, produced a list of required changes that later proved itself almost a recipe for the Single European Act. It said how they should be effected, calling for an intergovernmental conference to negotiate a Treaty of European Union and invoking the Stuttgart declaration and the Spinelli initiative. The particular power of the Dooge Committee, noted by an impressive authority on the Single European Act, the Belgian diplomat Jean de Ruyt, was that it made no attempt to achieve a bland consensus:

it laid out a majority view and allowed those who disagreed with it to demur by way of footnotes. Most members were in favour of majority voting and for the conference to discuss a new treaty; the minority — Britain, Denmark and Greece — were opposed. At the time, cynics could say that the message of the Dooge report was defined by its footnotes; after all the EC was run by unanimity. But with hindsight it is clear that Britain's Dooge representative, Malcolm Rifkind, sat through a trial run of Milan and the intergovernmental conference that followed.

Spurred by Britain's image, in the final Dooge report, as the "footnote European" and anxious to stress Britain's pragmatic commitment to Europe, Sir Geoffrey Howe, the British foreign secretary, led a vigorous diplomatic offensive in the early summer of 1985 to boost the Community's use of majority voting. He wanted to make it harder to invoke the 1966 Luxembourg compromise forced through by General de Gaulle. Britain suggested that the new rules on voting should be by agreement that did not alter the Rome Treaty; but that EC foreign policy cooperation should be enshrined in a specific treaty change. As the Milan summit approached this "pragmatic solution" found widespread favour, except with Italy and the Benelux countries which wanted more.

Drama in Milan

On the eve of the summit in June 1985 France and West Germany unveiled a surprise — a proposal for a "Treaty of European Union" which consisted mainly of a beefed-up version of Britain's own proposals for foreign policy cooperation. There were furious telephone calls between Downing Street and the Kanzleramt in Bonn. It soon became clear that this late bid to reassert the primacy of the Bonn-Paris axis in the EC had annoyed most of the other members rather than inspired them. The summit thus got off to a bad-tempered start.

The first day saw much airing of different points of view about whether and how the Community's rules of decision-taking should be changed, leading to further fruitless discussions between the foreign ministers over dinner. It was during that evening that Bettino Craxi and his foreign minister, Giulio Andreotti, began to wonder for the first time about forcing the pace with a straight vote on a conference on treaty changes that would be left intentionally ill-defined. Somehow, on that and the succeeding day, the British team frittered away the support that its pragmatic approach had accumulated in previous weeks. There are those who say that Mrs Thatcher was too dogmatic for her own good about what should, and should not, be included in any treaty amendment. At any rate, the nub of Craxi's technique was to avoid pinning things down: let the conference get on with it, he argued. The vote was called. The majority agreed. The conference was launched.

The European Commission was thus handed an unexpected bonus. Its president, Jacques Delors, had come to the summit hoping mainly for its blessing for the grand plan to create a single European market drawn up by his British colleague in the Commission, Lord Cockfield, and for much more European spending on research and technology. His hopes for reform of the encrusted way in which the EC took its decisions were modest. He walked away without his research money, but with the potent blend of a commitment to the 280 law changes required in the internal market's White Paper, and the prospect of changes to the Treaty of Rome to push that White Paper through.

As soon as Luxembourg, the president of the Community in the second half of 1985, had launched the conference it was clear that this conference had become a pantechnicon into which the accumulated frustrations of the 1970s and 1980s would be stuffed from all sides. At the start, the conference's brief for the revision of the Treaty of Rome was already a handsome one: improve the way the Community reaches its decisions; strengthen the Commission's ability to manage; increase the powers of the European Parliament; and expand Community policies to include new spheres of action. By the end, the pantechnicon's axles were creaking under new rules for decision-taking by the Council; deeper involvement for the European Parliament; a strengthened European Court; a commitment to complete Europe's great market by the end of 1992; a prod towards further development of Europe's monetary system; goals for social policy, mainly relating to the health and safety of workers; a commitment to help Europe's poorer regions (under the unlovely name of "social cohesion"); Community involvement in research and development; its role in protecting the environment; and rules for European cooperation in foreign policy.

A Singular Success

This was a cargo which, recalled today, immediately prompts the question: how was it ever allowed to grow under the eyes of reticent governments which had power of veto over its final passage? Luxembourg, a small but enthusiastic founding member of the Community, certainly presided skillfully over the conference, protecting those drafting the treaty texts from too much quibbling by worried governments. The Commission, too, seized its chance well. It brought on board the environment and technology without anybody seeming to mind. It cited the concerns of the poorer countries to squeeze regional development on board as well, and it helped the conference's drafting committee along with a series of clear position-papers.

But above all the Commission could brandish its prize exhibit, the single market. The genesis of this project is a tale in itself which will be told later, but in the drafting of the Single European Act, the daunting White Paper on the completion of this market suddenly came into its own. Since June it had lain around as an almost laughable challenge to governments to pass the 280 laws and measures needed to produce what they had insisted they wanted. Now it was laughable no longer. The means to get those laws passed was being devised right now. Britain, in particular, found itself bounced into surrenders of sovereignty that it would never have conceded had they been presented as abstract ideas. Britain was the member which, through the long wrangling over budgets and farm prices, had always insisted that Europe should concentrate pragmatically on completing its common market rather than dream airy-fairily of European Union. Touched by the single market, the treaty amendment was transformed: it was no longer Altiero Spinelli's dream, it was Arthur Cockfield's toolkit.

Mrs Thatcher's government, served by three particularly adept civil servants, Sir Michael Butler, Sir David Hannay, and David Williamson – now secretary-general of the Commission – was guided artfully through the negotiations towards what Mrs Thatcher had not realized she needed, and later forgot she had needed, and then perhaps regretted having asked for. This was the double surrender of sovereignty, outlined at the start, that was necessary to make the single market a reality. As for all the extras that were packed aboard, some, like the environment, were logical or inevitable aspects of the great market. Some like regional policy or social policy, were bargaining chips required to soothe members that feared the rigour of the open market that was promised. Others, such as the powers of the Parliament or economic and monetary union, were parts of the grander visions of Europe that had inspired the Act. Here the doubters could console themselves with two thoughts: first, that they had often intoned allegiance to European Union and to Economic and Monetary Union (EMU) in the past, so a fresh intonation would be nothing new; second, that the Euro-enthusiasts would have achieved far more at the Luxembourg conference and summit but for the doubters' vigilance.

One example of such vigilance concerned the clever formulation of the Delors team: "Europe without frontiers". Lord Cockfield insisted that if any sort of frontier controls remained within Europe they would be used to fragment the great market. Note how the project for a market was here being used to push for much more than a market. The British and the Danes insisted that the Single Act called for free movement for goods, people, services and capital "in accordance with this treaty (of Rome)". The Rome Treaty calls only for the creation of a common market, though it also wants "closer relations between the states belonging to it". Thus the doubters could feel their doubts protected, while the visionaries could see their visions projected.

Creaking across the Line

It was with such influences at work that the Single Act pantechnicon was stuffed to its load-bearing limit. The Luxembourg summit in early December 1985 was preceded by twelve hours of discussions between foreign ministers and then took twenty-eight hours of talks involving heads of government. The main sticking points were the crucial move to majority voting to pass the laws necessary for the opening up of the great market, and a vague, but still significant, section on economic and monetary union. For a time the summit seemed on the brink of breakdown, but the Franco-German axis reasserted itself, and Britain acquiesced for the sake of the great market it had so often demanded. Texts on nine different themes were agreed by the summit. These were the elements of the bundle that came to be known as the Single European Act.

Even then the brinksmanship had not ended. The final text agreed between foreign ministers on December 19th 1985 had to make it through the twelve national parliaments. The British parliament was sensitive to the threat to its own pre-emininence implied by the Act, but Mrs Thatcher's government was able to insist that it could not tinker with the text, that it had to take it or leave it, and that to leave it would be to make Britain an EC outcast. The Danish parliament rejected the Act, so the Danish government resorted to a rapid referendum. This, too, was fought not on the merits of the Act but on whether or not Denmark wished to remain a member of the Community. At the end of February 1986, 56 per cent of Danes voted in favour. Only then did

Italy and Greece put their signatures to the Act. It took until the end of that year for the Act to be formally ratified by all but one of the Twelve, and because of a legal challenge to the Act in Ireland it did not finally take effect until July 1987.

Bouncing Europe Along

The history of the Single Act is instructive because it is built of elements that are typical of the way the European Community has developed, and is still developing. Europe tricks its way forward. Idealistic visions of the Comunity are intoned by governments: they get nowhere but with repetition start to warp governments' views of normality. Concrete needs for the development of the Community emerge. Some of those needs are met within the existing system: the Commission and the European Court gradually mould the EC to meet them. Some require the system to be changed, so unanimity has to be constructed out of a varying line-up of majorities. How? Let a committee of all the members study the matter, so that a majority and a minority become more clearly visible. Call an intergovernmental conference and dangle in front of it a stick and a carrot. The stick is the threat of breakdown in the Community, the carrot is a pragmatic programme, with a deadline, that deals with the concrete need. Load a bit of federalist vision aboard as well – to the point where unanimity is on the point of cracking up, but is still just achieved. Sell the result to national parliaments saying that the whole confection is now untouchably fragile and the best deal that each country can expect to achieve.

If that seems whimsical, consider the moves towards economic and monetary union that Jacques Delors extracted out of the Single Act and has made the main aim of his second four-year commission. Commitment to the goal of economic and monetary union in Europe has been repeated by government leaders for years: there is the vision intoned. By the late-1980s the success of Europe's fixed exchange rate regime, the discomforts of floating currencies, and the prospect of the great market had created a perceived need for something still closer to "European money": there is the practical need. So the Delors Committee on Economic and Monetary Union (EMU) was set up and produced a possible blueprint for the way forward: there is the Dooge equivalent, but with quibbling footnotes remarkably absent. Then there was the vote, in Madrid in June 1989, for the intergovernmental conference on EMU to start sometime after the summer of 1990 – a date that was hardened up to late 1990 at the Strasbourg summit in December 1989. Already there is much talk of the other treaty amendments that may be loaded aboard this EMU pantechnicon – still more powers for the European parliament, and a further strengthening of the EC's abilities to forge a foreign policy to cope with the new situation in Eastern Europe.

The equivalence is not exact. The need for EMU is woollier than the need for a great market. The goal is a less subversive challenge to sovereignty than the great market was: it is an absolutely obvious one. The British government, in this matter, as usual, a Euro-doubter rather than Euro-promoter, is fully aware of the parallels and on its guard against being frogmarched down the same road twice. But the comparison shows how the Community system – the provisions of the original Treaty, the EC institutions, the ritual of EC councils, the special reports, and the ad hoc committees – can feed on a widespread presumption that the European peoples are united by more than divides them, and so engineer surrenders of national sovereignty that governments would normally be driven to only by high drama.

3

THE REBIRTH OF THE COMMON MARKET

Four Years of an Odd Couple

The essential ingredient of the magic that led to the Single European Act was a desire across the EC to rediscover the Common Market. During the early 1980s the lassitude with which Europeans had for ten years watched this market crumble before their eyes stiffened into frustration. At the end of 1982 the European Commission found itself inundated with 770 different examples of intra-European protectionism that it was duty-bound to investigate. Some twenty EC directives setting common technical standards for a variety of products, ranging from cars to thermometers, were deadlocked. France bore much of the blame: it was determined to keep such standards in play as weapons of national protection against over-zealous non-Europeans.

Anyone who suspects today that the EC's great-market project has been little more than a public-relations stunt should look back at the petty obsessions of Brussels only six years ago. It was counted a breakthrough then that the EC's members agreed to inform each other of any new industrial standards that they were developing. The idea that foreign products might be shown to satisfy national standards with a single European check-up was rejected as heresy. When, in 1983, the Commission presented a draft of a single customs document to simplify the paperwork on goods moving across the EC – a constant source of moans and groans in those days – the ten members tabled no less than 169 suggested amendments. It took six years for them to agree on a first directive governing the noise made by lawnmowers.

In 1979, at the opening of the first directly-elected European Parliament, the late Basil de Ferranti, a British member of the European Parliament and scion of the industrial dynasty of that name, met a fellow-member, Karl von Wogau, in a restaurant in Strasbourg, and swapped with him commercial horror-stories culled from their Euro-constituencies. Lancing Bagnall, a firm in de Ferranti's constituency, was having trouble selling fork-lift trucks in France because French rules demanded a particular layout of pedals in the cab. Von Wogau told of the time-wasting rituals a plumber in the Black Forest had regularly to endure when crossing the frontier with his toolbox to do jobs in France. The pair vowed to tackle such non-tariff barriers to trade in the EC. The "Kangaroo Group" that they founded drew parliamentarians from across the political spectrum of the European Parliament, and poured good-humoured scorn on Europe's petty protectionism.

By 1983, European industrialists, such as Wisse Dekker, the chairman of Philips, and Jacques Solvay, the chairman of Solvay, began to mount an increasingly energetic campaign for an end to Europe's economic divisions, and for European initiatives to finance expensive research and industrial projects. They saw these as part of the required answer to the challenge presented by Japan and the Asian "dragons". The campaign tied in – or at least the barrier-breaking parts of it did – with the new fashion for liberal economic policies that had flowed in from President Reagan's America and Thatcherite Britain.

On to the scene to satisfy these frustrations stepped the odd couple of the 1992 story: Jacques Delors and Arthur Cockfield. They achieved the sort of happy blending of total opposites that one can nod at wisely with hindsight but would be rash to prophesy in advance. Delors, a former French finance minister, charms people and understands their political constraints. He has a French appetite for visions and concepts, but shot through with common sense. He is prone to outbursts of emotion. He uses a good measure of guile, telling different audiences the version of European events that they want to hear. Lord Cockfield is awkward, unsubtle, formidably logical, completely undevious and undeviating. Both are men driven – Delors to come from nowhere and be president of all France, Cockfield by an austere sense of duty to see a job thoroughly done. Their Frenchness and their Englishness shine out of them, though in Lord Cockfield's case the aura has a ruddy, 18th century hue.

Public finance, the social order and the European Community have threaded their way through Delors's career. He started in 1945 at the Bank of France, moved into the social affairs part of the French national planning agency in the early 1960s, did a spell as a social affairs adviser to the Gaullist government of Jacques Chaban-Delmas in the early 1970s before formally transferring his loyalty to the Socialists in 1974. With the latter apparently doomed to perpetual opposition in France, he stood for the European Parliament, where he became the chairman of the economic and monetary committee. His success there made him a natural choice for finance minister when President Mitterrand won power in 1981.

Delors's common sense, and his familiarity with the European Monetary System, served him and France well as the Mitterrand government tried fruitlessly to apply the gravity-defying prescription it had so-long dreamed of in opposition – social spending, nationalisation, and shorter working hours. Delors did much to return France to the straight and narrow as the currency markets gave this vision a hammering. But Delors's ambition proved too much for President Mitterrand in 1984 when he wanted both to remain finance minister and to replace Pierre Mauroy as prime minister. The French president's suggestion that he exercise his talents elsewhere as the next president of the EC Commission made sense at home and was well received abroad.

In the late summer of 1984, Mrs Thatcher asked Cockfield to become one of the two British commissioners in Brussels at the start of the following year, with the near-certainty that this job would be the portfolio of the "internal market" that embodied Britain's European enthusiasms. Cockfield, then already sixty-eight, felt well set up to take on this job. He had been secretary of state for trade in 1982 and 1983, at the time when the Internal Market Council had first been set up in Brussels. He had been Britain's representative on that council and thus knew the portfolio. He wanted, characteristically, "to pick this particular thing up by the scruff of its neck and make it run".

By mid-December 1984 there was a feeling abroad that the Delors Commission in Brussels would be made of more sterling stuff than the rather lacklustre outgoing commission of Gaston Thorn. Delors had taken much care in allocating the jobs among his almost entirely new team of commissioners, and the traditionally tense day of appointments passed off smoothly. But there was little expectation at the time that the single market would be at the centre of any European relaunch. Indeed the appointment of Cockfield to the internal-market job was viewed as a mildly uninspiring sign of Mrs Thatcher's commitment to Europe. Other avenues of advance seemed more probable. The work of the Dooge Committee prompted hopes for more majority voting. Delors's own background suggested that he might choose to make the running in developing the European Monetary System.

In fact, Delors had made a tour of all the EC capitals that autumn, in the course of lining up his Commission, and had tried on governments four ways of jolting the EC out of its rut: closer collaboration on defence; development of the Community's system of government in line with the Dooge report; another move on the monetary front; or a renewed campaign for a proper European market. The internal market appealed to the (then) ten governments the most.

Cockfield promptly made his single biggest contribution to Europe's relaunch – one that is easy to take for granted today, but which was far from obvious at the time. He said that the Commission must set down all the law changes and measures that were needed to create a single market, and lay down a deadline for all of them to be completed by. What it should not do was choose a few priority areas and work on them into an unlimited future: that was bound, he argued, to lead to an argument about priorities. As for the deadline, he chose the lifespan of two commissions – eight years – conscious that the founders of the EC had given themselves, in 1957, three commissions to get the European customs union in place, and had beaten that deadline.

Pascal Lamy, the head of Delors's cabinet, says that the date 1992 came out of a cabinet discussion preparing Delors's speech to the European Parliament at the start of his reign as president. Later, as the mystique of the number took hold, elaborate theories were concocted that 1992 was a number of inherent psychological appeal, or was a European counterblast to the half-millenium of Christopher Columbus. "1992" in fact posed more and more of a problem as time went on: people assumed that the brave new world would dawn in 1992, whereas if there were any dawn at all, it would creep up from the beginning of 1993.

Whatever the origin of the magic figure, the upshot was that right from the start of the Delors Commission, the internal-market team was preparing the daunting list of 280 measures with the end of 1992 as their deadline. It was the vastness and tightness of this schedule that loomed over the Milan summit and the intergovernmental conference in 1985 and made the Single European Act so necessary. Cockfield says today that he was applying business principles here, drawn from his years as chief executive of Boots, a big British chain of pharmacists. Thus he started by planning the completion of his project – "You don't say, let's start building a factory. You decide when you want it running by" – and then worked backwards to create a timetable. Moreover he insisted on annual reports to the European Parliament on how his project was progressing, and on three progress reports in 1988, 1990 and 1992 to expose areas where progress was inadequate. It was all gloriously codified and unpolitical.

Cockfield had also been able to get a surprising number of the areas most immediately affected by the internal market under his direct command. These included the quagmire of industrial standards (see Chapter 7), all frontier controls on commerce, including those for tax-policing; the creation of an open market in finance, company law and company taxes, and responsibility for overseeing four industrial sectors – food, pharmaceuticals, textiles, and chemicals. The only important dossiers not ruled over by the market supremo were competition policy, regional policy and agriculture. The breadth of Cockfield's empire made it simpler for him and his cabinet to pull together the elements of the internal market White Paper. It also condemned Cockfield and his principal aides – Adrian Fortescue, Sebastian Birch and Michel Petite – to a workaholic existence. Cockfield says that he worked continuous six-day weeks and had never felt under such pressure in his life.

The White Paper was published on June 14th 1985, and bore the stamp of the Cockfield zeal. The introduction was heavy with reminders of the "clear and repeated commitment" to the great market made by successive summit conferences of European heads of state. It described how the White Paper would "set out the essential and logical consequences of accepting that commitment". It divided the impediments within the single market into three sorts: physical barriers at frontiers, technical barriers within different countries, and barriers designed to protect fiscal regimes.

These varieties will emerge, in exhausting measure, through the rest of this book. Suffice it to say here that the White Paper did three important things. First, it laid out the full scale of the single-market job, and the timetable to do it by. Second, it made sense of this long list of tasks by fitting them into a conceptual framework that any intelligent reader could understand. Third, it dared to broach two topics that were vital to the completion of the market, but anathema to governments: its implications for indirect taxes – that is taxes on things rather than people; and a claimed need to do away with all systematic frontier controls on people. The section of the White Paper on tax barriers was strikingly long and intricate compared with the prose devoted to other sorts of market impediment. Cockfield's own background as a tax collector played some part here, but he was chiefly guided by his instinct that tax was the matter over which the creation of a proper European market would run most solidly into national sovereignty. Cockfield wrote most of the section on taxes himself.

As for the rest of the job of putting together the White Paper, it was more one of trawling and sieving than of inventing. An immense amount – perhaps half – of the required European rule-making was already in draft form after years of effort by the Commission to construct pan-European regimes for this and that in piecemeal fashion. The Cockfield cabinet invited the different directorates of the Commission to submit what rules they regarded as vital to the internal market. A great number of draft would-be rules were pressed upon the authors of the White Paper, for it was by then already clear that project 1992 was a bandwagon worth boarding. The Cockfield cabinet sifted out much of what was gratuitously interventionist and kept what was logically need-ed for open borders. This technique made the White Paper, for the most part, a liberal document rather than an industrial policy masquerading as a market. In this sense it was an unspoken rebuff to the dirigiste instincts of many European civil servants. Remarkably, the socialist Delors acquiesced in this.

Cockfield's manner by the time the White Paper was published in June 1985 had become almost vindictive. "They want an open internal market," he said grimly of Europe's governments, "well, they've got it." The White Paper contained plenty to worry the government that had sent its author to Brussels. It went much farther than Mrs Thatcher wanted in insisting that the great market must involve "doing away with internal frontier controls in their entirety": she was determined that controls remain in place against illegal immigration, terrorism, drugs and rabies. It was much too explicit and interventionist in insist-ing that Brussels should impose a regime of value-added taxes. Already, Cockfield had, in British eyes, "gone native" in Brussels. The British had tried to steer him away from his pitiless tax-logic. But Cockfield was not for turning. At around this time the whisper went out from 10 Downing Street that Lord Cockfield was no longer "in favour" at the lady's court.

One can imagine the whistling through pursed lips in Whitehall that greeted Cockfield's conclusion to the White Paper. He asserted that 1992 was about "completing the integration of the economies of Europe" rather than building a mere free-trade area. The latter, said Cockfield, "would fail dismally to release the energies of the people of Europe" and "fail to satisfy their aspirations". Just as customs union had preceded economic integration, he argued, so economic integration had to precede European unity. Mrs Thatcher's turbulent taxman might indeed be her sort of plain-speaking, non-airy-fairy pragmatist. But once installed in Brussels he revealed that his pragmatism was dedicated to an ideal that was not her cup of tea at all – European Union. From that moment on Cockfield's days in Brussels were numbered.

A Slow-burning Fuse

The White Paper attracted little attention at its launch, and the idea of the great market took more than two years to burst upon the public's consciousness. The first impact of the plan was the way it helped the Single European Act into being. It then took the EC two years, between the summer of 1985 and the summer of 1987, to get that Act accepted by all its members and thus to change the paralysing way in which the EC took its law-making decisions. During that time the Commission was, in a sense, worse off in pushing its single market forward. It had won commitment to the idea, certainly, but it did not have majority voting, and was forced to take more notice of the European Parliament before the latter's strengthened involvement in European law-making technically came into force.

Meanwhile the EC's governments were bogged down in another grim argument about the EC's budget. The problem was, in essence, the same one that had launched the search for majority voting at the start of the 1980s – the way that agriculture gobbled up too much of the EC's budget and left too little for other, worthier programmes. But this time the crisis was provoked not by British demands for a fairer deal but by the prospect of the EC running out of cash unless its revenues were increased. Britain was determined to use this impasse to impose more discipline on farm spending. The French, having become net payers into the EC budget, were inclined to sympathise, while West Germany, which poured far more cash than any other country into the EC, remained ambivalent because of the politically powerful demands of its own farmers. At the same time, the poorest countries in the EC insisted that they could not face the rigours of the great market without a lot more help from the EC's regional fund.

A series of factors conspired to make the West German presidency of the EC, in the first half of 1988, the period when the 1992 project finally burst upon the world:

● **Publicity** Mitterrand led the way here in 1987, prompted partly by his close links with Delors. He saw to it that France took the abrasive, open-market prospect of 1992 seriously. The seriousness filtered down to industry from the top through the still-powerful links that exist in France between the bureaucracy and the private sector: the government commissioned a number of studies on the impact of 1992 from clever civil servants – among them Pierre Achard's on finance and Henri Froment-Meurice's on external relations and trade. The research for, and distribution of, these reports made the captains of French industry think 1992 through. That summer the French government launched a flashy television campaign to raise public awareness of 1992's challenge to France.

In the spring of 1988, Lord Young, Britain's secretary for trade and industry, and a man with a showroom instinct, launched a brassy advertising campaign aimed at making 90 per cent of British companies aware of the importance of 1992 by the end of the year. "Europe is open for business" ran the slogan, and the faces of some of Britain's best known executives stared out from newspapers and hoardings urging their compatriots to face up to the European challenge.

● **Research** During 1986 the Commission began to feel a keen need for numbers to illustrate the potential of a complete internal market. Adrian Fortescue, Cockfield's *chef de cabinet*, approached Paolo Cecchini, a senior official in the Commission who was heading for retirement, and asked him to coordinate research into the matter. With the Commission providing the funds, a steering committee for "research into the cost of non-Europe" pulled together around thirty different studies, some already under way, some specially commissioned, which examined the fragmentation of the European market sector by sector and estimated the total cost of what was nattily called "non-Europe". The results became available in the spring of 1988, in an impressive study of "The economics of 1992" put out by the Commission's directorate for economic affairs, and in a more popular and accessible book under Cecchini's name, "1992, the benefits of the single market".

This was clever consciousness-raising. It produced some big round numbers – of frankly dubious worth – to describe the costs of continuing in a divided market and the benefits of building an integrated one. More important, it spilled out a mass of anecdotes and examples of current nonsenses afflicting businesses trying to work across European frontiers. Its sector-by-sector approach triggered great curiosity among businessmen about what 1992 meant for their own trades, and an explosion of punditry, conferences and consultancy to tell them the answers. In the period from June 1988 to June 1989 barely a day went by without *The Economist* and the *Financial Times* receiving some invitation to a conference or some new work of research on 1992 by management consultants, lawyers or accountants. The Cecchini report provided the raw data that formed the basis of much of this pontification.

● **Mergers and Aquisitions** As awareness increased, project 1992 had the same effect on corporate strategists that a phase of deregulation has on any industry: it makes managements wonder whether they should be securing themselves a share of an opening market before their opponents do. There was a steadily rising curve of merger and acquisition activity. According to the Commission, the total number of outright takeovers, purchases of minority holdings and joint ventures – inside a single EC state, across EC frontiers and between Community and foreign firms – increased by 45 per cent in 1987–88 over the level a year earlier (when the rise was 27 per cent). Even within a single year, the increased tempo was evident. According to Translink's *European Deal Review*, the value of cross-border acquisitions virtually doubled each quarter during the first nine months of 1989.

It is hard to prove that these deals were due to the prospect of a great market, and would not have happened anyway as business became more international. But it is clear that from late 1987 onwards companies tended to cite 1992 as one of the reasons for their moves. They talked of concentrating their production in fewer sites; and those in businesses dependent upon governments as customers were particular anxious to spread themselves across the European market, knowing that they would be able to count less and less upon unchallenged government patronage.

The deals that attracted popular attention as examples of "1992 mergers" were: the takeover of Plessey of Britain by the Anglo-German duo of GEC-Siemens; Swedish Asea's link-up with Brown Boveri of Switzerland to compete in the great EC market; Carlo De Benedetti's raid on Société Générale de Belgique which eventually put the giant Belgian holding company in the hands of the Suez financial group of France; Deutsche Bank's move to snap up Morgan Grenfell, the British merchant bank; and CGE of France's purchase of ITT's Alcatel operation in Europe. All in all, after the end of 1988, business expectations of, and investment in, the prospect of an open European market was a political fact that governments could no longer treat lightly.

● **The Budget Solution** In February 1988, after an unsuccessful summit the previous December, the heads of EC governments managed to settle their dispiriting argument over the Community's money. Mrs Thatcher agreed to rather less discipline on farm spending than she would have liked. The West Germans agreed to stump up still more money. Aid to the EC's poorer regions was set to double by 1993. As a result of this deal the proportion of the EC members' cumulative GDP going on Community spending was set to rise from 1 per cent to 1.2 per cent by 1992 – (still not, it should be noted, a very high proportion in the hands of the fledgling central government of a would-be European Union). It was West German generosity that made this deal possible, and which thus allowed Germany to preside over the first real flowering of the 1992 programme. With the budget wrangling out of the way the pace of work on the White Paper picked up fast. The West Germans were able to end their stint having achieved nothing less than a sensation in negotiating a timetable for the removal of exchange controls in the EC by the end of 1992, and having themselves conceded that Germany's well-protected road-hauliers should open themselves to a more competitive European transport market.

The breakthrough on the budget and the new momentum towards the single market clinched for Jacques Delors the prospect of a second term as president of the Commission. He could put behind him the days of budgetary despond, when he had sometimes become too emotional for his own good. As a temporary obsession with 1992 developed across Europe, he walked ever taller, and raised his eyes to the goal of European Union that lay beyond the pragmatic market. He laid more emphasis on the "social dimension" – the attempt to lay down the rights of workers in the great market. He warned that "80 per cent of economic legislation and perhaps tax and social legislation would be of Community origin within ten years", seeking by this to point out that the EC's political institutions would have to be made more accountable if such a concentration of power was to be kept democratic. He began to plan for a new push in his second four-year term towards Economic and Monetary Union – a European market with one currency and one central bank.

But that is to run ahead of the story – into the pitfalls of tax, into the struggle over trade policy, into the quarrels over the social dimension, into the counter-attack against Delors's zeal of Mrs Thatcher at Bruges, into the contentious Delors blueprint for Economic and Monetary Union. By the end of the first of the two four-year terms that lay between Delors's arrival and the 1992 deadline, the great market was half-designed – in terms of draft directives presented by the Commission to the Council; and one-third built – in terms of directives passed by the Council. Whatever the provisos, caveats and problems still ahead, that achievement made those four years remarkable. For the entire programme had been conceived during that time, the means of implementing it had been created, and a vast public had been steeped in it to the point where "1992" had become almost a new reality.

But the odd couple who had pulled off this trick could not go on together. While Delors remained in Brussels, Lord Cockfield was brought by Mrs Thatcher back to London and to retirement from government service. His fief in Brussels was divided. His uncomfortable logic in the matter of tax was gently buried. For a time it seemed that this might have been an apt move – that the time for visionaries had passed and that the time for political fixers had arrived. But today, as Europe's taxmen look down in satisfaction at the still-divisive tax regime they are in the process of foisting on the great market, one is less sure.

4

THE INSTITUTIONS

Proposers, Disposers and Debaters

For the most part, the people who run the European Community are faceless. The European-in-the-street would be hard pushed to name many of Jacques Delors's 16 colleagues in the European Commission, let alone any of the 10,000 Eurocrats who work under them, or any of the 518 Members of the European Parliament, or even his own MEP. He would recognise his own national politicians in the EC Council of Ministers, but would have little idea of what they get up to in Brussels. More influence is now in prospect for these faceless ones as a result of the forthcoming negotiations among the Twelve about Economic and Monetary Union (EMU). These may give the Commission power to recommend, and the Council of Ministers to impose, national macro-economic policies, and may also ordain a European System of Central Banks to report to the European Parliament, much as the US Federal Reserve reports to the US Congress.

The Community's strange decision-making machinery already had a Heath Robinson air (see diagram on page 41) before the Single European Act made it more powerful and changed the balance of its component parts. By introducing majority voting in the Council of Ministers, it gave the Commission the opportunity to push far more legislation through the Council than it had ever done before. It also gave the Commission more policies to manage and more powers to do the managing. The simultaneous enlargement of the Community to twelve may have made negotiations inside the Council more complex, but it thus enhanced the referee role of the Commission, the one body able to take a bird's-eye view of the states' warring interests. As for the Parliament, the Single Act emerged as its Magna Carta giving it for the first time a real say in legislation beyond the EC budget. The Parliament also acquired a right of veto over new members of the Community and over certain kinds of Community agreements with other countries.

The Council of Ministers still retains the last legislative word. But it has become much harder to predict what that word will be, following the Single Act's shifting of more power to the two "federal" bodies, the Commission and the Parliament. Take, for instance, the emotive issue of the exhaust emissions of cars. The majority of national environment ministers within the Council were outgunned in the spring of 1989 by a newly forged (and probably lasting) "green axis" between Parliament and Commission. The upshot was that the Council found itself passing into law US-style exhaust controls far more radical than those it had approved only the previous November. Suddenly, people – not just European carmakers faced with big additional bills for pollution control – woke up to the changes wrought by the Single Act.

More insidious, but for the national legislatures of the Twelve more important, is the way that majority voting has undermined their control over what their ministers do in the Council. Even the most exacting national scrutiny, like that by the Danish parliament's EC committee which keeps Danish ministers on the tightest of reins, is of little avail when those ministers can simply be outvoted in the Council. Even before the Single Act, there was angry muttering about the "democratic deficit" created by the way in which ministers horse-traded behind closed doors in the Council with precious little monitoring by their national parliaments. With the Single Act, the muttering has become a growl. And when logicians suggest that the European Parliament be given still more power to fill that democratic deficit the growl moves up an octave into a howl.

The Berlaymont Brigade

The 10,000 Eurocrats headquartered in the large cruciform building in the centre of Brussels known as the Berlaymont have always felt themselves a breed apart – distinct from mere national civil servants and supposedly independent of the twelve national governments. Unlike other civil services – national or international – they have a monopoly in proposing European legislation: the Council of Ministers cannot do it directly, nor can the Parliament. The Treaty of Rome gave them this power to prevent any one member country being seen to dominate the law-making for its own national ends. So it is the Commission that starts the legislative ball rolling by making a proposal which goes first to the Council and then to Parliament. The Council cannot legislate without a Commission proposal in front of it. The Single Act gave the Commission nothing new in terms of power to propose. But by endorsing the Cockfield White Paper and its 280 proposals it gave the Commission a political impetus to get on with law-making that it hadn't had since the early 1960s.

This has spurred the Commission on in its other activities. One of these is the exercise of semi-autonomous powers (subject only to the European Court of Justice) in running the Community's competition policy. Inherited partly from the original Coal and Steel Community these powers include the right to fine companies for operating restrictive cartels, and to force governments to reclaim trade-distorting subsidies given to companies. Brussels has been increasingly tough in both these areas (see Chapter 12) not only because it has had a series of effective competition commissioners but also because cartels and, particularly, state aid are viewed as a particular menace to a truly open market.

Yet these powers by the Commission to act on its own authority have their limits. The Commission is currently in the dock of the Court of Justice in Luxembourg accused by France of going too far in forcing an opening-up of telecommunications markets without due reference to national governments. Ironically, it was under the French presidency of the EC that the Council agreed in December 1989 to the gist of what the Commission is trying to achieve in freeing-up the telecommunications business.

Another of the Commission's roles is as Euro-cop (see Chapter 11). Whenever it feels that a member is flouting EC law or, more often, dragging its feet in reflecting EC directives in national law, it can start legal proceedings against the state in question. In 1988 it served 569 "letters of formal notice" on states (which basically tell a government "we think you have a problem with EC law"); it delivered 227 "reasoned opinions" (which say "we know you have a problem"); and launched 73 cases ("you have a problem") against governments in the European Court of Justice. Such has been the recent tempo of the Commission's suit-launching that some in the European Court complain that Brussels is overloading the EC's legal machinery. But such is the abysmal general record of translating single-market law into national law that the hyperactive lawyers of the Berlaymont show no sign of letting up.

The Single Act gave the Community more responsibility for economic aid to poorer regions, social policy, the environment, research and technology programmes. These, too, have thrust the Commission deeper into management. This is not a happy development, if the degree of

The Legislative Roller Ball

An elaborate balance of lawmaking power has been created between the Commission, the Council of Ministers and the European Parliament since the Single European Act was passed. This rigmarole is called the "cooperation procedure". The picture shows what happens every time a 1992 directive or regulation goes through the Brussels-Strasbourg works. The legislation must be imagined as a ball rolling down and between the tubes of a structure looking faintly like an oil-rig. The tubes are the Commission, the Parliament, and the Council. Time moves down the vertical axis from the top. When a tube is shaded it means that that institution is working on a measure.

First the Commission consults national civil servants and businessmen and draws up a "proposal", which it ships to the Council, which in turn passes it to Parliament for an "opinion". A relevant committee of the Parliament considers the proposal and suggests changes to it. Parliament then decides in its "first reading", after a majority vote, to reject, accept or amend the proposal. It informs the Council and Commission of its decision, which each can choose to ignore if it likes. But if the Commission changes its own proposal to reflect the Parliament's wishes, the Council is then bound to try to reach its own "common position" on the basis of this changed proposal. The "common position" is the breakthrough that European law is looking for: it means that the twelve governments have licked the draft law into a shape that all, or a qualified majority, of them can accept (depending upon the matter in hand).

The process is then broadly repeated in a second reading. The parliamentary committee looks at the common position and recommends to the house to accept, reject or accept with amendments. The Commission then re-examines the common position and decides whether or not to build Parliament's amendments into it. If it does, the Council must then vote on that amended common position using qualified majority voting: it needs unanimity to amend the common-position back again.

The upshot of all this is that the Commission proposes and the Council disposes, while the Parliament, thanks to the chivvying value of the second reading is able to affect the outcome via the Commission, but is ultimately dependent upon the Commission for the effectiveness of its views. In practice, there is an unspoken deal between Commission and Parliament (both of which will often be in Euro-cahoots against representatives of national governments). So the Commission respects the Parliament's first-reading amendments, and the Parliament, in return, shows restraint in tampering with the "common position".

The vital time for individuals or national parliaments to alter the shape of European legislation is during the Commission's initial ruminations; because once a proposal is rolling down the tubes it begins to develop an institutional momentum that is hard to deflect. But lobbying the Parliament and its committees can help too, because there is a good chance that amendments recommended by Parliament after its first reading will receive the Commission's fairly powerful blessing.

Cooperation procedure

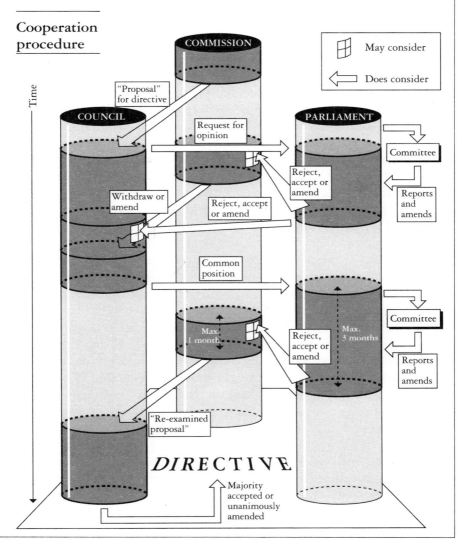

fraud in the long-established Common Agricultural Policy is any guide (though governments are also deeply to blame here). Part of the problem is the Commission's lack of manpower. Its services are often regarded as overstaffed, as well as overpaid. But at 10,000, the whole Commission has less than half the people in, say, Britain's Department of Trade and Industry. In certain areas it is ludicrously over-stretched. A mere half-dozen Eurocrats check for fair play in the public purchasing that amounts to 15 per cent of Europe's gross domestic product. Two and a half Eurocrats (one is part-time) supervise the EC's water purity regime. The Commission thus has to rely on national civil services not only for expertise in developing new policies but also for manpower to enforce them.

Despite such skeleton-staffing the Berlaymont brigade still retains a robust desire to increase its own importance. This ambition brings it into conflict with member states on two fronts. The first concerns, in the Euro-jargon, "subsidiarity" – the degree to which policy should be made at Community level rather than left to the members, and the degree to which supervision of EC policies should be left in the Berlaymont's hands. The latter leads to the second front. There is constant guerrilla warfare over what is known, in another piece of jargon, as "comitology" – the nature of supervising committees composed of national and Commission civil servants. The Single Act said that in single-market matters priority should be given to purely advisory committees. The Commission likes, and almost always proposes, such advisory bodies, which it chairs and whose advice it can ignore. Member governments prefer "management" committees such as those which oversee EC farm policies, whose opinions are more or less binding on the Commission.

The success of project 1992 has boosted morale inside the Berlaymont to an all-time high. For this, Jacques Delors must take credit. He wields more influence inside and outside the Berlaymont than any Commission president since the first one, Walter Hallstein in the late 1950s. Delors is the first since Hallstein to be reappointed to a second term. He is a supreme fixer – witness the way he presided over the events of Chapters 2 and 3, and over tales of Economic and Monetary Union yet to come. He is not, however, a particularly good team player, and since the start of his second presidential term in 1989 has tended to make policy on his own. For instance, he recently suggested a new EC relationship with EFTA without first clearing the initiative with Frans Andriessen, the Dutch commissioner in charge of external relations and the only one who predates Delors's arrival in Brussels. He also tends to keep formal Commission discussion of such momentous issues as EMU to a minimum. People with experience of Mrs Thatcher's cabinet may recognise the symptoms.

Luckily, the first Delors commission (1985–88) contained some strong figures who stiffened the president where he was initially weakest. A formative clash came in 1986 with Peter Sutherland, a doughty Irishman who was competition commissioner at the time. Sutherland put down a clear marker of his intent to take much tougher attitude towards trade-distorting state aid, by proposing that the French government be ordered to recover FFr300 million in aid it had paid to Boussac, an ailing textile company. Delors vainly opposed the demand, not least because he had been the French finance minister who had helped Boussac. But Sutherland got his way, and was ruefully, but respectfully, dubbed "the little sheriff" by Delors thereafter. The lasting effect of this incident was apparent when in late 1989 Delors acquiesced in a far bigger action against France by Sir Leon Brittan to recover most of FFr12 billion paid out to Renault, the state-owned carmaker.

The eight-year project of 1992 has given the Commission an unusually long period of cohesiveness. But the seventeen commissioners who form the Commission's management board don't always pull together. Nor can they be easily forced together. True, the Commission has a highly influential secretary-general, at present an ebullient Briton, David Williamson; but his role is akin to a British cabinet secretary, oiling the machinery rather than ordering the seventeen board-members into line. A Commission president cannot behave like the president or prime minister of a nation. He can neither choose nor dismiss his commissioners, who are appointed by their governments for fixed four-year terms. He has a considerable say in deciding at the start of those terms what jobs they should fill. For his second term, Delors was well able to rig the distribution of jobs. But unlike a national leader, a Commission president cannot reshuffle his cabinet mid-way through its term. It is by no means certain that the transformation of the Commission wrought by 1992 and Delors will outlast the project and the man.

The Council – a European government in embryo

The Council is the forum in which the EC's twelve member governments battle for their national interests. It has the final say on Community policies and legislation. While the Commission proposes and the Parliament amends, the Council disposes. Its multifaceted role is well summed up by Sir Michael Butler, a former British permanent representative (ambassador) to the Community. "In one sense, the Council and COREPER (the French acronym for the group of the Twelve's permanent representatives) are a forum for a permanent negotiation between the member states on a wide range of issues simultaneously. In another they are the legislature of the Community. In a third they are the senior board of directors taking many of the day-to-day decisions on its policies." But to the extent that the Council is a legislature it is an odd one: it consists only of experts in the legislation in question. Thus tax matters are decided in a Council of finance ministers; farm prices in a Council of agriculture ministers, etc. Only twice a year do heads of government get together in the European Council to take a broader view and break impasses.

The big change to the Council brought about by the Single Act was to formalise the use of majority voting on proposals "which have as their object the establishment and functioning of the internal market". This was what the row at the 1985 Milan summit was all about. The search for unanimity in the Council, leading to endless Council marathons and the nasty practice of agreement by sleep-deprivation, had by the mid-1980s become so ingrained that the majority at Milan were right to think that a formal treaty-change was needed to jolt the Community into reforming its ways.

The Single Act still provides for veto by requiring unanimity among the members on proposals relating to tax, the free movement of people, and the rights and interests of workers. These areas are granted special protection because they so deeply touch economic sovereignty, physical security and the organisation of societies. Unsurprisingly, it is in just these areas that the least progress towards a single market has been made. Since the Single Act there has been much legal wrangling over whether a measure is really related to the internal market or not, and thus whether its approval in the Council will be by majority or unanimity. For instance, in 1989 the Commission proposed a European Company Statute designed to make cross-border mergers easier but also calling for a degree of worker participation in the running of such "European" companies. The Commission said this was an internal-market measure, and therefore approvable by majority. Britain argued for unanimity because worker participation amounted to social legislation, requiring unanimous approval. The argument is still unresolved.

Despite such tiffs, the Single Act has broken the logjam. Much more

European law is now made by qualified majority, with votes weighted according to a country's population. The total number of votes is 76. The four biggest members – West Germany, France, Britain and Italy – have ten apiece. Spain has eight; the Netherlands, Belgium, Greece and Portugal five each; Ireland and Denmark three each; and Luxembourg two. A qualified majority is set at 54 votes, making a blocking minority 23. The latter can be assembled by two of the largest countries, plus any one of the smaller members bar Luxembourg (this does not greatly matter to the duchy, whose main worry is about having its appeal as a tax-haven harmonised away; and in tax matters, unanimity still reigns).

The new threat of being outvoted is potent. It forces countries to make alliances and compromises, to deal and negotiate with each other, in a way that easy reliance on the veto did not. One tactic, particularly used in agricultural councils, is the "indicative" vote. This is essentially a show of force. It is not binding. As such it allows outvoted governments to change their vote later on without loss of face. There remains, however, a certain gentlemanliness among the members. They do not like rubbing the losers' noses in their loss of sovereignty: after all, winners on one vote know that they may be among the losers next time around. So there is still a tendency, particularly on the big issues, to seek consensus before deciding. It is as though the ghost of de Gaulle still hovers above the Council table.

Such was the case in June 1988's decision to lift exchange controls – arguably the most important single directive in the 1992 programme. It concerned money, not tax, and therefore could have been passed by majority. France had, and still has, deep worries about this directive causing capital flight. So the other states took care to assuage French concerns to the point where the measure could be approved by consensus.

Majority voting occurs most frequently in "internal market" Councils which take place almost every month between trade/industry ministers. It is less prevalent among foreign, finance and agriculture ministers, who hold Councils just as frequently, because of what they do. In all, there are some 80–90 ministerial Councils a year. There is also, largely invisible to the public, constant activity among diplomats and officials of the Twelve, whose job is to prepare matters for ministerial decision/vote. COREPER – the forum of national delegations to the EC – meets every week, split into three groups. Ambassadors deal with foreign policy and anything touching on Community institutions. Their deputies deal with industry and internal-market issues. And a breed-apart of farm experts forms the Special Committee on

Agriculture. There are also about 150 "working groups". Some of these may meet only twice a year with officials coming from national capitals. But on an average day there are some 10–14 working groups meeting at the Council's charmless Charlemagne building near the Berlaymont in Brussels. To service this ant-heap of diplomatic activity, the Council has a secretariat of some 2,100 (70 per cent of them interpreters and translators), headed by a secretary-general, Niels Ersboell, himself once Denmark's man in COREPER.

There are no permanent alliances in the Council, which is just as well for its survival. It is said to be a Franco-German motor which drives the Community along. This is true for some big decisions. It was Helmut Schmidt and Valery Giscard d'Estaing who created the European Monetary System in 1978–9, and it is only through cooperation between President Mitterrand and Chancellor Helmut Kohl that Economic and Monetary Union (EMU) will ever come about. But on trade, for instance, Paris and Bonn usually find themselves on different sides, while the issue of aid from rich to poor parts of the EC tends to create a north-south divide. For all the talk of Britain being isolated in Europe, it happens to be part of a pair of countries (with the Netherlands) that have in recent years most consistently voted with each other in the Council, and is, in single-market matters, a less frequent dissenter than West Germany.

As well as shifting alliances, the Council has a shifting chairmanship. In alphabetical order (in countries' own language – hence Deutschland, Ellas, Espana etc) the presidency of the Council rotates every six months. The president sets the timetable, and influences the agenda, conduct and outcome of discussions in the Council. Over the medium and long term, much of the Council's agenda is, as we have seen, set by the Commission. But over a six-month period, it is for the president-member to decide which Councils will meet when and how long they will sit to reach agreement. Project 1992 has led to unspoken competition between presidencies to see how many internal-market agreements they can chalk up during their time in the chair. Thus, towards the end of every stint presidents of the various Councils tend to extend sessions into the night with cheese and salami sandwiches in order to hammer out agreements. The competition is good for the Community's health: that of ministers, and the quality of European law, sometimes suffers.

Each holder of the presidency has its own priorities, within and beyond the 1992 programme. West Germany, for instance, pushed capital liberalisation through during its presidency in the first half of 1988, and really got 1992 rolling. The two successive (socialist) presidencies of Greece and Spain shifted the emphasis to social policy. France, in the last half of 1989, used its presidency to corral the Community into formal negotiations on EMU by the end of 1990.

Equally, however, the presidency often inhibits the president-member: it cannot bang the table for its national interest when in the chair. Governments sometimes deliberately block progress in the period immediately before their spells in the chair, so that by unblocking it later they can beautify their own presidency. In late 1983, for instance, efforts during the Greek presidency to resolve the British budget row were blocked by France, which then took the chair and crowned its 1984 presidency with the Fontainebleau deal giving Britain a rebate. Similarly, Helmut Kohl basically wrecked the Danish presidency's efforts at the December 1987 summit in Copenhagen to reform the Community budget, and less than two months later exerted enormous pressure as president to get agreement on precisely the lines he had earlier sabotaged.

The Parliament – a symbol of not-quite Europe

No EC institution has had its power more increased by the Single Act – and is more likely to acquire still more clout as a result of negotiations over EMU – than the European Parliament. It is in the nature of parliaments to grab power from the executives wherever and whenever they can. But Enrique Baron, the Spanish socialist who is the Parliament's president, took many government leaders and the Commission aback at the December 1989 summit when he told them that the intergovernmental conference over EMU should give the 518 Members of the European Parliament (MEPs):

● The right to initiate legislation. Hitherto this, as we have seen, has been the jealously guarded monopoly of the Commission.

● The right to amend or reject legislation going beyond the 1992 programme. At present, on proposals unrelated to the internal market, the Parliament can only give opinions, which the Council and Commission are free to ignore.

● The power of joint decision-taking in any new areas of Community competence introduced under a new EMU-creating treaty. This would wipe out the Commission's discretion, even in the single-market matters, to ignore Parliament's amendments, and the Council's ultimate power to overrule both Parliament and Commission if it can muster unanimity among all twelve governments.

● A "decisive role" in the investiture of a new Commission, presumably meaning that a new Commission, or just its president, would have to get majority approval in the Parliament before it or they could take office. At present Commissioners are appointed by governments. The Parliament already can, in theory, kick out the whole Commission (not just individuals in it) by a vote of censure. Only a couple of (unsuccessful) attempts have ever been made to fire this blunderbuss weapon.

In short, Mr Baron and his fellow MEPs want to be treated like a real parliament. For the moment, the Strasbourg assembly isn't one, because it has no executive directly responsible to it. The Council of Ministers does not stand or fall on whether or not it can command a majority in the European Parliament. The powers of the Parliament are applied to the Commission, not the Council. However, some governments have signalled their readiness to see a big increase in the Parliament's powers before the next of its five-yearly elections, in 1994. Indeed Chancellor Helmut Kohl is positively gung-ho that this should happen. His motives are something of a mystery, since Germany, of all countries, is keenest that any European central bank should follow the example of its Bundesbank in being insulated from the vagaries of political control. It may be that the German chancellor foresees the need for more control over the EC Council of finance ministers, whose powers, Bonn feels, should be increased to match those of the governors of the new European central bank. Or it may be that West Germany already has reassuring experience, in its own *länder* system, of government by cascade-of-legislatures. In contrast, Margaret Thatcher has set her face against a bigger role for the Strasbourg parliament, arguing passionately that the seat of sovereignty in the Community must lie with its twelve national legislatures. She may get support on this from sovereignty-sensitive countries such as Denmark.

For a long time, both before and after it was first directly elected in 1979, the Parliament has often seemed to justify the contempt of its detractors. Bored by having to deal with minutiae like tractor roll-bar dimensions, and frustrated at having no control over the Council, MEPs have frequently tended to behave in a way that has underlined their own powerlessness, passing motions on East Timor refugees or deforestation of the Amazon – problems way outside the scope of their influence. This has, unfairly, reinforced the impression that MEPs are more interested in the not-inconsiderable perks of their posts and in the gastronomy of Strasbourg and Brussels than in real power.

A certain feeling of chaos is inevitable in an institution that functions with two alphabets, in three working places, in nine languages, with ten political groupings fitted around twelve nationalities. The Parliament is condemned, too, to be a travelling circus because EC governments refuse to give it a single seat. At present most of its staff live in Luxembourg, all its committee hearings (for three weeks out of every month) take place in Brussels, and its twelve plenary sessions a year are held in Strasbourg. Hundreds of tin boxes full of documents are shipped by the pantechnicon-load from Brussels and Luxembourg to Strasbourg, for the one week in every month that the Parliament inhabits its enormous premises in the Alsatian capital.

Here is a scandalous waste of time and money, which most MEPs would like to end by settling once and for all in Brussels, next to the Commission and Council. But it is a waste to which the French and Luxembourg governments, keen to keep the prestige and jobs of hosting a big Community institution, refuse to put a clear end. As a result, the Parliament has had to resort to subterfuge. Private developers are currently digging a large hole next to the Parliament's offices in Brussels. By some time in 1991 this hole will become a building with a not-very-mysterious hemicycle seating some 600 people. The Parliament has taken a long lease on the planned building. One day in the early 1990s, therefore, Europe's parliamentary nomads may take their fate into their own hands by pitching their tents for good in the Belgian capital.

Before the Single Act, the power of the Parliament related chiefly to money – the traditional lever by which parliaments have won themselves power in national politics. Once a draft budget has been drawn up by the Commission, it goes to Parliament and the Council to wrangle over. Parliament has a right of co-decision over the budget, since the budget cannot be adopted without its agreement. But MEPs have power over less than half the Community's spending. They cannot alter anything in the budget that is termed "compulsory" expenditure; since this includes farm spending, it amounts to two-thirds of the whole. MEPs' scope for changing (usually increasing) the rest, the "non-compulsory" expenditure, is also limited, too. (Bear in mind, though, that many national parliaments are effectively unable to alter the shape of national budgets presented to them). Budget battles, so much a feature of the 1970s and early 1980s, are unlikely to figure much in the immediate future – up to 1992. Until then, the EC budget is covered by a so-called "inter-institutional agreement", reached as part of the 1988 budget deal by which the Council, Commission and Parliament all undertook to abide by certain guidelines constraining farm spending and boosting regional aid for a five-year period. After 1992 the gloves will come off again.

The Single Act gave the Parliament much scope to amend or reject a draft for single-market legislation agreed by the Council – a "common position" – provided it can get the necessary 260-vote majority to do so. Whether the Parliament then prevails with its desired changes depends very much on the Commission, which acts as a kind of transmission belt between Council and Parliament. If the Commission backs the Parliament's amendments, it takes unanimity among all twelve governments for the Council's original view to win through. Since that initial Council position was probably only adopted by majority, such unanimity can be extremely hard to muster. Such a Commission-Parliament alliance was, as we have seen, decisive in the recent car-exhaust case. A Commission refusal to back a Parliamentary amendment, however, stacks the odds against MEPs; the Council simply needs to find a majority to overrule the amendment.

When the Single Act was signed, and broadly pooh-poohed as too little too late, the critics underestimated the power it had given the Parliament through this so-called cooperation procedure. Another miscalculation by governments was the "assent procedure", giving the Parliament the right to approve new members of the Community or new association agreements with outsiders. Governments, underrating the appeal abroad of 1992, did not foresee new members or new associates coming forward. But Turkey and Austria subsequently applied for membership, and Cyprus and Malta may yet do so, and now the Eastern Europeans want special relationships too. In the short term, governments may welcome this parliamentary assent as an extra hurdle for would-be entrants to vault. Later they may regret ceding to the Parliament something akin to the US Senate's right to assent to foreign treaties.

A further effect of 1992 on the parliament is that it has made rather more relevant the way MEPs align themselves by ideology, rather than by nationality as they do in the Council. MEPs divide into groups, ranging from Communists on the left, through the big battalions of the Socialists and Christian Democrats in the centre, to the neo-fascist far-right. Despite this, and for as long as issues like agricultural policy dominated the debate (with British Tory and Labour MEPs united for reform and all French MEPs united against reform) the Parliament tended merely to replicate the national clashes taking place in the Council.

Increasingly, issues like the "pro-business" single-market project, the "pro-workers" Social Charter, even environment and consumer protection are dividing MEPs along left-right lines. The result of the European elections in June 1989 reinforced this tendency. The British Labour Group supplanted the British Tories as the largest one-party grouping from a single country, and have given the Socialist Group a sharper left-wing edge. This in turn has rendered informal cooperation between the Socialists and the Christian Democrats harder. Overall, the Euro-elections produced, for the first time, a narrow majority for the broad left: Socialists, Communists and Greens.

An Appetite for reform

A feeling is growing, among parliamentarians both national and European, that somehow the European colossus is slipping out of the grasp of the people's representatives. The frustration is most obvious among national MPs, particularly those whose national parliaments are, like Westminster, ill-adapted to scrutinise EC legislation. Even those parliaments like the Danish Folketing, which rigorously monitors EC legislation and the conduct of Danish ministers in the Council, have had their control over what goes on in Brussels undermined by majority voting. Keeping ministers on the tightest of reins, as the Folketing does, is of no avail if those ministers can be outvoted. MEPs, for their part, have an established role to play in the making of at least some Euro-decisions. But they want a bigger one. They also chafe at the contrast between the openness of the Strasbourg assembly and the secrecy with which the Council does its deals behind closed doors. This lack of democratic accountability has come to be known, in the Community of mountainous surpluses, as "the democratic deficit".

One way of filling this "deficit" – we air another later – is to increase the European Parliament's powers. This is logical and, in the long term, probably inevitable. The more that the EC emerges as a community of European people rather than one of European nations, the greater will be the need for a directly-elected parliament with real powers. As the single market develops, the question of that market's implicit ideology – between left-wing liberalism and right-wing interventionism – will become harder to leave to a vote between governments. If and when EMU emerges, it will almost certainly require a greater concentration of

European public spending in the hands of Brussels. This is because automatic fiscal redistribution of wealth makes the rigours of being the depressed part of a one-currency area politically easier to live with. A growing central budget, too, argues for a growing central parliament to control it.

Will national parliaments stand for this? No, says Mrs Thatcher. She is supported in this view from a surprising quarter, Jacques Delors. His most famous, or infamous, prediction (in 1988) that in ten years' time 80 per cent of economic policy decisions would be made at the Community level needled the British premier. But had she read his words more carefully she would have seen that the context was a warning that unless national parliaments became more involved in Community decision-making, there could be a tremendous backlash. Shared though their concerns may be: the outcomes they want in their hearts are diametrically different.

Beyond saying "a plague on all Brussels's works", there are steps which national parliaments could take here. One is simply to devote more time to discussing EC business; the British House of Commons spends less than 5 per cent of its time on Community matters, and then usually at late-night, ill-attended sessions. Another is for national MPs to make more use of their Strasbourg colleagues' knowledge of the EC. The Belgian, Dutch, German, French, Italian and Irish parliaments regularly invite their MEPs into committee discussions of EC issues, while until recently British MEPs had no greater access to Westminster than the average citizen. Michael Heseltine, the dissident Tory politician who has been beating a pro-Europe drum in an eventual bid for his party's leadership, has suggested something more radical – the creation of a second chamber to the European Parliament, composed of MPs from national parliaments. His model is the US Senate, but with the representation of individual EC states weighted by their size.

Delors likes the Heseltine plan, but has an even more radical complementary suggestion – that member states should station deputy prime ministers in Brussels to represent them full-time in the Council. Of course, for the Commission president, this would be a welcome step towards a European government in the context of the European Union he openly espouses. But it would have the side-attraction for national parliaments that their permanent national representative would not be a faceless diplomat, but a well-established politician whom they could summon to account for his conduct.

The way forward into the mire of institutional reform is anything but clear. But the degree of mutual intrusiveness already implicit in the 1992 project – let alone the farther horizons of EMU and a wider EC membership – makes further change to the Community's peculiar institutions inevitable.

5

BARRIERS AGAINST THINGS

Tax and Other Problems

"Europe without frontiers"; the phrase trips nicely off the tongue, and that is what Jacques Delors and his cabinet liked about it when they coined it in the summer of 1985. They were looking for words less grey-sounding than "the completion of Europe's internal market" and they were, as usual, looking for a way of putting a bit of top-spin on their project: they wanted to use the 1992 campaign to help along the more idealistic notion of a "citizens' Europe" and, with it, European Union.

Ever since the White Paper on the internal market was presented in June 1985 the Commission has remained adamant that frontiers are the most potent symbols of the EC's divisions, and insistent that if frontier posts remain for any good reason at all they will be used, willy-nilly, as a means for carrying out less justifiable checks. One of the Commission's senior economists, Michael Emerson, put it succinctly: "the removal of frontier posts would be the proof that governments were disarming themselves in the shaping of intra-European trade".

In fact, they would be disarming themselves more seriously than that. Frontiers do not mark just the physical limits of countries, where commerce becomes trade; they mark the boundaries between different jurisdictions, and they are often the least intrusive way of containing and sustaining those jurisdictions. Eliminating frontiers is tantamount to stating that jurisdictions will be merged, and probably at the most permissive level. For example, West Germany and the Netherlands have a different approach to drugs. Laws against soft drugs are enforced loosely in the Netherlands, toughly in West Germany. Non-existent frontiers mean flows of soft drugs into Germany.

Of course, the German toughness could be exercised within its frontiers – by making possession illegal, snooping a lot and prosecuting rigorously. But what, in that case, would be gained by removing frontiers? The enforcement of the ban would then require internal checks just as disruptive to commerce as the ones that previously took place at the border, and probably much less efficient. In the end, it is the differences in jurisdictions which divide markets, not the means of enforcing them. Just as the principle of "mutual recognition" of rules is eroding the ability of EC governments to make their own commercial laws, so the notion of "Europe without frontiers" is equally insidious. It is a way of exerting pressure for the equalising of laws without actually saying so. That is why getting European governments to agree to worthy-sounding ends rather than daunting means has proved such a clever tactic.

So what is going to happen at European frontiers in the 1990s? This chapter looks at the flows of goods and services, which are of direct relevance to a common market. The following chapter looks at the flows of people, which are consistent with a "citizens' Europe" and which will become more economically vital as and when the Community moves towards economic and monetary union. For convenience, checks for illegal goods such as guns or drugs or explosives are covered in the next chapter.

Wherefore those Booms?

European customs controls carry out six commerce-distorting functions, all of which will have to be abolished or replaced if the frontiers in Europe's great market are to open. Frontier checks make Europe's current system of value-added tax workable. They control flows of farm products to allow different price levels for the same products to exist across the Community – the Common Agricultural Policy is not "common". They check plants and animals to preserve different health standards in different countries and to keep parts of Europe free of certain diseases. They check trucks for road transport licences – the right to carry cargo in Europe has been strictly controlled for years. They collect the trade statistics of the member countries. They protect the trade regimes that individual countries may have with states beyond the EC: for example, Italy's virtual exclusion of Japanese cars. Their seventh job has all but disappeared: the use of frontier controls to stop wealth flowing out of nations which still do not dare to allow their citizens to invest their money where they want.

Intra-Community trade amounts to 15 per cent of the EC's GDP, or rather more than half of the total trade that the Community's individual members do. The Commission, in its heavy-weight Cecchini study of the cost of Europe's trade barriers, found that frontier formalities were ranked third, behind technical standards and red-tape within countries, among the eight obstacles to trade within the Community that industrialists perceived (see table below). It estimated that the cost of undergoing border checks amounted to almost 2 per cent of intra-Community trade, but found that the cost was much higher than that for small companies. It cited the example of two truck trips of 750 miles (1,200 km). The first, wholly inside Britain, took 36 hours. The second, from London to Milan, took 58 hours, excluding the time it took to cross the Channel. In other words, frontier delays made an Italian delivery more than 50 per cent more expensive than a British one.

To the free-market faithful it is intuitively clear that the impact of frontier controls on the European economy is greater than such spare figures suggest. The mere existence of frontier officials, frontier documents, travellers' allowances and the like inhibits the shopping-around-on-whim in different countries that puts European products and prices into true competition. It frustrates a huge potential trade in, say, second-hand industrial equipment: imagine the paperwork on a job-lot of cement mixers that a British construction company hears is on sale in

Ranking of market barriers by business*

Total industry	B	DK	F	FRG	GR	IRL	I	L	NL	P	S	UK	EC 12
National standards and regulations	2	1	1	1	7	2	4	2	3	4	6	1	2
Government procurement	6	8	7/8	8	8	7	2	8	7	3	8	4	8
Administrative barriers	1	2	2	2	1	1	1	1	1	1	1	2	1
Physical frontier delays and costs	3	3	4	4	3	3	3	3	2	2	2	3	3
Differences in VAT	8	7	3	5/6	4/5	6	7	7	8	8	7	8	6/7
Regulations of freight transport	5	4/5	5	5/6	4/5	4	8	5	4	5	3	5	6/7
Restrictions in capital market	4	6	7/8	7	2	5	5	4	6	6	5	7	5
Community law	7	4/5	6	3	6	8	6	6	5	7	4	6	4

*This table is compiled from answers given by 11,000 businessmen to the question "How important do you consider this barrier to be removed?" Range of ranks: 1 (most important) to 8 (least important).
Source: European Commission

the Netherlands. They are needed on site tomorrow? Forget them. It hinders something that has rocketed many small American companies to greatness: the ability to deliver new products by mail-order across a great continent without tax complications and without having to set up physically in different states.

Tax Riddles

Customs posts are above all a matter of tax. There is no issue like tax to show how the good intentions and simple vision of the 1992 project have run into the sands of sovereignty. Tax is, after all, the main civilian perquisite of sovereignty, the matter over which parliaments have justified their existence and nations their right to independence. Despite the thirty-year evolution of the Common Market, it has been run until now in a way that has allowed the member governments to remain broadly unhindered in choosing whether to tax people's income or their spending, and in deciding where for the good of society to make life artificially cheap or artificially expensive.

A customs-post-free internal market would put an end to much of that. Border controls have insulated the tax regime on goods and services – the indirect taxes – in one country from the regimes of its European neighbours. If there were to be a Europe without customs halls, EC's governments would have to live with heavy diversions of revenue and distortions of businesses in areas near frontiers – unless, one way or another, they move their rates of indirect tax close enough for such tax-dodging to become uninteresting. The experience of the United States shows that contiguous states can maintain differences in sales taxes of up to about five percentage points without tax leakage becoming unbearable. With customs-free frontiers, Europe would, either by allowing competition between regimes to do its painful work, or by negotiations in advance, have to accept a similar order of tax-sameness if it were to get rid of its tax frontiers.

Of all the problems of creating an open market, the tax issue was the one on which the 1985 White Paper lavished the most attention. In fact the Commission's approach here departed from the general 1992 tactic of getting members committed to a simple-sounding goal, chivvying them towards it, and letting them cope with the consequences later. Rather than opt for a fiscal version of "mutual recognition" – you charge your tax; I'll charge my tax; and we'll see how we manage – the Commission went straight for pre-emptive harmonisation. Why?

Tax revenues as % of GDP

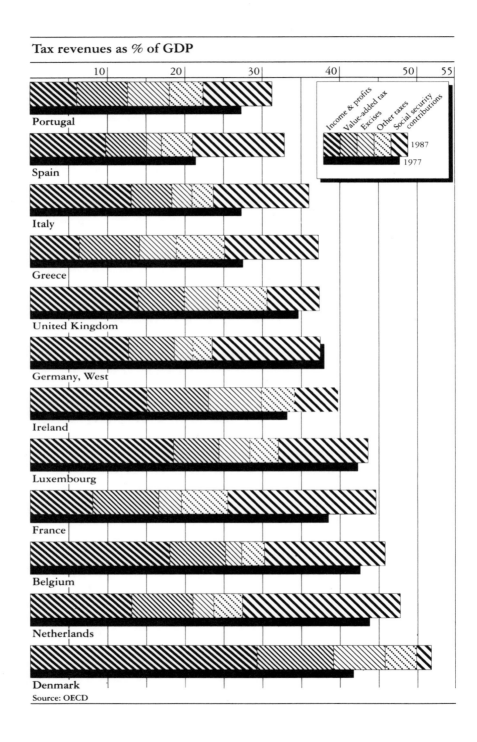

Source: OECD

Undoubtedly there were those within the Commission who saw direct influence over tax rates as a powerful lever in the creation of European federalism. This was not a chance to grasp at power that could be missed. There were others in whom the old Euro-habit of harmonisation for harmonisation's sake lingered on. But Lord Cockfield did not see things that way. He was a former, senior British tax official, so this was a field in which he could see with particular clarity beyond the frontier-free goal to the practical consequences. His detailed tax-blueprint in the White Paper was the product of a remorseless logic of the sort that makes politicians squirm and seethe. He could see what fiscal pressures governments would be under when the border booms went and he was determined to create a system that would honour the goal of a single market and protect politicians from themselves.

He feared, for a start, that far from allowing market forces to determine what tax differences could be sustained as the British government urged, high-taxing countries with land frontiers like Denmark, Ireland or even France would not lift their barriers to let those forces do their work. EC citizens already have an allowance of 350 ecus-worth (roughly $400) of tax-paid goods that they can take across frontiers without tax paperwork and payments. This amount alone prompted Ireland and Denmark illegally (under European law) to restrict their allowances to "genuine" travellers: that is those travelling outside their country for more than some arbitrary length of time, or those lugging suitcases but not washing-machines. The amount of tax lost was already more than these two governments were willing to shrug off. It thus seemed wishful thinking to rely on them removing their customs barriers when those allowances become infinite.

Render Unto Cockfield

So Lord Cockfield proposed a practical form of harmonisation. He started with the American example of the spread of tax rates that seemed sustainable. Then he tried to fit this spread, as best he could, around the scatter-shot pattern of European tax rates. This was a challenge. As the table on page 60 shows, the standard rates of value-added tax (VAT) range from 22 per cent in Denmark and 20 per cent in the Netherlands down to 12 per cent in Spain and Luxembourg. The Italians charge a hefty 38 per cent on consumer gadgetry: the Netherlands and Britain do not have a luxury rate at all. Britain does not charge any tax on a range of things including books, food and children's clothes. (These

Rates of VAT* (%)

	Low rate	Standard rate	High rate
Belgium	1 and 6	19	25 and 33
Denmark	None	22	None
France	2.1, 4, 5.5 and 7	18.6	28
Germany, West	7	14	None
Greece	6	18	36
Ireland	2.4	10	25
Italy	2 and 9	18	38
Luxembourg	3 and 6	12	None
Netherlands	6	20	None
Portugal	8	16	30
Spain	6	12	33
United Kingdom	0	15	None
Commission proposal	4 to 9	14 to 20	None

*April 1st 1989
Source: European Commission

exceptions were the political concessions needed to get the VAT system accepted in Britain by Westminster.) Denmark taxes food at 22 per cent.

The Commission's answer was to propose two VAT brackets – a normal rate of tax stretching between 14 per cent and 20 per cent and a reduced rate of between 4 per cent and 9 per cent that could apply to a list of basic goods and services. Countries would choose their rates within those brackets, and hope to sustain them despite open frontiers.

Alas, the Commission had to deal with more than just tax rates. The quest for a frontier-free tax system involves changes in the way the VAT on traded goods is levied. VAT is an odd hybrid: it is a consumption tax levied by countries bit by bit as value is added to a product en route to its final consumer. The way it is levied (each stage collects and owes full VAT on its sales but can deduct the VAT it paid on its inputs), has two great advantages over the normal levying of sales taxes. It is largely self-policing. And it does not require any arbitrary definition of final consumption – whoever keeps a product finds himself automatically having paid the full tax on it.

Problem: what happens if goods move outside a country in the course of their evolution? Answer: countries by common consent demand no VAT on export sales. They refund to the exporter the VAT it paid on the ingredients of those exports. Meanwhile an importing country levies full VAT at the border on the import price and then tops this up with more VAT when the imported item is finally sold to the consumer. So, border posts are vital both for tax-levying by the importing country, and for tax-policing by the exporting country. They make sure that the full VAT, at the local rate, accrues to the country of final consumption. They make sure that zero-rated goods-for-export really do leave the country.

This was a real puzzle for Lord Cockfield and his team. They wanted to make the European market equivalent to the market in one country – to remove the notion that a sale from Britain to France was an export; but they had to get the right tax to the country of final consumption. They had to keep the system fraud-proof; but they also had to make it unobtrusive, otherwise what was the point of getting rid of frontier controls? The Commission thought up, and then refined, an intellectually elegant answer. VAT would be collected just as though EC goods were being traded within one country. Export fraud would be eliminated by VAT's self-policing qualities. The revenues would then be put into the hands of the country of final consumption by a clearing system that would use net trade flows to see which country owed what to whom. The wheeze, admittedly complicated as first proposed, was greeted with whistling and upward-rolling eyes in every exchequer in the Community.

But before coming to the denouement, there is one remaining piece in the tax puzzle – the question of excise duties on things like cigarettes, alcohol and fuel. The problem here was even more intractable. The differences in duty across the EC are very large (see table below) and are compounded by VAT. A litre of pure alcohol in Britain would carry 25

Excise duty rates*

	Pure Alcohol (ecus per litre)	Wine (ecus per litre)	Beer (ecus per litre)	Petrol (ecus per litre)	Cigarettes (ecus per 1,000)
Belgium	12.52	0.33	0.10	0.261	2.5
Denmark	34.99	1.57	0.56	0.473	77.5
France	11.49	0.03	0.03	0.369	1.3
Germany, West	11.74	0.20	0.07	0.256	27.3
Greece	0.48	0.00	0.10	0.349	0.6
Ireland	27.22	2.79	0.82	0.362	48.9
Italy	2.30	0.00	0.17	0.557	1.8
Luxembourg	8.42	0.13	0.05	0.209	1.7
Netherlands	12.98	0.33	0.20	0.340	26.0
Portugal	2.48	0.00	0.09	0.352	2.2
Spain	3.09	0.00	0.03	0.254	0.7
United Kingdom	24.83	1.54	0.49	0.271	42.8
Commission proposal	12.71	0.17	0.17	0.34	19.5

*April 1st 1987
Source: European Commission

ecus duty compared with 11.5 ecus in France and 0.5 ecus in Greece. What is more, excise-bearing goods tend to be eminently smugglable. The Commission decided, rashly, that the only way forwards was to harmonise the taxes completely at one EC level for each product. Tell that to the British chancellor at one end of the Community, or to the ouzo-sipping Greek at the other.

Finance ministers had a depressing first three years discussing these proposals. They formed committee after committee to study them (ie, make them go away for a time), but no committee could find any elegant escape from what was intuitively plain – the open market was going to be fiscally painful in different ways for different members. The British feared for their tax sovereignty and for the politically potent symbol of its zero VAT-rates on food, books and baby clothes. The Danes, the tax junkies of the Community (see chart on page 58), faced the prospect of losing 6 per cent of GDP's worth of tax: their VAT rate is 8 per cent higher than neighbouring West Germany's. France was staring at a single-market-imposed reshaping of its fiscal policy and knew it. The income tax system in France is loophole-ridden and a political football: millions of voters don't pay the tax and will vote only for those who promise that they will continue not to. France has feared for its savings and wealth taxes once exchange controls are lifted (see Chapter 8). The French government is used to spending money. It cannot print this money any longer because the franc has accepted the German discipline of the European Monetary System. Revenues from VAT are its only dependable source of spendable cash.

Thus Lord Cockfield found himself under fire from all sides. The French insisted on very tight tax bands. The British, with low taxes and from behind a stretch of sea that would do its old duty of keeping continental forces at bay, demanded no bands at all: let there be open competition between tax systems, they said, except, of course, in the matter of excise where British rates were high "for health reasons" and must therefore be protected. As for the Commission's clearing-house proposals, they were never popular because they meant that national tax-collectors would no longer be wholly in charge of their own revenue collection. The debate was made all the more sterile because Lord Cockfield had a particularly scathing way with the finance ministers' inconsistencies. Relations between him and the British chancellor of the exchequer, Nigel Lawson, at gatherings of finance ministers became damagingly tense.

Dropping the Draftsman

By the end of the first Delors Commission in December 1988, little had been achieved. But then Mrs Thatcher removed the over-zealous Cockfield as British commissioner in Brussels, and Jacques Delors gave the tax portfolio to a pragmatic French lady, Christiane Scrivener. The atmosphere improved at once. The British became less offhand about the problem, and readier to honour the commitment to remove fiscal controls at frontiers. They hinted that minimum rates for tax might be needed to stop competition driving all rates down to zero. The French became less insistent about tight tax bands. The Commission realised that harmonising excise duties was a non-starter: the answer here was an "anti-bootlegging regime" of tax stamps to stop commercial sale of liquor at the wrong tax rates.

The main remaining rift was over the system. The Commission wanted very badly to see the end of zero-rating on intra-Community "exports" with the negation of a single market that this implied. It was also convinced that its system was the least intrusive and the least fraud-prone. But the governments were united in having none of this. They proposed continued zero-rating with the use of bureaucratic checks, rather than frontier ones, to beat the fraudsters and to gather trade statistics. Mrs Scrivener was instructed by Jacques Delors to hold out against this proposal. But she had no allies in the Council of finance ministers and the French wanted to wrap up the matter during their presidency of the Council in the second half of 1989. So in the autumn of that year the Council agreed to continue with zero-rating for a "limited" transition period of indefinite length.

Lots of details remain to be worked out. But the following elements are now visible for fiscal frontiers after 1992, though still far from certain:

● Organisations registered for VAT, usually companies, will pay home VAT on their purchases from abroad. The VAT will be collected from them as a result of their invoicing, rather than when the goods cross frontiers. They will still pay home VAT even if they physically go and buy something abroad and bring it home, or get a subsidiary abroad to buy it for them. In effect, there will be no tax-paid border allowances for businesses, though how this will be policed without frontier checks has yet to be worked out.

● The system of zero-rating exports within the Community will remain. Policing against phony zero-rating (ie, on goods that never leave the country) will rely on comparative spot-checking of invoices between, say, the VAT authorities of France and those of Britain. It remains uncertain what amount of international paperwork this will involve, and whether exports/imports will involve a discouraging extra administrative burden for companies. The governments bravely say it won't.

● There will be no limits on the quantity of VAT-paid goods carried across frontiers by private travellers. Ireland and Denmark will be pushing for exceptions in particular cases. There may therefore be some officially sanctioned laggards here.

● Tax rates will be brought either within the bands originally laid down by the Commission (14–20 per cent and 4–9 per cent), or held above agreed minimums. Existing zero rates will be allowed – but no new ones – providing that they do not lead to marked distortions of trade. In other words, both national governments and the Commission appear to have relaxed on the matter of VAT rates.

● There will be a special regime for mail-order business. This will probably involve the vendor selling via a representative in each country who will be VAT-registered and thus collect VAT at the local rate. The details have not yet been worked out, but it is hard to see direct selling by small enterprises thriving unless an imaginative way of collecting tax in the buyer's country is worked out. There will also be a special regime for the purchase of registered vehicles.

● Some minimum excise duties will be set by the Commission to reduce the present range of duties a little. There will be much larger limits to the amount of excise-bearing goods that individuals can take across frontiers provided they are not for resale. Policing within countries will be stepped up to guard against commercial fraud, and will probably be reinforced by a system of tax stamps or seals required in each country to make goods legally sellable.

● All of this will be a "temporary" regime pending a "desirable" move to one where zero-rating is scrapped and VAT is collected as though the EC was one country.

All in all, the story is a nice demonstration of the point made at the start of this chapter: that it is not frontiers that divide markets but the different regimes that they protect. Governments are here sticking to the letter of the 1992 project, but not its spirit. They are removing border controls by seeking substitutes for them, not by removing the underlying need for them. It is hard to call a single market "single" with a straight face when sales that cross intra-European frontiers have a special tax-regime applied to them, or to imagine a single market in which firms still cannot send things to non-VAT-registered customers without tax complications. Mrs Scrivener may have improved the atmosphere of the tax talks, but it was by letting the national governments wriggle off their own hook.

Nevertheless, the deal is better than nothing. Lorries will not need to stop at frontiers for tax checks after 1992. Tax-policing will become retroactive, rather than trade-delaying. The presumption that people can buy anything anywhere in Europe at the local tax-rate will become very strong. This will tend to drive governments to align their tax rates more closely, particularly on the continent. The crucial unknowns remain the amount of extra paperwork that exports/imports will involve, and the extent to which pan-European direct-selling will remain suffocated by tax difficulties.

One Out of Six

So much for tax. It is only the first, but much the most important, of the six trade-hindering roles played by frontiers. All the hard work on eliminating that role will be for nothing if the others remain.

The gathering of trade statistics will not be a frontier-affair after 1992: the statistics will be compiled from the same information that will be used to police the tax system. Some Europhiles dream of the day when trade statistics between European countries are not deemed necessary, any more than they now are between England and Scotland. That day will not dawn until the Community is deeply into economic and monetary union. Until it gets there the tax system will provide the numbers.

The problem of the foreign-trade regimes of individual countries is tougher. The goal of a customs-free Europe does not sit well with Article 115 of the Treaty of Rome, under which a member state with a long-standing quota on imports from outside the EC can prevent them sneaking in via another Community country. This Article underpins a number of trade blockages that are inconsistent with project 1992, though not necessarily with GATT. There are some 700 different national quantitative restrictions (QRs), many of them allowed under Article 115.

The future of Europe's external-trade regime is discussed more fully later (see Chapter 15), but the presumption, as far as the EC's internal frontiers are concerned, is that the Commission will end Article 115-protection for QRs in future and that the vast majority of them will have to be scrapped. The exceptions most often cited are shoes, textiles, cars, televisions, bananas and sheep-meat. These remaining areas of national sensitivity may be protected, at least for a while after 1992, either by EC-wide import restraint (textiles and, perhaps, cars) or by internal controls within member countries. The assumption is that they will prove hard to sustain.

Agriculture creates two needs for frontiers which look still harder to remove. The official support-prices of farm products under the Common Agricultural Policy vary from country to country, and profitable arbitrage between them is stopped by a system of levies and rebates imposed at frontiers. These "monetary compensatory amounts" are supposed to be obsolete by 1993. Yet governments have barely started thinking about doing away with them. The same is true of health checks for diseased plants and animals where the required standardisation of rules accounted, in September 1989, for 28 of the 43 directives in the White Paper which the Commission had not yet been able to draft. The way the Common Agricultural Policy and the single market affect each other is dealt with in greater detail in Chapter 9.

Finally, and on a more hopeful note, there are currently two types of frontier checks on lorries. The first, to see whether a lorry is allowed under the protectionist transport quota system to carry freight in the country it is entering, should be obsolete by 1993. Transport quotas will be lifted completely, at least for international transport. The second type of check is for the lorry's safety under rules that are more draconian in some countries than in others. These checks will probably be allowed to continue, provided that they are carried out selectively and not as a matter-of-course.

A Bounce that Worked

Adding all those elements together, it seems that governments now regard their commitment to remove frontier checks used for what one might term "economic insulation" as unduckable. But they will distinguish between these sorts of checks and the ones on people and criminal activities dealt with in the next chapter. These will remain. The functions carried out at frontiers will not necessarily evaporate, but those that remain will be adapted so as not to be frontier-dependent.

A cynic might say that nothing will thereby be achieved except bureaucratic unwieldiness. This would be too harsh. Certainly, the envisaged tax regime creates a grudging version of what most people would understand by a single market. Yet the removal of frontier controls will make the national regimes that divide up the European market harder to enforce. These national regimes will therefore be more likely to drift towards European norms proposed by the Commission and agreed by the Council. The beguiling goal of "Europe without frontiers" will have beguiled, even if it remains beyond reach. Untouchable national habits will have been touched.

6

BARRIERS AGAINST PEOPLE

The Wilder Shores of 1992

For many of Europe's 320 million citizens, project 1992 will fall flatter than a failed soufflé if it does not make it easier for them to travel around the Community of twelve countries. They see European unity much as Ernest Bevin, the post-war British Labour foreign secretary, did in 1951 when he said he hoped one day to be able to buy a ticket at London's Victoria Station and go anywhere he pleased in Europe without further ado.

This vision is easy to grasp and to proclaim, but requires a vast political undertaking. The questions of crime and of immigration control that it raises touch the core of sovereignty for all member states, and each such question tends to beg a bigger one. Does a common policy on immigration require a common policy on visas for citizens from a given country outside the Community? And does a common visa policy imply a common foreign policy towards that country? Would policing of borderless Europe require cross-border operations by police forces of the Twelve? And would that therefore mean harmonisation of national criminal law and its enforcement? Is this, along with Helmut Kohl's suggestion of a European FBI, conceivable without a true European government? Would strengthening the Community's external frontiers mean an end to Western Europe's traditional role as a haven for refugees?

Equal Concern, Differing Reactions

These questions exercise all EC countries; but they react with varying degrees of anxiety. Countries separated from the EC's continental heartland – Britain, Ireland, Greece and to a great extent Denmark – want to retain the security of their relatively self-contained territories. For Margaret Thatcher, it is "a matter of plain common sense that we cannot totally abolish frontier controls if we are to protect our people". Her common sense tells her to continue to exploit a sea barrier that has shaped Britain's history. Countries without such natural borders feel less strongly about dropping systematic checks on people coming in from other EC countries.

In reality, it is not an all-or-nothing argument between these two groups of EC members. In signing the Single Act they all were pledged to create an internal market without internal frontiers so that people, as well as goods, services and capital could circulate freely. To achieve such free travel they also promised to help each other deal with immigration from outside the Community, terrorism, drug trafficking and illicit trading in works of art and antiques. But they entered a clear caveat that nothing in the Single Act would affect any member state's right to deal with these problems as it sees fit. Against this legal background the European Commission, in its role as guarantor of the Treaty of Rome, insists that the Single Act calls for total removal (not just reduction) of internal border controls. But the Commission concedes that the issues involved in removing them lie largely outside the traditional sphere of the Community as laid down in the Rome Treaty and are thus for member states themselves to sort out.

Trevi and other groups

The national governments have not been idle. Action is being discussed at three levels. In 1986 the Twelve set up a working group on immigration with the task of "easing and ultimately abolishing" the checking of people at internal EC borders; though the initiator of this group, the British government, insists that this freedom of movement is intended to benefit only EC citizens. The Trevi Group of EC interior ministers, set up in 1975 to swap information on, and join forces against, international crime, drug trafficking and terrorism, has been far more active in the late 1980s than it was in the first ten years of its existence. Within the wider Pompidou Group that brings together interior ministers of the twenty-three member states of the Council of Europe, the Twelve have discussed ways of getting at the money-laundering activities of drug dealers. But progress has been slow, for reasons as much to do with the constraints on and the characters of institutional players as the nature of the game. One problem is that the Commission cannot perform its normal role of chivvying governments along with proposals to the Council of Ministers and exhortations to the European Parliament.

It is allowed to be present at most of these discussions only as an observer and, in the case of the Trevi Group, is deliberately excluded. More important, the tempo of negotiation is set by security and immigration professionals from interior ministries, people who are not inclined to rush their work in order to meet a political deadline like 1992.

The Schengen Five

A catalyst to speedier progress has been the Schengen Agreement. In June 1985 five countries – France, West Germany and the three Benelux nations – set themselves a tight timetable. Meeting in the Luxembourg village of Schengen, they decided to abolish border controls between themselves by the beginning of 1990. The Schengen Agreement predated the Single European Act, stemming from a series of events in 1984 which included protests by lorry drivers at frontier delays, desultory discussions in the EC Council of Ministers about easing border crossings and a bilateral pact signed at Saarbrücken between France and West Germany to reduce formalities on their common border. Within months, the Benelux countries were clamouring for inclusion in this arrangement, given their generally happy experience with a common travel area since the early 1970s, and given the importance to them of the French and German markets. The Saarbrücken Two became the Schengen Five in June 1985.

Their first stab at freer travel was largely symbolic. For instance, cars crossing Schengenland's internal borders were henceforth to be subjected only to random checks, provided they displayed a green disc confirming that all passengers were EC nationals obeying duty-free goods and currency rules. In practice, few motorists travelling through Schengenland sport these discs because, perversely, most feel that a disc tends to attract the unwelcome attention of immigration and customs officers.

But Schengen's envisaged second stage is very far-reaching indeed. The Five have been working on a convention that will allow free movement of all people (including non-EC citizens) between the five countries, set up a common visa policy, harmonise rules for extraditing suspected criminals and penalties for carrying illegal drugs and guns, and establish rules for cross-border operations and surveillance by the police forces of the Five. Schengen's finest would all be linked by a central computerised data bank.

Even if the Schengen Five now reach speedy agreement on all this in

1990, they are unlikely to have their free-travel area ready before 1992. They came close to agreement in December 1989. The day before ministers of the Five were supposed to gather in Schengen to sign the convention, Chancellor Helmut Kohl asked for more time to consider the implications of his country's newly-opened border with the other Germany. The practical problem raised for Schengen by the historic puncturing of the Berlin Wall is the need to combine free travel by East German citizens to West Germany (which Bonn insists on, and its Schengen partners accept) with screening of non-East Germans travelling into Schengenland through East Germany.

In truth, there were other problems too. Only Belgium and Luxembourg were ready to sign the convention on immigration and police cooperation before Christmas 1989. The Dutch government was fussing about inadequate intra-Schengen cooperation against tax evasion (a complaint directed at Luxembourg's bank secrecy), and the Dutch parliament about protecting data from the planned Schengen computerised crime-bank. France, too, in a temporary scare about Arab terrorism, suddenly asked for tighter safeguards allowing suspension of Schengen's free-travel arrangements in certain circumstances.

Any convention will have to be set before the five national parliaments, which inevitably will want to scrutinise closely the details of the pact. In addition, the Schengen Information System, a key element in policing the new rules, will take one or two years to set up once the Five have decided which country will house its central computer.

If the Five do finally succeed, there is an outside chance that the Twelve will one day follow suit. If they fail, the wider enterprise of Europe without frontiers is almost certainly doomed. The Schengen Five have all the advantages of long-standing cooperation: three of them are in the Benelux customs union, and all of them are founder members of the EC. They all have similar legal systems and well-developed police cooperation, and form a compact geographic whole. Without this common heritage, the Twelve will find it much harder to resolve the issues that follow.

Border Definitions

The more the controls at the Community's external frontiers can be tightened and made consistent, the freer travel within the Community can be. All EC member states accept this logic. But there is no agreed distinction between what is an "external" frontier and what is an "internal" one. Clearly land borders between France and Germany, say, or Belgium and the Netherlands are internal ones. But what about airports, with transit facilities for people arriving from outside the Community who do not need to clear customs and immigration controls before catching a connecting flight to another EC state?

This problem worried the Dutch in the Schengen talks. Schipol airport outside Amsterdam handles a lot of transit traffic – people arriving from outside the EC and going straight on to an EC country other than Holland. Making everyone flying into Schipol from outside the Community go through Dutch customs and immigration at the airport would make Schipol much less attractive to the weary transit passenger.

This is just what the Dutch found their Schengen partners insisting upon: that passengers, arriving at Schipol from beyond the Community, should be regarded as crossing an "external" EC frontier, and vetted accordingly, even if they were not legally stepping onto Dutch soil. The likely upshot is a distinction between transit passengers who get back on the same plane and who will not undergo frontier formalities until reaching their final EC destination, and passengers who change planes and who will have to clear customs and immigration controls on arrival at their first EC landing point.

The problem is less acute for the other Schengen countries, because none have airports for which flights outside Europe represent a large share of their activity. But it would be a real headache for Britain because of the millions of North Americans who fly to continental Europe via Heathrow and Gatwick.

Sea traffic is less closely monitored than air traffic, and harder to control because the Community has very long coastlines conducive to the smuggling of people and goods; a boat from Naples to London can nip undetected into all manner of coves en route, picking up and dropping illegal immigrants at dead of night, which an aircraft on the same journey cannot.

So the Commission thinks that all ports should be regarded as "external" frontiers, except where a regular ferry service is plying an intra-EC route. Cross-channel ferries would thus be exempted; but the British government doesn't want them exempted, thank you. It is determined to keep patrolling all its frontiers. Indeed it even argues that the rail tunnel being built under the Channel between England and France will still constitute a sea, not a land, frontier-crossing. So Chunnel passengers will have to clear customs and immigration controls just like those on the ferries above them, even though they could not conceivably have come from anywhere but France.

The importance of this almost theological argument over the differences between "external" and "internal" borders becomes clearer when you realise that it is impossible to check non-EC nationals without also checking EC nationals. Some checks must be made on the latter to distinguish them from the former. EC states agree with the logic of this, but draw opposite conclusions. The Schengen Five do not propose to impose checks on anyone within Schengenland, while the British government intends to keep checking EC and non-EC citizen alike at all its borders.

Defining the Undesirables

If and when the Community ever decides where its external border really lies – an increasingly distant day given the recent pace of change in Eastern Europe – it will be possible to consider how to strengthen that frontier. Talk of stronger external border controls has, not surprisingly, stirred fears that the Community will harden its attitude to refugees and asylum-seekers and become a "fortress Europe" against people. This might happen, but the EC's real problem lies not in an argument about toughness, but in absence of mutual trust. The Twelve must set up reliable and uniform external checks and trust each other to enforce them efficiently, for in a free-travel zone each state's defence against crime or illegal immigration will only be as good as the controls operated by the other eleven. This is a tall order: the fears of EC member states are different and their historic links with the rest of the world incompatible.

The views of the Twelve about who should be allowed to enter the Community, and who should not, are just as varied. But the need for as common a Community policy as possible on visitors' visas is accepted by all, even by the British, who want to simplify, though not abolish, their frontier checks.

So the Twelve have set out to agree upon a list of third countries whose citizens will be required to get visas before travelling to the Community. This is what the Benelux countries did in the early 1970s. But the task of the Schengen Five, and of the Twelve, was considerably complicated in 1986. In reaction to a rash of street bombings in Paris, France decided to impose visa requirements on visitors from every country, with the exception of its EC partners and Switzerland. It has since scaled down this visa list, removing the requirement for citizens of the USA and most of its other European partners in the Council of Europe to have visas. But the scare has still left France with a much longer list than more liberal states like Denmark and Britain. However, as a result of protracted negotiations, the Community Twelve are nearing agreement on a common "negative" list of some 60–70 countries on which visa requirements will be imposed by all. If this is finally agreed, it will force tougher action from countries such as Britain, which has recently imposed visas on visiting Turks, and Spain, which may come under pressure to do the same for a few Latin American countries.

The negative list would seem to require a relaxation of French policy. The French have signalled a possible compromise: they would retain visa requirements for some countries, over and above the Community-agreed negative list, but allow the non-EC nationals in question to get the visas from other EC states before crossing into France. If they were picked up in France without the required visa they would be liable to expulsion.

It is a sad fact for many non-EC nationals that a Community agreement on visas might require them to get more visas to go to European countries than they need now. This is the prospect for nationals of North African countries, Yugoslavia and Turkey – traditional sources of emigration to the EC – and of Eastern Europe. It will be ironic, not to say politically insensitive, if Western Europe brings down its shutters just as the East begins to heed the West's long-standing demands to let its peoples go. West Germany is starting to press for visa requirements to be dropped for visitors from Hungary. This is being resisted by other EC states. If the 1992 project puts the dampers on Bonn's newly-rediscovered ties with Eastern Europe, it will also force Denmark to break away from a long-established passport union and free-travel zone with its fellow Scandinavian countries. The simple idea of removing travel restrictions begs an uncomfortable lot of emotional questions.

The debate over visa policy is quite separate from the question of right of residence. Imposing visa requirements on citizens from certain countries is an extra check on visitors; it does not confer on them even an implicit right to settle or work. Nor has there been any discussion between the Twelve over the granting of nationality. It remains for individual states to decide to whom to give their passports. Thus, the British decision to give some Hong Kong citizens full passport and residence rights in the UK is accepted by its partners, just as Bonn's right to offer its passports to all East Germans goes unquestioned. Possession of an EC country passport gives its holder a right to travel and work anywhere in the other eleven Community countries, but not (so far) an unqualified right to live in them indefinitely.

However, there is the related issue of granting political refugees asylum. The criteria under which asylum is granted does not, strictly speaking, need to be re-examined as a result of 1992. They are set out in various United Nations conventions to which all EC states subscribe. But some member states, notably Denmark, have been more liberal than others in applying these criteria. In addition, an increasing number of refugees are nowadays fleeing for "economic" reasons and simply seeking a better life in Western Europe, where wealthy states such as West Germany have particular appeal. As a result, refugees have begun to arrive in the Community and to shop around among the member states for a home. The concern of EC governments has been that the 1992 project will make such "asylum-shopping" easier. Therefore – and this is one of the few agreements on people-frontiers so far reached – the Twelve have agreed on a complicated set of rules to decide which state should be responsible for examining the applications of individuals seeking asylum. The general principle, though with many exceptions, is that the onus will fall on the EC state that first admits the asylum-seeker into the Community. Thus, a Sri Lankan whose first Community port of call is Rome, but who does not file his request for asylum until he reaches Copenhagen, would be sent back to Rome.

Policing the Twelve

It would be wonderfully convenient if the threat of international crime, terrorism and drug trafficking were entirely external to the Community, and all the Twelve had to do to sleep as soundly as the Swiss was erect a sound perimeter fence. But criminals come in all disguises, some even carrying the new Community passports. There is thus much concern that the frontier-free internal market will give Euro-mobsters and racketeers a wider playground.

Few of today's international criminals and terrorists are in fact caught at frontiers. Most arrests of such are made away from borders and on the basis of intelligence and tip-offs. It is said, for instance, that the nearest that Carlos, the notorious international terrorist of the 1970s, came to getting caught was when he aroused suspicion when on a shopping binge at Harrods. Nevertheless, police say that borders are vital to them – the only place where an identity check and car-search can be carried out without evidence of crime being required. They claim it would be a significant loss if, as one senior British policeman has put it, they could no longer "monitor the progress of suspects through these points, perhaps at a time before there is sufficient evidence to effect an arrest but where the whereabouts of the individual are very important to the inquiry".

The police do not and cannot prove the intelligence value they place on border checks. Drugs are another matter. Customs officers, particularly in Britain, vaunt their success in spotting the large consignments of illegal drugs at borderpoints, before they are broken up for distribution inland. The British Customs and Excise says that between one-quarter and one-third of illegal drugs seized in Britain come from, or via, another EC state – with South American cocaine coming in via Spain and the Netherlands, cannabis crossing the Community from North Africa, and heroin arriving overland from Iran.

At the same time, the Community's internal frontiers also hinder crime detection within the Twelve. Europe's police forces face increasingly "international" policing problems, be they drug-smuggling, terrorism, hooliganism at international soccer matches, or even demonstrations; one example of the latter occurred during recent protests in Belgium caused by that country's endemic language problem when the demonstrators slipped across the Dutch border to evade Belgian police. Interpol, the Paris-based police organisation which operates worldwide, is too bureaucratic and is held, by Sir Peter Imbert, London's chief of police, to be no substitute for "direct personal contacts" between EC police forces. Such contacts exist in regional organisations linking, for instance, the German, Dutch and Belgian police, or in the Cross-Channel Conference between the British police and their nearest counterparts on mainland Europe. But these contacts may need to be widened and deepened with project 1992. If, for instance, the Schengen Five set up their computer data bank, the British police will certainly hope to make use of this massive stock of information.

The politicians, too, are beginning to work together. The Trevi Group of interior ministers pledged in 1986 to speed up exchanges of information on terrorist activities, agreed in 1987 to streamline their extradition procedures, and undertook in 1988 to try to get at the bank accounts financing international crime. Such cooperation was dealt a well-publicised blow in 1988 when Belgium refused a British request to extradite a suspected IRA activist, Father Patrick Ryan, and sent him in hurried secrecy to Ireland instead. But, generally, the Community partnership-against-crime is developing well.

What has helped make this possible is the way in which the Twelve have increasingly aligned their foreign policies, particularly towards some countries that have proved breeding grounds for terrorist or anti-Western villains. Thus, they have at various points taken common diplomatic and/or trade sanctions against Libya and Iran. This process has some way to go, however, before it can be called the basis of a "twelve for one, and one for twelve" crime prevention regime. Differing attitudes towards Israel and the PLO within the Twelve mean, for example, that the EC cannot yet claim a shared policy towards the lively terrorist hotbed of the Middle East.

Three Problem Areas

Inevitably it is where the general project of cooperation focuses upon particulars that the problems arise. Take, for instance, three issues with which the Schengen Five have been wrestling.

● **Drugs** The uniquely permissive attitude which the Dutch authorities have towards users of soft drugs has underlined a need for common enforcement of laws, not just common laws. The Netherlands has roughly the same laws on the possession of marijuana and cannabis as the other four Schengenites. But it is much more lenient on individual users, be they Dutch or foreign; it would rather catch the big drug-pushers. However, this is not an attitude that endears the Dutch authorities to their immediate neighbours.

● **Data Protection** The Schengen computer could put a lot of information about people at the disposal of the authorities of five countries, not all of which have the same laws to protect such data from misuse – in the case of Belgium, no law at all. This prospect disturbs some politicians and civil rights groups, particularly in the Netherlands which, in addition, is the only continental EC state not to require identity cards of its citizens. Dutch sensitivity stems from memories of German wartime occupation. British nationals and residents do not carry identity cards either; and driving licences are a poor substitute because – unlike in the Netherlands – they have no photographs.

● **Hot Pursuit** Police forces in the three Benelux countries have long had an arrangement whereby in "hot pursuit" of a suspect they can drive up to 10km (6.25 miles) into each other's territory. However, the French have a problem – not so much with hot pursuit itself, but with limits on what hotly pursuant police officers can do if they catch up with their suspect. Not surprisingly, the French still shy away from the prospect of German police arresting French nationals in the middle of Strasbourg.

A Bounce too Far?

In the matter of people, therefore, the powerful concept of "Europe without frontiers" brings both advantage and risk. The advantage is that it forces European countries to take a hard look at the jurisdictional differences that divide them, and ask if these are really that important. Few differences get left unexplored and, to the extent that they are either harmonised away or left at the mercy of open frontiers, the ideal of an open Europe is advanced. The danger is that national differences won't fade away, and that the quest for the frontier-free ideal leads to more expensive, bureaucratic and generally inconvenient ways of enforcing them than the frontiers were in the first place.

The European Community will not be frontier-free by 1992: the last two chapters have made that seem a fairly safe bet. But, so far, the gamble of promoting the idea of Europe without frontiers seems to have paid off. In other words: the advances made towards free flows of people and things across the EC have been worth the risk that such a promise would only leave the promisers looking foolish.

7

THE BARRIERS
WITHIN

Free Trade Redefined

Crème de cassis, the blackcurrant elixir which transforms white wine into kir, also transformed the nature of Europe's common market. It is largely due to a famous European Court case involving this liqueur that the 1992 single-market initiative has been able to do so much to restore progress to the European Community, but also to arouse such unease in member states about loss of sovereignty.

In the late 1970s, Rewe Zentral AG, a West German food importer and retailer, wanted to import Cassis de Dijon into Germany. The West German authorities demurred: under West German law crème de cassis had too low an alcohol content to be classed as a liqueur but too high an alcohol content to be considered a wine. Rewe thought this a nonsense and took the matter to court. It could get no redress in the national courts because the German rules were clear, so in 1978 it took its case to the European Court of Justice in Luxembourg. The West German government tried to defend its rules as consistent with the Treaty of Rome, arguing that they were not protectionist because they applied to Germans and foreigners alike.

The case begged the question: What does free trade really mean? Does it mean that, say, French companies have a right to sell anything in Germany that conforms to German rules – the commercial equivalent of "When in Rome do as the Romans do"? Or does it mean that French companies can sell in West Germany whatever they happily sell at home? Article 36 of the Treaty of Rome is ambivalent on which of these two interpretations of free trade the Common Market's regime should be. On the one hand, it allows governments to block imports on grounds of "public policy"; on the other hand, it says such bans must not amount to "arbitrary discrimination or disguised restrictions on trade".

79

The Cassis Judgment

The European Court went for the liberal interpretation. It ruled in 1979 that West Germany had no right to block sales of Cassis de Dijon unless it could show that the rules blocking it were needed for reasons of health, tax policing, fair trading within Germany or consumer protection. The Germans are dab-hands at such finessing – for a time Bonn blocked the import of still mineral waters arguing that bubbles were needed to kill microbes – but even they could not convince the Court that the ban on cassis was needed for any of these reasons.

The case was little noticed at the time, but it turned out to be a powerful blow against jurisdictional sovereignty and in favour of a supranational European Community. For it meant that a European country's product laws could be undermined by nonconformist products from another European country. A government could stop that undermining only if it could show that morality, health, safety or the environment were at risk. That in turn meant that some central adjudicator would have to decide whether or not those values were endangered. The Cassis de Dijon ruling thus implied that Europe's democratic governments would no longer be masters of many of the rules of their own societies.

The Technical Barriers

This judgment, and the European consensus that accepted it, changed the whole perspective of the Common Market. It had long been clear to Europe's industrialists that the real barriers to their business across Europe were not frontiers and the customs-dues, paperwork and quotas traditionally enforced at them. The real villains were the rules, licences and permits within countries that stopped or hindered them from selling there – the standard for windscreens that stops a car built to West German standards being automatically sellable in France; the particular way headlights and sidelights must be wired in cars sold in Britain; the way French buildings are uninsurable unless tiled with French standard tiles; the national favouritism in government procurement which so often means that foreign companies' tenders are unsuccessful; the local banking rule banning the service that a foreign bank is adept at providing.

These are the obstacles that keep some of the most modern industries in Europe fragmented and that preserve price differences in them of 20 per cent or more. Take cars, a product whose price is crucially important to individuals and companies throughout Europe. Technical barriers are one of the three main reasons why the European car market remains divided along national lines. The other two are border controls, which are chiefly to do with differing tax regimes, and the way cars are sold through networks of exclusive dealerships – a particular concession to this business made in the face of what European competition law would normally demand. This system allows car companies and their dealers to adapt their model-ranges and prices country-by-country with little fear that these differences will be undermined by competition from other enterprising retailers. The net result of these national divisions is that car prices were, in 1983, 42 per cent higher in Britain than in Belgium for the same model of car, without tax rates playing any part in this calculation. The difference in price between even West Germany and Belgium – contiguous countries – was around 20 per cent. By 1989 cross-border competition had reduced these differences somewhat. But the British-Belgium difference was still 31 per cent, and the German-Belgium difference 11 per cent.

Until the Cassis de Dijon ruling there was a presumption that such technical "barriers within" were part of European life. After it, there was the prospect of all of them being challengeable. The scene was set for a much more demanding single-market regime: the business rules of European countries would be forced to compete for survival across open frontiers, with only certain essential standards being enforced by common consent from the centre. Above and beyond these standards, consumers would be free to decide what qualities they were ready to pay for. They would not be bossed into paying for them by governments.

The Cultural Divisions

This change, lurking little-noticed beneath the benign words "single market", was a move towards a world alien to German eyes or to French tradition, and uncomfortable even for the British. The extreme reluctance of the supposedly centre-right government of Helmut Kohl in Germany to trim the technical rules that cocoon the West German economy shows how attached that society is to precise norms and standards, and how unwilling it is to see them undermined by those of less fastidious nations. The process of collectively raising standards, whether for the ingredients of beers or for the depth of tread on worn tyres, is for the German people an accepted wisdom: misguided individuals should not be allowed to opt for something shoddier and cheaper.

For France, with its long-established tradition of unchallenged *dirigisme* from the centre, the prospect of "competition-between-rules" seems insidious in a different way. Rules are essential to the binding together of this large and diverse country. Political loyalty to France's central government has long been bought with special regimes for special interests – a protected market for this type of farmer, or a special exemption for that sort of *petit commerçant*. The price the French paid for getting Cassis de Dijon into Germany was the prospect that such political favours would henceforth be challenged by European judges in Luxembourg. This prospect has made some French keen to curb the power of those judges with a more powerful European Parliament and executive.

Idiosyncratic Britons find deregulation easier to swallow, and they are accustomed to the legal framework of their lives being shaped by the practical evolution of common law. What worries Britain about the fallout of the Cassis de Dijon case is the notion that a few people across the Channel should be empowered to say that Britain's water is polluted, its beaches dirty or its rules on pornography in television unnecessarily strict.

Hopeless Harmony

These perspectives are unfolding only gradually. One result of the Cassis de Dijon case was that the numbing business of "harmonising" Europe's different national regulations could be abandoned. Since 1957 it had been forlornly hoped that all national product rules, to which all imports had to conform, would gradually be merged as skilled negotiators settled national differences over what constituted pasta, beer or properly-made pressure vessels. By the start of 1985, some eighteen years of work had produced 177 product directives and 56 amending directives, but with the emphasis very much on the motor industry and on weights-and-measures. The average gestation time for the last 15 product directives had been ten years: some draft directives were having to be junked in the early 1980s, before they had been considered by member governments, because technological advances had already made them obsolete.

Such was the mounting frustration over this impasse that a new approach to the problem, based on the Cassis de Dijon principle, had been brewing even before the Delors Commission launched its renewed bid for a real common market at the start of 1985. In March 1983, the

EC Council of Ministers agreed that all new national standards must be registered with the Commission before coming into force: across Europe these standards were proliferating at a rate of five thousand per year and thus creating new obstacles to trade far faster than the harmonisers could harmonise them away. The very fact that the Commission would be vetting new standards implied that it had to develop some principles to vet them by. In February 1985 the internal market commissioner, Lord Cockfield, sold the concept of "mutual recognition" to trade ministers. This was based squarely on the Cassis de Dijon ruling. EC countries would recognise each other's rules for a given product provided those rules met safety criteria agreed upon between the Commission and national governments. If a government wanted to block the import of a widget it would have to persuade a committee of all the member states that it did not meet the central requirements. This committee would rule by qualified majority voting.

This new approach was reinforced by the changes wrought by the Single European Act. The Act's amendments to Article 100 of the Treaty of Rome ordained that the laws needed to complete the internal market, with the exception of those on tax, employment and the movement of people, were to be passed by qualified majority voting. It also explicitly stated that the Council of Ministers "may decide that the provisions in force in a member state must be recognised as being equivalent to those being applied by another member state".

So, by taking the Cassis de Dijon ruling, adding the mounting frustration felt at lack of progress towards a common market, stir in the Single European Act, and the Community was equipped with a powerful new agent to dissolve the "barriers within". The impossible task of reconciling thousands of national rules – embodying thousands of national traditions, hang-ups and special interests – by unanimous vote was abandoned. Its successor was less daunting: devising underlying standards, agreed by qualified majority vote, and accepting each others' rules provided they satisfied these standards. Less daunting but still not easy: Article 100A of the Single European Act also insists that "proposals involving health, safety, environmental protection and consumer protection will take as base a high level of protection". The scope for argument over how pernickety the central rules should be was obvious from the start.

To hold this argument in check, the Commission introduced an elegant distinction between regulations and standards. Regulations, it argued, are there to achieve ends – chiefly safety. Standards are there for convenience, and to provide one standard means of meeting those ends – but not necessarily the only means. Hitherto, the two concepts had become muddled up, so that an attempt to forge a European product regulation became an attempt to create a complex European standard.

Under the Commission's "new approach" legislators legislate and standardisers standardise. The legislators stick as far as possible to ends: viz, the pressure vessel shall not explode even under extreme conditions. They do not concern themselves with how these aims are met – wisely, because technology changes the ways of doing so continuously. The standard-setters may then set about providing the convenience of a standard European pattern of pressure vessels that are interchangeable, connect with one another, conform to international standards, etc – and also satisfy those European safety requirements.

The new approach has done wonders for the pace of creating basic product law for the single market. Half of the directives needed to remove national product rules as a means of stopping imports have already been passed by the EC Council of Ministers. The essential requirements have now been set out for pressure vessels, toys, construction materials, electrical interference, low voltage machinery, and machine safety. The machinery directive is just sixty pages long. It lays down the obligatory qualities for up to four thousand different types of industrial machine whose manufacture makes up an industry with an annual turnover in the European Community of 120 billion ecus, or roughly half the output of Community's mechanical engineering industry. European regulations for motor vehicles cannot be far away, too. An immense amount of standardising work was done upon them under the old harmonisation regime and the fiddly differences that remain are there mainly because France and Italy have wished to retain some way of stopping Japanese cars flowing into their markets via, say, West Germany.

Protectionism: Dulled but not Dead

Inevitably, the tangled web of technical rules and standards has not yielded cleanly to the tidy logic of the Commission's new approach. Plenty of potentially protectionist problems remain.

● The habit of writing product regulations in terms of ends (the machine should not catch fire even at full power) rather than means (use the following fireproofing techniques) remains hard to instil.

● The existence of a basic European regulation for a product does not necessarily give it a passport across the Community. It can in theory be sold, but won't be if, say, it is incompatible with local usage rules.

● The "certification" system which allows manufacturers to demonstrate that their products meet European safety rules is inadequate. The British are pushing for self-certification by manufacturers: machines would be presumed Euro-safe if their makers say so. The Germans want testing laboratories, white-coated testers, certificates, rubber stamps.

● European product standards created under the aegis of the European standards bodies – the European Committee for Standardisation (CEN) and the European Committee for Electro-technical Standardisation (CENELEC) – do not always replace national standards, as they are meant to, but are incorporated into national standards. The national standard-setters often remain free to add additional national virtues to their standards. Once again, a non-national standard product may have a theoretical right of entry into a country, but no one can force a private buyer not to stipulate whatever standard he is accustomed to.

Despite the theoretical separation of mandatory rules and optional standards, the business of standard-setting remains vital to the prospect of a great European market. CEN and CENELEC are coordinating the work of some 160 technical committees attempting to turn national standards into European ones. Not far short of half of these committees are headed by representatives of the Deutsches Institut für Normung (DIN), the West German organisation that is Europe's undisputed standards-setting champion with some twenty thousand different standards already on its books. The flow of directives, coupled with the Commission's efforts to create Europe-wide procurement by governments has created a relentless new pressure for harmonised standards, which CEN and CENELEC are hard-pressed to satisfy. CEN has three council meetings a year and each of these has, of late, set up as many as twenty new technical committees.

The committees operate by consensus so there has to be much give and take between countries as to whose standards should form the basis of the new European ones. Their recommendations have then to be adopted by a vote within CEN using qualified majority voting. If they agree upon a full European standard, this is adopted, identically, by all member states as their new national standard. The desire to retain harmonised national standards rather than replace them with a full Euro-standard, remains strong, however, and inconvenient. Manufacturers of small products sometime cannot find the space on their widgets to print on them all the national standards that they satisfy.

Often, agreement upon a full European standard remains elusive. This can be because one country insists that one of its laws will be infringed by the new standard – which in theory should not happen under the "new approach" but in practice still does, pending someone challenging the law in question before the European Court – or because a country pleads for time to adapt to the envisaged standard, or because the technical committee is deadlocked. In such cases, the committee can pass up to CEN a "harmonisation document" in order to make the most of the common ground achieved. If CEN adopts it, this common ground must be incorporated into national standards, but without any need for these to become identical.

The good news in this wearisome process is that in the space of some five years the standards-setting habits of European countries have become largely Europeanised; indeed, internationalised, because CEN and CENELEC are themselves heavily influenced by the International Standards Organisation. It is also encouraging that CEN has agreed upon the standards required of certificating laboratories, which will do much to dissuade countries from discriminating against the goods of others on the grounds that they don't trust their tests. Already European manufacturers are finding that they can speed certification for a new product in one country by threatening to get it certified elsewhere.

The bad news is that full European standards will emerge only slowly and that while national standards linger, commercial reality will keep them an obstacle to trade. It is a brave company which tries to sell in West Germany without meeting DIN norms: not because it will be doing something illegal if it doesn't, but because, rightly or wrongly, DIN is the proof of quality that West German consumers and insurers insist on.

Governments: the Greatest Customers of All

European countries typically see one-third or more of their gross national product flow through the coffers of central government, local government and the services they provide. So the behaviour of the government-as-customer is clearly crucial to the prospect of a single European market. So far, governments have let the Common Market down. The EC's public sectors have been theoretically compelled to put large construction contracts (any worth over 1 million ecus) out to

Europe-wide tender since 1971, and to do the same with big purchases of equipment and supplies (above 200,000 ecus) since 1977. Yet there has been little to show for it. Just 2 per cent of orders in each category flow across European frontiers. Indeed, in 1986 American construction companies managed to win 6 billion ecus-worth of public orders in Europe while all European firms together won only one-tenth as much in parts of the EC outside their home markets.

These figures tell of the deeply ingrained habit that the European Commission is trying to break. A carefully cultivated old-boy network binds national suppliers and national buyers together. Outside suppliers are loath to complain about discrimination: they know this to be a sure-fire way to ditch the small chance that they might get some business. Governments, under obvious political pressure to "buy national", are most unlikely to pick up the cudgels for an unfairly excluded foreigner. Quite a lot of this public buying is from what can be called "strategic" industries – because they supply things either so basic to an economy that it seems risky to buy them from foreigners, or so expensive and crammed with technology that their producers qualify as "national champions". And wherever there is one national champion there must, of course, be two or more to preserve some show of competition in what is often a cosy and lucrative business.

The Tide is Turning

Procurement accounts for 15 per cent of the EC's GDP, but this includes the buying by bodies administering the telecommunications, transport, energy and water-and-sewage sectors, which are not necessarily in government hands. These "excluded sectors" – so-called because they were excluded from the EC's early directives on Europe-wide procurement – take about half of that share. In trying to prise this one-sixth of the European economy out of its national compartments, the Commission does have a tide of fashion flowing with it. Some of the most eyecatching European mergers, or would-be mergers, of the past two years – such as the link-up between Siemens of West Germany and GEC and Plessey of Britain, or the purchases of stakes in European telecommunication equipment makers by AT&T of America and Northern Telecom of Canada – have been based upon the expectation of more open government procurement after 1992.

That tide notwithstanding, the economic case for open procurement exactly matches the political counter-pressures that will be aroused by

European industries

	Value of EEC market billion ecus	Intra-EC trade	Number of EC producers	Number of US producers
Boilermaking	2	little	12	6
Turbine generators	2	little	10	2
Locomotives	0.1	little	16	2
Mainframe computers	10	extensive	5	9
Telephone exchanges	7	moderate	11	4
Telephone handsets	5	little	12	17

Source: European Commission

it. The table above shows what scope there seems to be for a shake-out in the industries that serve the excluded sectors. It is based upon research in the mid-1980s by W.S. Atkins Management Consultants and it makes the large number of European producers, compared with the number surviving in the more integrated US market, strikingly obvious. The notable exception is mainframe computers – but it is an exception that reinforces the underlying point. The computer industry is not dependent upon procurement for its survival. It serves customers of many sorts and has thus been shaped by pan-European competitive pressures, not by government patronage. Moreover, IBM has risen above the national-champion pattern that rules in the other businesses listed and has thus stopped the usual inefficiencies from emerging.

The Commission's Challenge

The Commission has had four main aims in the procurement part of the 1992 campaign. They are: to broaden the scope of the obligations that already supposedly exist and to block the loopholes in them; to equip itself with greater powers to enforce those obligations; to improve the redress that disappointed bidders will have if they feel themselves unfairly excluded; and to extend open procurement to businesses that have remained exempt from it till now – the "excluded sectors" mentioned earlier.

The "supplies" and "works" directives, enshrining the existing obligations that date from the 1970s, have been revamped and are already law or nearly law. The "remedies" directive, designed to enforce these principles, is having a much tougher passage. Under the pre-1992 regime a company that feels it has been illegally deprived of a contract can only complain to the Commission which first investigates and then complains to the national government in question, wielding the ultimate sanction of action in the European Court. The government then, in theory, remonstrates with the public authority that shopped around so poorly. Not much hope of justice here: the system amounts to a protracted way for the would-be supplier to infuriate an important potential customer.

The Commission's early drafts of the remedies directive attempted to install a far more abrasive regime. It wanted each member country to set up some form of independent tribunal, usually the national courts, to which would-be suppliers could appeal if jilted. No strong objections there. But the Commission also wanted the right to intercede in such cases if it felt that the procurement directives were being too weakly interpreted. Still more contentiously, it wanted power to suspend, for up to three months, the award of contracts if it decided that the right procedures – the rules that contracts must be advertised fully and long enough in advance – were not being followed. This was too peremptory for the taste of most governments: the rights of the Commission to apply the law over their heads were judged excessive, and the obligations on project managers too inflexible to be coped with in real life ("We needed twenty more cement-mixers, fast. How could we possibly advertise?"). Since then the directive has been progressively watered down. The main result has been to shift the job of enforcing the law squarely back to national governments, leaving the Commission with a right to tell them of infringements and to demand action within fifteen days.

The Commission has found the going heavy, too, in its attempt to bring the excluded sectors of energy, water, transport and telecommunications within the pan-European procurement regime. The problem is that these activities are businesses serving customers, not forms of government spending, and the pattern of their ownership, whether state or private, varies from country to country. Why should Gaz de France, which is state-run, have to go through a Euro-procurement rigmarole when British Gas, now a private company, can buy where it wants?

So the Commission is hoping to replace ownership with other criteria that will determine whether an enterprise has to procure openly. Is it operating behind barriers to entry, whether legal or technical? Is it a natural monopoly like telecommunications was once thought to be? Does it operate through an unchallengeable network like a railway? Is it working closely with government either because it is government-regulated or holds a government concession of some sort? The gas and electricity industries will ring most of these bells, telecommunications and railway companies rather fewer, bus companies fewer still, and oil companies barely any.

The economic logic of tackling these bastions of procurement-nationalism is strong. Yet the Commission's venture into the exempt areas has a quicksand feel to it. If the resulting regime is tough, privatised companies will be up in arms about their right to manage; if it is lax, it will not make much difference. How can any rule book cope with the blend of patriotism, government persuasion, tactical gesture and straight thriftiness that moves, say, Lord King when he orders Rolls-Royce engines for British Airways? The West Germans maintain that where types of excluded sectors compete – as gas vies with electricity to provide heat, for example – fair procurement should be entrusted to the rigours of that competition. Many countries have pet sectors to protect from open procurement: the oil and gas equipment industry that Britain built to extract North Sea oil; the heavily-rigged buying of coal by power stations in West Germany; the mandatory flow of orders to the Mezzogiorno in Italy. Managers in the excluded sectors fear the paperwork that will be needed to comply with the open procurement rules: British Gas estimates the cost of its compliance at £24 million a year.

There are as yet no proposals for refereeing this complicated private-public sector game. And because the GATT's fair-trade rules do not apply to these "excluded sectors" there is a foreign-trade component to the problem, too. The Commission has suggested that tenderers should have to add at least 50 per cent of their value in Europe to count as European (though the buyer does not have to insist on such content if he wants to buy cheaply abroad) and that a European bid can be given precedence provided its price is not more than 3 per cent above a foreign one. The prime object of these rules is to try to prise more open excluded-sector procurement concessions out of the Americans and the Japanese. The Americans, in particular, will find the attempt to lay down buying-rules for private sector utility companies distinctly at odds with their tradition of clinching deals down at the country-club.

All in all, the prospect that pan-European procurement will lead to a moment of horrid truth for some of Europe's best known "national champions" is not as grim as in theory it should be. A mixture of world-wide business ambition, gradually spreading privatisation and budgetary rigour will probably drive the emergence of Euro-procurement, not vice versa.

Migrating Professionals

The most satisfying example, in the 1992 project, of the principle of the mutual recognition of rules is the emerging right of Europe's professionals to work across the EC without having to requalify. In mid-1988 the EC governments agreed a directive requiring governments to recognise each other's diplomas, obtained after at least three year's study, for such jobs as accountancy, the law, engineering and teaching. Such professionals will not merely have their national diplomas accepted as valid for practice: they will have the right to put after their name the diploma of the country to which they have moved, provided that they take a test covering any lack of skills implicit in the transfer, or go through a period of supervised practice in the new country. The point is that they do not have to take the entire exam for the diploma of their new home. This involved a lot of heart-searching by the institutes of Chartered Accountants in Britain, for instance. On the continent, professional qualifications tend to be provided by the higher-education system, but in Britain and Ireland, the right to be a barrister or solicitor or accountant comes out of something analogous to a system of private guilds. These professional associations had to accept that they too must swallow their crème de cassis like good Europeans.

The next step will be to extend the same principle to two-year qualifications for such workers as plumbers, electricians and social workers. Thus, bit by bit, the "barriers within" will be swept away until all that remains to stop Western Europe from being one great market and workplace will be the powerful instinct of buyers, sellers, professionals and workers not to think of it that way.

8

PANDORA'S
MONEY BOX

Profits and Pain in the
Financial Services Industry

The business of financial services accounts for 3 per cent of jobs in the EC and 6 per cent of its pay. Finance is the sector in which project 1992 has moved most impressively forwards – in a surge that promises to create in the next half-decade more benefits, pain and general upheaval for an industry and its customers than any other business will experience as a result of the internal-market campaign.

Why the momentum? There are two reasons. First, because in the matter of money 1992 is flowing with the current of developments worldwide. Financiers deal in promises to pay or repay. A promise is information, and nothing moves faster than information in a telecommunications world. Frontier posts have become irrelevant to the movement of money. Internal rules still affect it, but promises can change their form with quicksilver ease. The mood in the Western world in the 1970s was to resist the drowning of sovereign power by money-market power – to try to create life-rafts of monetary independence in a floating-currency world. The mood of the 1980s was to go with the flow and make the best of it. The financial provisions of 1992 thrive upon that change of mood.

The second reason derives from the first. Painful object-lessons in the 1970s, notably the collapse of Herstatt Bank in West Germany and of the Franklin National Bank in the United States, made it clear to governments that national systems for assessing and controlling the soundness of banks badly needed to be coordinated and "harmonised" into an international system. The process of sorting out who should police which banks for what standards got under way in the mid-1970s, and moved in the 1980s towards common rules on such vital things as how much capital a bank should have to support different sorts of loans. So, in banking at least, the EC governments could call upon much prior, hard thinking about the essential standards for an open market in

92

banking. Such groundwork was lacking in the businesses of insurance and securities, and the 1992 financial revolution has been held up accordingly.

Lifting Exchange Controls

An absolute precondition for an open European market in financial services is that money should be able to move freely across Europe. This became thinkable only during the 1980s. Despite Article 67 of the Rome Treaty calling for the free movement of capital across Europe, little was achieved in the progressive 1960s, and much of what was achieved was reversed in the oil-slump years of the 1970s. It was only in 1979 that Britain felt able, in one of the first dramatic gestures of Thatcherism, to sweep away its exchange controls and thus match West Germany whose financial freedom had been instilled after the Second World War by the Americans. France remained convinced – as it had been throughout the negotiation of the Rome Treaty – that exchange controls were an essential feature of sovereignty, to be relaxed with utmost caution so that the dreaded speculator should not get the upper hand.

The financial momentum of project 1992 would not have been possible without a remarkable change of attitude by the French. After the country's ill-fated attempt to go it alone with socialist reflation in the early 1980s, France abandoned the right of its government to allocate credit within the economy, opened up the *chasses gardées* of its financial system and committed itself to removing all exchange controls. The go-with-the-flow thinking that lay behind this switch was made clear in a report on 1992's impact on the French financial system by Pierre Achard, an *Inspecteur Général de Finance*. He concluded: "Mergers, regrouping and mutations are inevitable. Better to anticipate them and help them, for the competitiveness of our financial firms ought to be judged against that of Japanese or US giants, rather than against those of our European competitors". So the prescription of more open competition, which had been grudgingly accepted as right for French industry when the Treaty of Rome was negotiated thirty years before, was accepted as right for French finance, too.

Italy, the other big EC economy with exchange controls, nervously followed, with the result that eight EC members have agreed to remove all exchange controls by mid-1990, while Spain and Ireland have the right to retain theirs until 1992 and Portugal and Greece until 1995.

Logical though the development was, the agreement of the French in June 1988 to go along with the removal of exchange controls was something that went to the core of French perceptions of sovereignty. The French insisted upon a pre-condition: that the Commission suggest ways of preventing tax evasion on interest income by newly-liberated depositors.

The Commission duly responded, without much relish, proposing a uniform minimum withholding tax on interest income of 15 per cent. Britain never liked this idea. Part of London's attraction as a financial centre is its lack of tax on large deposits (small deposits do have tax-on-interest levied automatically or "withheld". Despite the lack of exchange controls, there has been no mass-emigration of bank accounts, which suggests that the small depositor is not quite as light-footed as the French government fears). Yet when West Germany tried to impose a 10 per cent withholding tax in 1989 it was a disaster – partly because all the big West German banks have subsidiaries in tax-free Luxembourg which were set up to exploit just this sort of opportunity for lucrative side-stepping of German rules. The German government saw that even if Luxembourg harmonised its rules, Swiss banks would happily oblige those looking for an escape route. Bonn scrapped the tax, and with it any chance of Brussels getting Community agreement on such a tax-at-source. The Commission then proposed that the tax authorities of the Twelve should agree to furnish each other with information on anyone suspected of tax fraud. This, however, ran into predictable opposition from Luxembourg, which took care – just as Brussels was unveiling its plan for cooperation between "fiscs" – to reinforce its bank secrecy law. The duchy's basic problem is that it does not regard simple non-payment of taxes as serious enough to justify the lifting the curtain of bank secrecy; it also claims it can't let its banks provide more depositor information to foreign governments than they do to the Luxembourg authorities.

A Daring Directive

Building upon the assumed right to move money across Europe, the Community is composing its most daring variation on the 1992 theme of "mutual recognition" of rules established by the European Court in the Cassis de Dijon ruling (see Chapter 7). Broadly speaking, once essential standards for the soundness of financial firms and for the safety of their customers have been laid down in Brussels, EC governments will be asked to respect each others' interpretation of those rules and to allow financial firms to sell in each other's market whatever they can sell in the home country, and under control from home. This approach goes well beyond the "national treatment" which has, until now, been the usual basis of trade in services. National treatment demands that a US bank behaves in Canada like a Canadian bank, and vice versa: such an approach is in fact the basis of the free trade agreement between the United States and Canada. Mutual recognition of rules is equivalent to a far tougher trade demand: "equivalent access" – the right of a branch of a British bank to do in France what it is allowed to do in Britain.

So where until now a Greek bank had to make eleven different applications to open branches across the Community, a single EC banking licence will, after January 1993, allow it to open up in all of them, or to provide services to them across frontiers, as a matter of right. If the Greek bank decides to open a subsidiary in another EC country, in contrast, that subsidiary will have to be established under the law of the country in question.

Each branch in the EC will be supervised by authorities in the head-office country, which must follow a set of Euro-rules for bank soundness. It will be allowed to do abroad any of a wide-ranging list of banking activities provided its parent bank does them at home. This list, set down in the Second Banking Coordination Directive, includes the securities business.

Boldly Going

Already this directive promises to make Europe's banks far freer than their US counterparts, whose access to consumers in other American states and to a full range of financial services is still strictly limited. But how free will a freely-established bank branch really be? Will the bold principles laid out in the directive be honoured in practice? For they are, without doubt, bold. They effectively allow a foreign bank branch to do things in a given country that the home banks of that country are not allowed to do. Here is the banking counterpart of the "competition between rules" that the Cassis de Dijon case established for goods. But national governments are understandably more neuralgic about allowing such a free-for-all to develop in banking, where they stand as lender of last resort and through which they sometimes hope to shape their economies.

In practice, the principle of "home-country control" of financial institutions operating in other countries of the Community will not be straightforwardly applied. There will be a blend of home control and "host control" – ie, control by the authorities in the country where the branch is operating. In the case of the Greek bank, the branch abroad will have to abide by local consumer protection rules – covering for instance, opening hours or deposit insurance; by any banking regulations to do with local monetary policy; and by rules relating to liquidity (the amount of ready cash banks have on hand to pay withdrawals). It will also have to heed a – worryingly vague – clause in the banking directive that prevents the sale of financial services that might damage the "public interest" in the country in question. There is, moreover, a chance that its style will be cramped in time by additional directives harmonising the European qualities required of products such as mortgages or leasing-contracts.

Here is a tug-of-war between the Commission, which wants to stop spurious demands for financial safety being used as a pretext to thwart healthy competition, and local regulators and vested interests reluctant to abandon the national habits and procedures with which they feel comfortable. Part of the outcome will be decided by the European Court, as financiers try to offer this and that service but find themselves thwarted by local rules of questionable Euro-legality.

The Court has already taken decisions that have shaped the regime in financial services. In four important cases about insurance in the late 1980s the Court decided that the Cassis de Dijon principle did, indeed, extend to finance, and that West Germany was wrong to insist that the sale of insurance required the presence of a permanent office in the country of sale. But the Court also argued that while a bottle of crème de cassis could be safely consumed even if its bottler had gone bust, the same would not hold true for an insurance policy. An insurance policy dies with the company that issued it. So, until the EC evolved European standards for the soundness of insurance companies and insurance policies, trans-border selling should be limited to customers big enough to decide whether a foreign insurance company was sound or not. Some impatience with this gradualist approach has set in. In late 1989, Sir Leon Brittan, commissioner responsible for financial services, said he wanted faster across-the-board progesss in insurance, citing the public impact of lower premia for ordinary policy-holders. But an open market in insurance policies for the man-in-the-street will take another some years to evolve, whereas an open European market for commercial insurance is already emerging.

A Money-merchant's Charter

The cause of pan-European banking was helped by the amount of international regulatory brainstorming that preceded the 1992 project. A relative lack of such, though, has held up the creation of an equivalent market in securities and investment services. The Commission is trying to create an adequate European regime for brokers, dealers, fund managers, underwriters and investment advisers to allow the same principle to apply and to open branches in other EC countries with "home-country control". Two different sets of Euro-rules are needed here: the first for the soundness of the firms involved and the second for the products that they sell and the markets on which they are quoted.

The first of these – the regulation of financial firms – is a veritable monkey-puzzle: not least because national regulatory systems have been evolving fast of late to cope with a tide of innovations and cross-frontier influence that is changing the nature of the business. Two sample problems. Will financial centres on the continent accept as "home-country control" the odd mixture of regulation and self-regulation that the City of London has devised for itself? And what will be the accepted rules for risk (the risk that the prices of shares or bonds held by firms will move up and down), and the capital that is supposed to cushion firms against that risk? In order for financial firms across the continent to compete fairly the capital adequacy rules that they live by must be uniform. This is true not only within the investment services and securities industry, but for banks too – to the extent that they become involved in securities. An Anglo-Saxon/continental divide in attitude to securities risk has to be bridged here.

As for the financial-product rules, much was achieved in this area before the year 1992 acquired significance, driven by the general internationalisation of financial markets. Directives already exist to ensure Europe-wide recognition of the national prospectuses and listing requirements that allow shares and bonds to be quoted upon Europe's stock exchanges. In October 1989 a directive for the minimum standards of mutual funds/unit trusts came into force, allowing these to be sold freely throughout the Community. This early manifestation of 1992 in financial services will give a foretaste of two thorny problems ahead. First, while the products (the unit trusts) may be legally sellable, the rules and methods for selling them across Europe will still vary dauntingly. Europe-wide distribution will be very expensive to establish. Hence the scope for deals between those who manage funds and those, say banks or insurance companies, that have established selling networks in given European countries. Dresdner Bank has bought the British fund management firm Thornton, for instance, as Société Générale of France has bought Touche Remnant.

Second, Europe-wide unit trusts will put particular pressure on investment-income tax regimes. Already Luxembourg, which levies no withholding tax, has six hundred funds on its books with the number rising fast. If other financial centres are to compete as the bases for Euro-unit trusts (UCITS as they are known in the jargon) they are going to have to make their tax regimes friendlier for investors from other EC countries.

All in all, the prospects for 1992 in finance remain encouraging. The conceptual blueprint for the pan-European market has been thought out and accepted – a courageous one which allows national systems to infect one another rather than be insulated from each other. The basic legal framework of the structure is taking shape. What remains to be set in place are the fixtures and fittings. National systems must be altered to fit into the framework; the rules on exactly what can be prohibited in "host" countries will have to be tediously redefined. There will also be a constant tendency for national authorities to demand that fully-harmonised definitions of financial products – whether types of loans or types of securities – be worked out. It will be a real challenge for the Commission to resist this tendency, while at the same time seeing that "diversity in safety" is the outcome, rather than diversity with steadily slipping standards.

Banks: Opportunities and Pitfalls

The three new financial liberties – freedom to establish branches abroad, freedom to sell across frontiers, freedom to move money – will alter the nature of the market for the banking, securities and insurance industries. Deregulation of this sort creates opportunities and discomfort in equal measure – opportunities for obvious reasons, and discomfort because market shares and profit margins based upon the existence of national markets and national customs are suddenly eroded by international competition. The Cecchini report (see table opposite) provided startling evidence of the price differences to be found in Europe's financial markets. Bank loans to consumers in Britain, for instance, carry more than three times the margin over money-market interest rates that they do in Belgium. On the other hand mortgages in France and West Germany carry twice the spread over money-market rates of mortgages

European prices for financial services

Per cent above or below the average of the lowest four national prices found

	B	FRG	S	F	I	L	N	UK
BANKING SERVICES								
Consumer credit Annual cost of consumer loan of 500 ecus. Excess interest rate over money-market rates	-41	136	39	na	121	-26	31	121
Mortgages Annual cost of home loan of 25,000 ecus. Excess interest rate over money-market rates	31	57	118	78	-4	na	-6	-20
Foreign-exchange drafts Cost to a large commercial client of purchasing a commercial draft for 30,000 ecus.	6	31	196	56	23	33	-46	16
Commercial loans Annual cost (including commissions and charges to a medium-sized firm of a commercial loan of 250,000 ecus.	-5	6	19	-7	9	6	43	46
INSURANCE SERVICES								
Life insurance Average annual cost of term (life) insurance.	78	5	37	33	83	66	-9	-30
Home insurance Annual cost of fire and theft cover for house valued at 70,000 ecus with 28,000 ecus contents.	-16	3	-4	39	81	57	17	90
Commercial fire and theft Annual cover for premises valued at 39,000 ecus & stock at 230,000 ecus.	-9	43	24	153	245	-15	-1	27
BROKERAGE SERVICES								
Private-equity transactions Commission costs of cash bargain of 1,440 ecus.	36	7	65	-13	-3	7	114	123
Institutional-equity transactions Commission costs of cash bargain of 288,000 ecus.	26	69	153	-5	47	68	26	-47

Source: European Commission

in Britain. (The spread is the banker's "price" to his customer: the over-all interest rate is set by factors beyond his control.)

The single-market campaign has created an urge to "do something about 1992" among financiers similar to the urge to buy something that possessed the City of London before its so-called "Big Bang". Financiers have an additional, endemic, motive to buy: it is harder to sell services across frontiers than it is to sell goods. In order to succeed a service company really needs to have a presence in the country in which it wants to operate, and buying "a presence" is often much simpler than setting one up.

In the background to such strategy-making sits a nasty truth. Europe is over-banked. Dr Ulrich Cartellieri, a board member of Deutsche Bank, made a telling speech to a conference on 1992 run by *The Economist*. He described how the EC has one banking office for every 1,900 people – one-fifth more than the USA (1 per 2,300) and 50 per cent more than in Japan where the ratio is 1 to 2,800. Yet the share of the financial industry in Europe's GDP is roughly the same as in the United States and less than it is in Japan. Moreover the fragmentation of the industry is striking not just because there are 10,000 deposit-taking institutions in the EC – many industries have many "niche" players – but because a large and powerful bank like Deutsche Bank, the largest in West Germany, has just 2 per cent of the European banking market. There is, on the face of it, huge scope for mergers and acquisitions.

Yet, partly because the directives on banking do not take effect until the start of 1993, and perhaps because of the fingers burned in "Big Bang" and earlier ambitious banking moves abroad, no wave of banking mergers and takeovers has yet begun to roll. Indeed, one spectacular move towards merger between Belgium's biggest bank, Générale de Banque, and Amsterdam Rotterdam Bank (Amro) came to nothing. The idea had been to create one fully-merged bank. But as the two faced

Financial services as % of GNP* (banking and insurance)		Population per banking office*	
Britain	12.6	Italy	4,398
Japan	6.5	Japan	2,800
Italy	5.6	Britain	2,310
United States	5.0	United States	2,300
EEC average	5.0	EEC average	1,900
Germany, West	5.0	Germany, West	1,541
France	4.5	France	1,524

*1985
Source: European Commission

*1985
Source: BIS

up to the different traditions of banking in the two countries and to the different fiscal and legal frameworks they got cold feet. The prospect of redundancies in the Netherlands played a role too. "Lord make me competitive; but not yet," as St Augustine might have remarked.

One market in banking that has been identified as a prime candidate for "Europeanisation" is the one serving the rich individual. The late Alfred Herrhausen, the former head of Deutsche Bank, explained that wholesale commercial banking was the first slice of banking to become international – to the point where it is now no longer a particularly attractive business to be in. Then investment banking – advice and raising money on the capital markets for companies – followed, and it too has experienced a crisis of profitability. Banking for rich individuals would be the next, he thought. Deutsche Bank's recent moves seem consistent with that perception. In 1986 it bought Banca d'America d'Italia with its hundred or so branches and good customer base of medium-sized enterprises, and in 1989 it strengthened its capacity in international corporate finance by buying control of Morgan Grenfell, a London merchant bank. The beginnings of a Europe-wide corporate bank are emerging here – but Deutsche Bank is still chary of moving as a full scale bank into retail markets such as Britain, France or Belgium where the home banking business is dominated by three or four banks. Midland Bank of Britain is following the same path, building upon its network of local investment banks such as Trinkaus & Burkhardt in West Germany and Euromobiliare in Italy. Chase Manhattan, too, has decided to go for rich private and corporate customers across Europe – but by focusing upon them the skills of its existing operations across Europe.

Europe-wide banking for the man-in-the-street remains the great unknown. Consumer banking has long proved a dangerous sector for ambitious international banks which think that they can transplant successful home-grown systems abroad. Citibank's forays into it proved a disappointment. Midland Bank's adventure in American consumer banking was worse than disappointing. The habits of different markets take so much learning; and existing oligopolistic branch networks are so very difficult to challenge.

Yet there are those who maintain that banking is set to be transformed by the same mass-market packaging that gave Europe fast food chains such as McDonald's, or furniture retailers such as Ikea. They will provide standardised savings schemes, loans, mortages, retirement plans, on attractive terms. And some of these will be marketed directly across frontiers — by mail-order, as it were. The notion is superficially appealing, and certainly American Express is one of Europe's most successful sellers of banking services to a particular clientele and achieves this with a very modest physical presence in the markets it serves. One constraint will, for some time, be the regulatory regimes in the different countries: they will be slow to allow uniform products for the masses to emerge. The underlying fact remains that most banking products involve — unlike McDonald's hamburgers or Ikea's furniture — a continuing relationship with the customer. He or she has to maintain a stream of investment payments, or pay off the loan at some future date. Will one mortgage contract fit all? We doubt it.

Meanwhile, the advisers, arrangers and dealmakers of the finance industry — investment banks, corporate lawyers, accountants — must prepare themselves to serve customers newly inclined to think in European terms. It will no longer be adequate for British advisers not to understand French takeover rules or the West German property market. Such firms need either to open offices throughout Europe, or to form partnerships with local firms. Shearson, Lehman Hutton, a big US investment bank, is doing the first — hiring local talent to give its operations abroad local competence. Hambros provides a British example of the second approach: it is spinning a fee-sharing network of banks across Europe that includes Bayerische Vereinsbank in West Germany, Banco de Bilbao in Spain, and Instituto Bancario San Paolo di Torino in Italy. Nomura, the Japanese investment banking giant, is pursuing the same course. It has bought a 10 per cent stake in the investment banking arm of Banco Santander in Spain, a 10 per cent stake in François-Dufour Kervern, a French stockbroker, and a stake of 5 per cent or more in the Matuschka Group, a West German investment bank.

Covering Europe Slowly

Banking has been becoming a multinational business for many years. Insurance — except that of large risks and reinsurance — has lagged behind. The national markets in direct insurance — that is, policies sold directly to the customer — have remained largely national. Striking differences in the patterns of ownership, in the sizes of insurance companies, and in the types of product that predominate across Europe testify to this habitual isolation. The prospect of 1992 in insurance promises to unfold rather more slowly than in banking, mainly because, as already explained, the Cassis de Dijon principle is being applied more warily, with much insistence that proper European standards are worked out before the man-in-the-street is exposed to foreign insurance salesmen.

There have thus been relatively few eye-opening insurance mergers that could be labelled as resulting from project 1992, although nine of the smaller insurance companies in nine EC countries have signed an agreement to form a network called NEXO through which they will seek to cooperate in selling life insurance.

The new business opportunities are emerging as follows. Reinsurance has no need of further deregulation having had a European directive to abide by since 1964. For non-life insurance (commercial, fire and theft insurance) there has been a directive since 1973 allowing companies to establish themselves in other member states and laying down some common prudential rules for company soundness. The Second Non-life Services Directive (to take effect in mid-1990) will allow the cross-border sales of insurance for large risks, on the theory that buyers of such insurance are sophisticated enough to assess the soundness of a foreign insurer controlled by a foreign regulator. Personal insurance, such as fire insurance for the home, will continue to be available only from an insurance company established in the customer's country. The same logic will apply in motor insurance by 1992: fleet-operators will be able to shop abroad, individuals will insure their cars at home.

As for life insurance an "establishment directive" was adopted in 1979 that allowed foreign insurers to set up branches in other EC countries. But cross-border selling still remains very much on the drawing board. The Commission is trying to satisfy the reservations of the European Court with a directive that distinguishes between "actively" and "passively" marketed insurance: a French customer would be allowed to buy life insurance in West Germany on his own initiative, but the West German insurer would only be allowed to market its policies in France under French rules and supervision. This would not lead to much of a boom in cross-border life insurance; but it would be a more liberal order than the current one where it is actually illegal in six member states to buy life insurance abroad.

As for the effect of all this on the industry, it seems most probable that it will be similar to, but lag behind, the evolution of pan-European banking. The competition for commercial risks insured by professional customers will become Europeanised first. Mass (consumer) risks will follow some way behind. The points in favour of pan-European mass insurance are economies of scale, the attraction to consumers of the name of a large, pan-European insurance success story, and the fact that most insurance customers have, unlike in banking, only a postal relationship with their insurers anyway. On the other hand, language, differing customs and differing tax rules will probably be more complicated for insurers to deal with than for bankers. The currency factor will add both a complication and an opportunity. Michel Albert, the head of Assurance Générale de France, is already thinking of offering his French customers life insurance-savings schemes denominated in Deutschmarks after French exchange controls are lifted. He argues that a nation used to keeping gold under its bed will embrace the chance to save for the future in the dependable German mark.

The Outsiders' Chances

The external trade policy of the integrated European market has loomed large as an issue in the business of financial services. This is partly because the regime being assembled has been particularly testing – and therefore, in some eyes, protection-worthy – for European governments, and partly because US and Japanese financial firms had a lot of interest already vested in Europe before the single-market initiative was dreamed up. Added piquancy was guaranteed by the wide difference between France, with its long tradition of financial protectionism, and Britain with one-eighth of its GDP stemming from the open and relatively-liberal City of London.

The core of the argument was the "reciprocity clause" in the Second Banking Coordination Directive, which had been inserted to give the Commission some bargaining leverage in the current negotiations about financial services in the GATT, and to reassure the Euro-doubters that the brave new European financial market would not be wide open to banks from countries that remained no-go areas for European banks. The initial proposal on banking reciprocity was worryingly tough both for outsiders and for the City of London. The toughness lay both in the treatment of EC banks demanded of foreign countries – the exact words were "reciprocal treatment" – which implied to fearful outsiders "equivalent treatment" to that meted out in Europe, and in the way the Commission would have blocked any foreign application to open a new bank in a European country until it had made sure that all eleven other EC countries were not having trouble getting banks established in the applicant country in question.

These concepts are rather a mouthful. In essence, London was frightened that it would no longer be able to run an allcomers' banking centre; and Washington was worried that new US banks would not be able to open up in Europe unless the USA agreed to allow European banks to do things in the United States that would break US banking law. A great fuss was made and in the end, after much hard bargaining within the Commission, the reciprocity clause was watered down to make the obligatory vetting by the Commission much less intrusive but to allow the Commission to threaten sanctions to ensure "national treatment that gives effective access" abroad. This demand for "effective access" might require a mild bending of rules in foreign centres to allow European banks to gain entry, but it would not require that they be able to cock a snoot at local banking practice.

What is more, the phrase "effective access" is incorporated in the guidelines, agreed in Montreal in 1988, for the current (1986–90) round of GATT negotiations on trade in services. The GATT's aim is a "progressively higher degree of liberalisation taking due account of the level of development of individual signatories". In short, the EC's pioneering application of "mutual recognition" to the financial rules of countries within Europe is being echoed, in a weaker way, in the principles that the GATT hopes to apply to services worldwide. What is more, the reciprocity rule, which the Commission stresses is needed only until there is a GATT regime for trade in services to match that for trade in goods, is roughly consistent with that emerging regime.

The EC can thus make a reasonable claim to be acting as a research laboratory both for trade in financial services between countries and for the deregulation of finance within them. The Americans, who only five years ago, were telling Europe that it suffered from a "Eurosclerosis" of rules and traditional demarcations, must now admit that Europe has commissioned a regime for finance that is much less constraining than their own. The blueprint is largely drawn up and accepted. Construction, with many an argument, go-slow and court case along the way, will last well into the next century.

9

FRONTIER-FREE FARMING

A Serious Challenge to the Great Market

In the summer of 1989 the Spanish were rumbled. They had kept the world, and their Community partners, in the dark about an outbreak of a highly unpleasant, and notifiable, disease called contagious bovine pleuropneumonia (CBP). Cattle in the region of Leon y Castilla had begun to come down with the disease three years earlier, in 1986. Fearful for their beef exports, the regional authorities in Castille tried to keep the outbreak secret from Madrid and from the rest of Europe. They managed to keep the lid on it for three years, but in the end their secret came out, damaging something much more important than their beef exports – namely, the mutual trust of veterinary authorities of the Twelve.

Nothing in commerce is more emotive to the citizens of one country than the idea of a hazard to their health being imported from another country. And nothing is more likely to make EC governments resist the lifting of their national frontier controls – on animal and plant diseases as well as many other hazards – than the feeling that they cannot trust each other to tell the truth. Project 1992 is designed to increase the free movement of many things, but not animal diseases, bugs that destroy crops and hazards to public health.

This is just one of the hidden tripwires to the progress of 1992 that lie waiting in the matter of agriculture. Such tripwires were temporarily forgotten in the euphoric glow that still lingers around the reforms of February 1988, through which the EC leaders finally summoned the collective will to bring spending on the Common Agricultural Policy (CAP) back under some sort of control. They put price "stabilisers" on important farm products to discourage expensive surpluses, placed a lid on the overall growth of the farm budget, and reached a four-year budget deal with the European Parliament.

A smaller size of CAP

Gone, for the moment, are the midnight wrangles in Brussels over surpluses, butter mountains, wine lakes, farm spending overruns, and the related and bitter issue of the British contribution to the Community budget, so much a feature of the 1970s and 1980s. Britain argued that it shouldered an unfairly (for a medium income country) large share of the budget burden, because as a major importer from outside the EC it paid Brussels a substantial amount in customs duties but, having a small farm sector relative to its home food market, it got little in return from the Community's biggest cash cow, the CAP (see Chapter 2).

Since spring 1988, the EC's food surpluses have been shrinking rapidly, albeit thanks to a huge and expensive disposal programme: a butter mountain of 1.3 million tonnes was reduced to 200,000 tonnes within a year. EC farm spending in 1989 was well within its newly-prescribed overall limit, and for the first time the share of the EC budget devoted to propping up farm prices fell to below 60 per cent of the total.

But a jury could not yet give its verdict on the adequacy of the reforms, for several reasons. One is that these "stabilisers" – which provide for automatic price cuts when a certain threshold of output is reached – are designed to persuade farmers to produce less, but cannot force them to do so. If they choose to go on producing at lower prices, the Community still has a legal commitment to buy their crops. In addition, the structure of the farming industry is unusually fragmented. Even the largest of the Community's ten million farmers, such as an agro-business mogul of East Anglia or the Loire, produces no more than one hundredth of 1 per cent of a Community crop. He knows he alone cannot keep general prices up by restraining his own output, so he is tempted by the likelihood of lower marginal prices, after 1988, to plant even more crops or rear even more animals to maintain his income. It is also most unlikely that the 1988 reforms constitute anything like the swingeing cuts in EC farm support which the United States is demanding in the Uruguay Round of GATT talks. The 1988 drought in America raised world prices, thus temporarily cutting back the degree to which Brussels has recently needed to subsidise EC farm exports to make them sellable on the world market, but the United States still lays most of the blame for distortions in world agricultural trade at the Community's doorstep. It is, however, equally doubtful that the EC is disposed to go much further than it did in 1988 to satisfy Washington.

Mixed Prospects for the 1992 Harvest

There will be at least one consolation if the farm budget nightmare returns in the early 1990s: it will not deprive 1992 of financial resources, as it would conventional European spending programmes like transport or technology research and development. The 1992 programme is rare among Commission initiatives in not being a direct charge on the Community budget; as a programme of business deregulation and Euro-regulation its "costs" are borne by companies and workers all around the Community. But just as the 1988 reforms released the political energies of EC leaders to tackle the internal market, so the return of farm squabbles could prove a serious political distraction in the early 1990s.

Set money to one side: agriculture still poses as serious a challenge to the full achievement of the great market as looms anywhere. There are many thorny questions still to be answered. How, in the absence of internal frontier controls, can EC member states maintain the funny-money system that has insulated their farmers for the past twenty years from changes in European currency rates? What is to replace the national import quotas that govern products as diverse as New Zealand lamb and Caribbean bananas? How, without checks at their borders, can national authorities be sure they won't be importing noxious diseases from the other eleven states? How far can there be a genuine common market in food products, given that each regards its foods as tastier, but more importantly, safer, than other countries' fare?

The MCA, or Mightily Confusing Arrangement

Currently, there are two main financial uses for borders in intra-Community trade. One is to check goods subject to value-added taxes and excise duties (see Chapter 5). The other is to administer monetary compensatory amounts (MCAs), a system of levies/subsidies designed to iron out currency-related distortions in cross-border agricultural trade. The removal of internal frontiers demanded in the Single European Act requires radical change in both areas.

The very existence of MCAs is a reminder of how uncommon the common market is, even in farm products. Certainly, in agriculture the Twelve do have common prices in European currency units (ecus), a common intervention system to prop up those prices, common finance to bankroll the intervention system, and common protection against cheaper third-country imports cutting away the price props. Why should the Community seek to provide a common price for farmers when it leaves the levelling of prices in other industries to the workings of the market? The political answer is that farmers were considered so subject to vagaries such as climate in their business, so strategically important and so dear to the pre-industrial folk memories of all Europeans, that they were specially catered for in the Treaty of Rome. Article 39 states that the aim of the CAP is to improve farming productivity and security of supply and "to ensure a fair standard of living for the agricultural community, in particular by increasing the individual earnings of persons employed in agriculture". The same article also whispers of the need to ensure that "supplies reach consumers at reasonable prices", but rather less is heard of this assertion.

Gradually the European public has become more hard-headed in its view of farming. According to Peter Pooley, a senior Brussels agriculture official, the new social contract between Europe's public and its farmers runs roughly thus: "We, the voters will carry on subsidising you the farmers, if necessary directly, provided you do not embarrass us with surpluses, or with scandalous frauds, and provided you keep the countryside sweet-smelling, clean-tasting and pretty to the eye, and your animals healthy and undrugged." Nonetheless, the commitment to support farmers is still firmly there, and to do it mainly in the time-honoured or dishonoured Community way of forcing consumers to pay high prices, buying up any surplus, and either storing it or dumping it on the world market. This rigging requires common prices; otherwise, all the Community's surplus crops and livestock would, in theory at least, end up in the state with the highest intervention price.

The next oddity is that common prices exist in the Community's hypothetical currency, the ecu, but not in the national currencies which farmers actually pocket. There was once a truly common price for each farm product, but only briefly in the late 1960s. Within two years of common guaranteed prices being introduced in 1967, they were hit by parity changes of the French franc and the Deutschmark. The franc was devalued by 11 per cent in August 1969. In theory, with the ecu (in which EC farm prices are set) worth more in franc terms, French food prices should have risen. But the French government decided it could do without such an additional boost to inflation, and its Community partners decided they could do without French farmers getting a bigger apparent price rise than their own. So, the dreaded monetary compensatory amounts came into the world. These took the form (in France's case) of "negative" MCAs or subsidies on imports into France and taxes on exports from France, so that French farmers lost the advantage created by currency devaluation, and producers in other countries were protected against competition from cheaper French products. Soon afterwards the Deutschmark was revalued and similar arguments were heard and adjustments made involving "positive" MCAs for West Germany.

At the time, there was faith that "normality" could be restored within a few years. The plan was for the "green franc" rate (the rigged conversion ratio of EC farm prices from ecus into real French francs) to be devalued over two years and the "green Deutschmark" to be revalued over four years. But this plan was killed by the monetary ructions that followed the 1971 unpegging of the dollar from gold, and was not revived the following year when Community currencies floated jointly into the "snake" – the forerunner of the European Monetary System. Ever since then, governments have used MCAs to protect their farmers from the direct impact of European currency realignments.

Some say that MCAs are the glue that has held the CAP together during twenty years of currency adjustments. They cushioned the impact on farmers of the changes in "real" currency parities that have compensated for differing rates of growth in industrial productivity and inflation. Others say: more's the pity. MCAs have undoubtedly led to much fraud. For instance, in 1986 when the UK had a higher negative MCA than Ireland, there was a lucrative trade in smuggling cattle from Northern Ireland into the Irish republic to avoid the MCA import tax. These cattle were then slaughtered in Ireland and the meat exported to the mainland UK with a handsome export subsidy. There has also been a technical quirk in MCA payments that has made it profitable for the French and Belgians to load farm goods at their own ports but declare them for export at a Dutch port.

More serious than minor trade deflections like these, however, is the way MCAs produce varying levels of support across the Community and thus distort investment in farming. Positive MCAs keep national prices in countries like West Germany higher even than they would be under the already price-boosting CAP. This preserves a particular German species, the three-cow, Mercedes-driving farmer. On the other hand, the "green money" system relatively discourages investment in weaker currency countries like France with natural farming advantages. This has two knock-on effects. It increases regional imbalances in the Community, because the poorer countries all happen to have negative MCAs. And the average European pays an even more unnecessarily high price for his food.

Enter 1992. The one certain thing about MCAs is that as a border levy/subsidy they cannot easily survive the removal of border controls. Elimination would obviously be the ideal, but so far this harsh option has barely been talked about. One phoney solution has been tried since 1984. Because positive MCAs are the hardest to dismantle (since this involves a farm price cut in national currency terms) it was decided no further positive MCAs would be created. The device agreed in 1984 was that in any future currency realignments MCAs would be based on the currency which was revalued the most, ie the Deutschmark. The effect of this has been to tie EC farm prices to the ever-rising German currency. Simply as a result of this the common price for Community farm goods in ecus was five years later nearly 14 per cent higher than it would have been in the absence of that 1984 ruse. Since 1987 there has been agreement on how to partially phase out negative MCAs, too. But perversely – and so much in EC agriculture is perverse – some states have cut their negative MCAs faster than agreed, precisely because this has raised their national prices and so enabled them to get around the Commission's attempt to freeze prices.

If MCAs are to live on after 1992, probably the only way of administering them will be by whatever means is found of checking VAT receipts (see Chapter 5). The eyes of agri-fraudsters will light up at the prospect. Beyond that, there remains a distant hope that the currency parities of the Twelve will be irrevocably locked together in a monetary union, and the perceived need for MCAs will thus disappear. This is one area where current rampantly illogical behaviour creates a straight logical link between a frontier-free single market and the need for monetary union.

Yes, We Have Too Many Bananas

Some of the toughest problems raised by the prospect of a frontier-free market from the Elbe to the Atlantic concern the national quotas which certain member states impose on imports. In the industrial arena the big quota issue involves Japanese cars; in agriculture the arguments revolve around the more mundane staples of butter, lamb, bananas and rum. Nonetheless, they are of great moment to their New Zealand, Caribbean and African producers, whose view of "fortress Europe" will be determined by what happens to their commodities. All these commodity exporters can do to force the outcome is to exploit the traditional ties with individual EC member states that gave rise to the quotas in the first place.

New Zealand's share of the EC lamb and butter market has been greatly reduced from what it was in the early 1970s, when much of Britain's effort in negotiating entry into the Community went into making sure it was not suddenly cut off from its long-standing Antipodean supplier. But despite many complaints from European farmers, New Zealand still retains a butter quota in the British market, as well as a Community-wide quota for lamb. It is just possible that this British quota could survive 1992, *de facto*, given that the salting of New Zealand butter deliberately caters more to British than to continental palates.

Bananas, however, are much the same everywhere, though their cost of production varies radically. That is precisely the problem facing the Caribbean producers who now have the jitters over 1992. The present regime governing bananas is perhaps the strangest trade fix of any in the Community. The market is split three ways. Some 20 per cent of bananas consumed in the EC comes – duty-free – from former British, French and Italian colonies in the Caribbean and Africa who are all members of the Community's Lomé Convention with Third World countries. These bananas go to the UK, France and Italy. Around 30 per cent comes from the tropical parts of the Community itself – France's overseas territories, Spain's Canary Islands, Portugal's Madeira and Greece's Crete – and are mainly eaten within these EC member states. The remaining 50 per cent comes from the huge plantations of Central America, whose so-called "dollar bananas" are eaten by those northern EC states without a tropical ex-colonial connection. But there is a further rift in this most fragmented of EC markets. Denmark, Ireland and the Benelux pay a 20 per import levy on their dollar bananas, but Germany, the biggest EC consumer of the fruit, does not. Quite why the Germans should have insisted during the Treaty of Rome negotiations on special treatment on bananas is not clear; it had no political rationale like Britain's demands on behalf of New Zealand produce. Perhaps it was the memory of having no bananas during the war that set the fruit on the same pedestal as coffee. At all events, Bonn wants to keep its large duty-free import quota of dollar bananas.

Unsnarling this historical tangle presents one of the more unexpected challenges of project 1992. A totally free market would suit banana peelers around the Community, and the plantation owners of Central America who would easily be able to undercut growers both inside the

Community and in the Caribbean and Africa. The latter, of course, want the continued shelter of their quotas in the British, French and Italian markets, and are appealing to their traditional ties with the Community, and to the Lomé Convention, that 1992 should not be an excuse for squeezing them out. One answer would be to extend the 20 per cent tariff to all dollar bananas, but West Germany won't agree to that. On the other hand, a post-1992 open market would make it as hard for West Germany to have a separate tariff arrangement as it would be for the UK, France and Italy to have separate quotas. If there is one commodity that puts 1992 on the skids, it will be the banana.

Bugs, Beasts, Borders

No symbol of a country's fear of foreign contamination is more graphic than the snarling poster of a rabid dog that greets anyone who lands at a British port. When the British government puts forward a raft of reasons why some checks will continue to be needed at internal EC borders after 1992, arguments about animal, and to a lesser extent plant, disease command the widest public support in Britain – much more than fear of terrorism or of drugs.

Of all the checks that take place at borders, those on animals and plants are perhaps the hardest for Brussels to play down. Not because these controls are always effective. Disease is no respecter of thin red lines drawn on the map of Europe. The difficulty is that the free circulation of animals and plants cannot be achieved by the same means found so successful in other sectors – ie, agreement by the Twelve to harmonise a bare minimum of common standards and then to tolerate each other's remaining product differences. States can't mutually recognise each other's habitual diseases in this way. ("I'll accept your foot-and-mouth disease, if you'll relax about my Colorado Beetle in potatoes.")

What the member states might, in time, come to accept is the efficacy of each other's disease control systems. They are, however, far from that position of mutual trust at the moment. Yet the Commission wants to phase out checks on animal and plant imports and to place the onus of health control on the exporting country. In the case of animals, member states would be allowed, for a transitional period, to carry out checks at the destination of the consignment (ie farm, abbatoir, processing plant); animals could be held in quarantine, but at their place of destination, not at frontiers. Each consignment of animals or meat would be accompanied by a veterinary certificate issued by the exporting country.

Something equivalent – "a plant passport" – would be issued for plants travelling across the Community, on the basis of an inspection carried out at the nursery or farm where the plants were grown. A Community Plant Inspectorate would be established, along the lines of the current Community Veterinary Inspectorate, to ensure that member states applied uniform disease controls on products circulating within the Community, as well as those coming in from outside. Such was the Commission's vision.

It was the Commission's bad luck that just when it was trying to sell these far-reaching changes to governments, the row over the outbreak of CBP in Spain occurred. The response of countries like Britain, Ireland and Denmark, with borders that consist wholly, or in part, of a natural disease-barrier like water, and which so far have less than the average EC quotient of animal and plant health problems, was predictable. "Let us keep our controls where they are most effective – at the frontiers – and do not force us to let potentially diseased animals and plants into the heart of our countries, possibly spreading infection along the way, before we can check them," they say.

To try to assuage these doubters, the Commission is proposing regional, as distinct from national, measures. On the outbreak of a serious notifiable animal disease, all movement of animals in and out of the infected area would be halted for thirty days. Brussels officials say they recognise that some animal and plant disease controls may also have to be introduced which cut across national borders. This occurs already in some countries; Northern Ireland, for instance, has a better animal health record than mainland Britain because it has certain extra restrictions. As for the health of plants, it would be abnormal for a landmass the size of the European Community not to have some internal controls, just as the United States does. For instance, there are certain diseases to which citrus fruit is prone, but, say EC officials, there would be no point in applying these controls outside citrus-growing areas of Europe. Thus, there might need to be controls on citrus pests spreading across Spain, Italy and Greece, just as similar controls separate citrus-growing Florida, Texas and California from the rest of the USA.

In time, protective zones defined by disease, rather than by political, frontiers might work. The doubting member states concede this. But far better, they contend, to wait until the Community has tougher and more harmonised disease controls. Total eradication is quite impractical for many plant pests which are embedded, literally, in the soil of certain regions. By contrast, most animal diseases could probably be wiped out.

And some progress is being made here. One reason why the UK, Ireland and Denmark have a better record than continental countries is that they slaughter livestock infected with serious diseases rather than vaccinate them. Ironically, relying on vaccination has led to further outbreaks from laboratories making vaccines. Vaccination is, for this reason, going out of fashion.

But it is very much in fashion as a possible means of wiping out rabies. This is because Switzerland has apparently rid itself of rabies by putting vaccinated bait out for wild foxes, the main carrier of the scourge. The Community is now trying to emulate the Swiss success, on a far bigger scale. Its target is the area stretching from Belgium and Luxembourg in the north, down through eastern France to southern Germany, throughout which rabies is endemic in foxes. Under a plan approved by EC farm ministers in the summer of 1989, the first bait was dropped in autumn of that year, and the operation is to be repeated in the spring and autumn of the next two years. "We could have a positive result by 1991," says an EC official, "and if so, the British and Irish can drop their quarantine." UK officials, for their part, say they welcome the plan, but doubt that nature will respond to the man-made deadline of 1992.

Eurobread is a Europain

There is, in contrast, every expectation that the Community will win its race for a single market of freely-circulating food products by 1992. Indeed no other area better shows how the new technique of minimal harmonisation can break an ancient legislative logjam.

Food, appropriately, has always been on the minds of commissioners and ministers whenever they have sat down in Brussels to try to advance the common market. The first directive the EC Council of Ministers ever adopted was that on food colouring in 1962. But food law not only blazed the trail in the 1960s for the single market; it also led the way in the 1970s up the cul-de-sac of product-by-product harmonisation. In answer to each country's myriad food content restrictions, there was the misguided attempt to create Euro-recipes so that the Euro-sausage and the Euro-beer might be freely sold throughout the Community, though perhaps eaten and drunk by no one. Painfully and slowly, some definitions were agreed, and directives passed, on such relatively simple items as instant coffee, chocolate and honey, but even some of these have had to be updated as food technology has evolved.

Then, in 1979, there was the Cassis de Dijon ruling (see Chapter 7). It is worth recalling that this landmark case, ending harmonisation for harmonisation's sake, came in the food and drink sector, and had its most immediate effect there. Well before the 1985 internal market White Paper, the Commission had pulled off the Council of Ministers' table its previous product composition proposals. "We had developed the new thinking before Cockfield arrived, though Cockfield was the general needed to grasp the strategy and push it through," one Brussels official explains. The "new thinking" was that the Community would only legislate so as to protect public health, ensure fair trading and inform consumers, and everything else in food could be left to the choice and taste of the consumer so informed.

Progress has since been rapid. More than forty-five directives were passed between 1985 and 1989. They are almost all horizontal in nature: that is to say, they deal, across the board, with the additives that can go into foods, the materials in which they are wrapped, or the labels that describe their ingredients. This last measure is the key to the whole new approach, because, as one EC official puts it: "The only way of reconciling the differences in people's ideas of a given food is to describe it more carefully and let the consumer choose." The European Court has continued to back this approach. It said, for instance, that Italy could not block imports of pasta simply because it was made of soft wheat rather than the classic Italian ingredient of durum wheat – provided that the type of wheat was clearly listed on the pasta package.

Each to His Own Taste

Acceptance of the new approach in food law has not been easy for all member states. Britain, for instance, has long been liberal – too liberal, some would retort – on what goes into its food, largely because food industrialisation arrived in Britain first. West Germany has sought to stick to some idiosyncratic standards, but much of the fight went out of its effort when it lost a European Court case to define the precise ingredients of all beer sold in Germany. France has, in the same court, lost bids to keep imported imitation dairy products and frozen yoghurts out of its shops.

According to the Cecchini report on 1992, the food industry stands to reap some of the clearest benefits from a freely-circulating single market – between 500 million and 1 billion ecus or 1–2 per cent of the food-processing sector's turnover. This will come, directly, from the march of cheaper products or ingredients into previously protected markets, and, indirectly through greater competition with US and Swiss rivals. Up to now, of the forty-six largest EC food companies, nearly half operate in only one EC member state in addition to their country of origin, and only five of them operate in four or more EC states.

However, one overriding caveat is in order. If food is to move more freely around the Community, so too may hazards to the health of those who eat it. A balance will have to be struck: public health controls must be applied properly, but not so zealously as to become the last non-tariff barrier available to governments. The Community has recently passed new food inspection rules, which will have, incidentally, the effect of bringing greater uniformity into Britain's exceptionally decentralised system (operated at the level of district and county council). But, where there are outbreaks of food poisoning, cooperation between states — through the Commission's fast alert system — becomes all the more important. Nothing could panic governments into cumbersome re-regulation of the market faster than public hysteria about listeria, or other food-borne pests, getting a free ride around the single market.

10

OPENING ARMS

The Special Case of Defence Procurement

Every year France and Britain now do something that would have been unthinkable until recently. Defence officials of the two countries get together to brief defence industry executives from both countries on forthcoming military contracts, and to invite companies from *both* countries to bid for the business.

The sight of France and Britain – cut-throat rivals in selling arms around the world, and the two countries with the largest and most self-centred military procurement in Europe – opening their markets even by a fraction to each other strains belief. Yet the contagion is infecting others, too. Britain and France already publish bulletins listing their coming military contracts, and from the start of 1990 eleven other European members of NATO are to follow their example in inviting foreign tenders for their defence buying.

Clearly defence procurement, in its own strange and halting way, is beginning to follow other forms of public purchasing (such as telecommunications) in being opened up to free cross-border competition and bidding. It would be odd indeed, if the defence sector were kept quite apart, since there is virtually no military manufacturer that does not produce something for the civilian economy too. Some of the biggest mergers attributed to project 1992 have occurred in defence-oriented companies – the Siemens-GEC takeover of Plessey, the West German "marriage of the elephants" between Daimler-Benz and MBB, Thomson-CSF's purchase of Philips's defence company HSA, and so on.

It almost sounds as though the 1992 programme has embraced defence. But it hasn't. What is happening in defence is parallel to project 1992, but separate from it. The European defence sector is still far from slipping into the grasp of the European Community, despite the avowed ambition of Jacques Delors, the Commission president, to get his hands on it. Rather, European states have left it to the thirteen-country

Independent European Programme Group (IEPG), which groups together all the European NATO members minus Iceland, to make the running in trying to forge a semblance of a common arms market, and to the nine-nation Western European Union (WEU) organisation to reconcile the views of most major European countries on defence policy.

The reason for this is as old as the Treaty of Rome and its Article 223 which specifically excludes "the production of, or trade in, arms, munitions and war material" from any EC rules. For some thirty years member states firmly kept defence off the Community agenda. This clear demarcation long suited most EC states which had no desire to let Brussels interfere in so sensitive an area of their national sovereignty as defence; it also prevented any compromise of the neutrality of Ireland, the Community's one non-NATO state. Having tried, and failed in 1954 to set up a European Defence Community (EDC), the Europeans were happy for many years to leave all defence matters to NATO. The one exception was, of course, France which opted out of NATO's integrated command structure in 1966 while remaining a political member of the alliance; this was ironic because it was the French parliament's failure to ratify the EDC treaty in 1954 that killed the proposed European organisation.

The New Ball-Game

By the mid-1980s, however, circumstances had changed. France was fretting to get as far back into the Western alliance as it could without putting its soldiers under NATO command; and its European partners were keen to accomodate France's desire. It so happened that there were two defence bodies of which France was a member – the IEPG set up in 1976 to promote European military research, development and production, and the WEU established in 1948, largely as a pre-NATO means of committing Britain to keeping troops on the continent. In 1983–84 both organisations were kicked back into life.

There was a transatlantic factor at work, too. Ronald Reagan had jolted the Europeans into action in a variety of ways. By his erratic policy towards the Soviet Union – first taking a tough arms control line and then, in his 1986 Reykjavik summit with Mikhail Gorbachev, raising the prospect of total nuclear disarmament – he made Europeans conscious of their different perspective. In addition, his Star Wars programme, though roundly criticised by West European politicians on doctrinal grounds, was regarded by European defence industrialists as a threat to their own ability to compete with the United States in high-tech weaponry.

Then the tide in East-West relations turned, as Mikhail Gorbachev got his peace-offensive fully under way and Ronald Reagan left office. Everything that has happened since has merely underlined the reasons why West Europeans should want to prepare themselves for greater military self-reliance: the 1987 Intermediate Nuclear Forces (INF) treaty has removed US as well as Soviet medium-range ground-based rockets from Europe; George Bush went into negotiations to reduce NATO and Warsaw Pact conventional forces in Europe with a proposal for a first-stage 20 per cent cut in US troops (and an even larger cut in Soviet troops); and Congress continues to press America's allies to do more in their defence so as to help reduce the US budget deficit.

Playing the Field Cautiously

In this unfolding drama, it would have been surprising if the European Community had not sought a part. It was given its cue in 1985, when the Twelve wrote into the Single European Act their desire for closer cooperation on security issues and their determination "to maintain the technological and industrial conditions necessary for their security". The Single Act was silent about whether this should be achieved through the Community; indeed the treaty-writers entered a specific caveat that nothing in the Act should impede cooperation for certain EC states through the WEU or NATO. And it is true that "security" is a broader, and vaguer, concept than defence. But even before the Single Act, the Commission had put down a marker of its intent to play a role.

Jacques Delors, with his Gallic desire to miss no opportunity to Europeanise defence, and Lord Cockfield, with his lawyer/accountant's determination to let no sector escape the logic of his market, used the June 1985 White Paper to label the defence industry as a suitable case for the single-market treatment. However, the Commission has yet to pronounce on defence. Its caution is understandable. Mr Delors became warier, after his call for a special EC summit on security policy issues, following the 1986 US-Soviet summit in Reykjavik, was heard in hollow silence by EC leaders. Even on the industrial side, an attempt by the Commission since 1988 to assert that the Community's common external tariff applies, at least in theory, as much to military as to civil imports, has left most EC states unimpressed, and the United States (Europe's main outside arms supplier) downright hostile.

The Commission may have left its say on the defence industry too late. Neutral Austria applied for EC membership in July 1989. Vienna's application is, to put it mildly, unwelcome to Jacques Delors and to a country like Belgium which believes that the Community's eventual destiny lies in a political union encompassing defence. With Austria as a member, it would be hard for the Community to develop policies on defence procurement, let alone defence strategy.

Rather more important than Belgium's objections to Austrian entry is the warning from West Germany about Eastern Europe. Politicians in Bonn are beginning to argue that the Community should not make reunification of the two Germanies, or eventual EC links with the newly democratic countries of Eastern Europe, more difficult by adding defence to its array of policies.

A Singular Market

Defence procurement is special, and will remain so. It can only be a candidate for partial deregulation, because governments generally define, pay for, and jealously guard, their military technology, and because governments are the sole customer for expensive pieces of weaponry. A heavy degree of government intervention is common in the defence industry the world over, whether it is in state or private hands.

But there is something very peculiar about the European defence market which Delors calls "the most immobile – because of its national vanities and captive markets". It is a curious fact that forty years after joining NATO, every member government, bar Luxembourg and Iceland, still tries to buy as much weaponry as possible within its own borders. Such autarky is understandable, if expensive, in neutral countries such as Sweden or Switzerland which don't want to have to rely on others for their means of defence. But it makes neither military nor economic sense within an alliance. Nevertheless, the gut instinct of governments not to trust foreigners when it comes to arms purchases remains strong. This attitude of governments makes things easy for their own domestic defence companies, which are delighted to be protected from outside competition, provided, that is, military spending stays stable or rises. The upshot of the fragmented market is that Europe has an amazing variety of weapons system and makers – 22 types of combat aircraft and 12 types of tank, and when it comes to, say, surface-to-air missiles, there are 18 companies in the seven European NATO countries that produce them.

Collaborators Cannot Compete

Collaboration by two or more member states on a given project to produce a specific weapon has been the much-vaunted way of getting long enough production-runs in the segmented European market to keep modern high-tech weaponry affordable. Even for the larger European countries, this is the only solution short of buying a weapon straight off someone else's shelf. The last fighter-aircraft which Britain made by itself was the Lightning in the 1950s. Today only France is left in the deeply uncomfortable position of choosing to fly solo with its Rafale fighter project. The three other major European countries – Britain, West Germany and Italy – teamed up to build the Tornado and are now wrestling (along with a fourth co-pilot, Spain) to try to get its successor, the European Fighter Aircraft (EFA) off the ground. But collaboration, as it has been most frequently practised in the military field, is the very antithesis of competition. Only with small projects have companies taken the initiative of developing a weapon on their own and with their own money, and run the risk that they might not interest either their own or any other country in buying it. Far more frequently, they have sat passively, like some Indian bride, waiting for their government to arrange a marriage with another equally passive commercial partner.

Such passivity, prevalent in the past, is hardly surprising. The share of the work that a company gets in a collaborative project is, in the last resort, determined by the amount of money its government is putting

Public procurement of weapons and missile systems* (billion ecus)

	B	FRG	F[1]	I	NL	UK	EC 6	EC 12
Defence budget	3.4	28.1	28.3	15.0	5.3	31.5	111.6	132.6
(as % of GDP)	(3.3)	(3.4)	(4.2)	(2.7)	(3.2)	(5.3)	(4.0)	(4.0)
Expenditure on weapons and missile systems	0.4	3.9	7.6	2.8	1.2	8.5	24.4	29.3
Potential savings[2]	-	-	-	-	-	-	-	6.2

[1] French expenditure on weapons and missile systems is assumed to be the same proportion of the defence budget as in the United Kingdom.

[2] Assuming that the potential savings on this type of defence procurement are comparable to those estimated in the Atkins study for transport equipment other than motor vehicles.

*1985

Source: NATO Commission

into the project, and the amount of hardware its government is getting out of that project, rather than the company's relative skills and competitiveness. As an example, in the EFA project British Aerospace is pretty well guaranteed one-third of the work on the airframe, no matter how it performs (relative to its EFA airframe partners, MBB of Germany, Aeritalia of Italy and CASA of Spain), simply because Her Majesty's government is putting up one-third of the money and the Royal Air Force will take one-third of the planes. Collaborative projects also tend to be management-heavy. They need to be. Every country wants to make sure it is not being cheated out of its fair work share (*juste retour* is the French catch-phrase for this in the jargon of European military contracting). In addition, projects which are not subject to normal commercial competition merit extra close observation, if they are not to go wrong.

New Brooms — with Harder Bristles

It was hardly surprising therefore that a certain disenchantment with this bureaucratic and highly regulated form of cross-border arms procurement should set in among Europe's more competition-minded defence ministries and aggressive defence companies. Prominent among these sceptics has been Peter Levene, who was in 1985 brought in from running a medium-size defence contractor to be Britain's chief of defence procurement. His brief was to get better value for money out of a defence budget strapped for cash by post-Falkland war spending and the Trident nuclear programme. Exploiting his position as British industry's largest single customer, Levene made himself very unpopular with many defence contractors, by making them compete for more contracts, and bear the cost of failure (and expect the fruits of success) through fixed-price contracts. Levene also gave the British defence industry as a whole a powerful shock with the decision in 1986 to abandon the Nimrod airborne early warning system, on which GEC had spent nearly £1 billion of British public money, in favour of the Boeing Awacs system from the United States. This was the biggest UK contract (apart from Trident, a special case) that had gone to a foreign bidder for many years, and, more effectively than any words, the award served notice on the UK defence industry that it could no longer count on a doting government.

More innovative, however, was the 1987 agreement which Levene reached with his French counterpart at the Delegation Générale pour

L'Armement (DGA) in Paris on reciprocal purchasing. The deal was that the defence ministries of Britain and France would first look at what weaponry the other country's industry had already on the shelf before going ahead to develop it itself. To make the innovation less painful, it was decided that reciprocal purchasing should be limited to contracts worth less than £50 million, and though there would be no precise accounting every year, a rough balance over a period of years would be sought. In addition, the two defence ministries agreed to hold annual industry-briefing conferences on forthcoming contracts, and the French defence ministry ended up imitating Britain in publishing a monthly contracts bulletin for would-be bidders.

The practical results so far have been few. But French taxpayers have been saved some francs by their army buying ready-made British tank range-finders and their navy some navigation radars, and British taxpayers were saved some pounds when the Royal Navy bought off-the-shelf French mine disposal equipment and sonars. More considerable has been the symbolism of Europe's two most autarkic defence industries looking outward for a change, with a view not only to collaboration, but also buying from each other. Britain purchases only about 10 per cent of its weaponry abroad, and the remaining 90 per cent from UK suppliers (though about 15 per cent is made in the UK under collaborative arrangements with foreign partners). The figures are roughly the same for France, but quite different for West Germany and smaller EC member states like the Netherlands which imports nearly half its weaponry. Indeed the reciprocal purchasing (or *achats croisés*) accord was made possible precisely because the French and British defence industries are roughly of the same size and competitiveness, and the two countries' armed forces have broadly the same needs. The fact that, due largely to being chief salesman of the collaboratively-produced Tornado to Saudi Arabia, Britain displaced France in the mid-late 1980s as number three in world arms exports (behind the superpowers) did not spoil the harmony. Indeed it made the once-fearful British more confident about opening up their market, and the once-cocky French readier to treat with a European neighbour.

Extending "Levenism"

On a broader stage, the British defence minister, Michael Heseltine, who brought Peter Levene into the UK defence ministry, was also instrumental in breathing the same sort of pro-competition and market-opening message into the IEPG. In late 1985 the IEPG commissioned a study from a group chaired by Henk Vredeling, a former Dutch defence minister and, significantly as it turned out, a man who had spent time in Brussels as an EC commissioner. The Vredeling Group effectively recommended that "Levenism" be extended on a European scale. It stressed that governments had it in their power to create a more open arms market by the general conditions on which they awarded their defence contracts. To this end, the Vredeling report said, the thirteen IEPG governments should first let collaborative contracts on the basis of competitive fixed-price tenders by rival international consortia, and second each publish tenders to inform companies of bidding opportunities beyond their home base, and establish a register of their defence contractors to help companies across Europe pick foreign partners.

The aim of the latter proposal was to fill the deliberate gap left in the Treaty of Rome exempting armaments from EC rules, and in particular from the requirement that big pubic-sector contracts be advertised across the EC. Small wonder, then, that the first reaction of most defence ministers was a sharp intake of breath. Indeed, by the end of 1987, Vredeling, an impatient man, was complaining (in a NATO publication) that defence ministers were ducking the challenge he had posed them, and arguing that the whole matter should be passed to the EC Commission. Gradually the message sunk in. In November 1988 the IEPG countries adopted an "action plan":

● Governments were to take steps to allow contracts to be placed "more readily with suppliers in other countries".

● In addition to more competitive bidding across frontiers, "comprehensive and systematic cooperation in research and technology will be the centrepiece for the creation of an European Armaments Market".

● However, "the introduction of cross-border competition depends on individual countries receiving a fair return" in the long run. To measure such fair returns, the IEPG would record the pattern of cross-border contracts. In addition, the fledgling defence industries of Greece, Portugal and Turkey would be allowed special protection.

A Brave but Flawed Attack

It was a brave start in a difficult field. By late 1989 the thirteen IEPG countries had all assigned special representatives in their defence ministries to the task of helping foreign bidders to tender for contracts in their countries, and had committed themselves to publishing their future contract details. But, clearly the IEPG action plan is no Single European Act. Nuclear contracts and, less excusably, warships are excluded from the action plan's scope. More important, inclusion of the *juste retour* principle – essential, as it was, to secure southern European acquiescence – may prove a fatal blow to the emergence of freer competition.

Another certain flaw is the impossibility of IEPG countries agreeing on a definition of what constitutes fair competition in the arms business, let alone the impossibility, without EC-style legal machinery, of enforcing any such definition. For instance, the Vredeling report said that the advantages of a single European defence equipment market – amounting to nearly half the size of the US market – "will only come in full if governments are prepared to allow real competition and do not distort the market, for example by hidden subsidies". But if, for instance, a British company competing for an Italian defence contract feels that it has lost out to a local Italian company which was helped by Italian state aid, the British company's only recourse is to appeal to the hardly neutral referee of the Italian defence ministry. There is no military equivalent of the European Commission to investigate complaints, nor military division of the European Court to rule on such complaints. Here is a nice example of the way free trade leads on to supranationalism.

But it would be utopian to suppose that there could soon be such institutions in Europe's defence industry. By attempting to set up a semi-single market in defence, Europe's defence ministers have, for some time to come, forestalled any more drastic action by the European Community. That might – tell it not in Gath, publish it not in the streets of Ashkelon – have even been part of their intent.

The Growing Overlap: Competition Policy

But the 1990s are likely to see the lines between Europe-in-uniform and Europe-in-civvies become increasingly blurred. There are three areas in which the overlap will occur. The first is in competition policy. The European Commission may not be about to intervene directly to settle wrangles over rules set by a body, the IEPG, two of whose members (Turkey and Norway) do not belong to the Community. But it is likely to take a growing interest in how Europe's big defence contractors comport themselves, particularly because few of these companies produce for the military market alone and some of them are beginning to carve out – by merger, acquisition or joint venture – larger shares of a smaller cake.

Many of the big mergers and takeovers attributed to project 1992 are, as already noted, occurring in the defence field. This is scarcely surprising, given the current prospect of East-West peace breaking out. Professor Roland Smith, the chairman of British Aerospace, forecast: "unless individual governments take it upon themselves to interfere with the progression of market forces, I cannot foresee more than three or four major European players in the European defence equipment industry by the mid-1990s". Up to a point, the creation of anything resembling a semi-common market in arms will make it easier to take a more relaxed attitude to mergers and takeovers, if the effective market increases along with size of the players. This was why the British defence ministry fought to block GEC's bid for Plessey in 1985–86, but was prepared to see it go through in 1988–89, especially because second time around GEC had a co-predator in Siemens.

Competition, it could be argued, was actually enhanced by the takeover because the giant German company was relatively new to defence in general, and to the UK defence market in particular. The same line of reasoning can be used, and is used, by German defence officials, to defend the Daimler-Benz-MBB merger. No matter that this grouping will now account for half of Bonn's military procurement, they say, adding that West Germany is simply emulating the national aerospace monopolies that already existed in Britain, France and Italy. The important thing, Bonn officials say, is that West German military procurement remains open to foreign bidders. And it is true that West Germany, whose defence industry was virtually outlawed between 1945 and 1955, has traditionally bought between 15–20 per cent of its defence equipment outright from abroad. This is double the share of imports in French or British procurement.

Letting defence-related mergers go unhindered is one thing. But it is quite another for governments actively to encourage them, as Professor Smith's colleague at British Aerospace, Admiral Sir Raymond Lygo, proposed when presenting joint proposals on behalf of BAe and five other major European defence contractors. The BAe chief executive set out his salty vision of a rationalised defence sector: "the big dogs will eat the little dogs, and spit the bones out". Governments may baulk at this, particularly if they pause to think what it bodes for their professed desire to have rival international consortia competing for their collaborative defence contracts. National monopolies would produce the farce of a country always fielding the same company in every competing bid. Nor should continued Brussels passivity in this area be assumed. The

Commission has signalled that it sees nothing in principle to prevent it from investigating the competitive nature of mergers involving defence companies, especially as the latter generally have some civil output.

More Overlap: Dual-use Technology

A second area of overlap occurs in technology, where the same scientists in white coats serve pinstriped executives and the military top brass equally. Some duplication is inevitable between the new so-called Euclid technology programme which the IEPG has just launched in the defence field, and the many industrial research programmes run by the European Commission. Among the latter supposedly civil programmes, there are research projects into computer software and composite materials with considerable potential spin-off to the defence sector. Defence contractors of the likes of Aerospatiale and British Aerospace already line up at the door in Brussels for involvement in these EC programmes, whose billion ecu kitties far outglitter the 120 million ecus planned for Euclid. And the appetite of defence companies and ministries for such EC funding may grow. If West and East reduce the quantity of troops and weapons in central Europe, they will probably compete even more in the sophistication of their weaponry.

The blurring of civil-military lines may upset some Communist or Green members of the European Parliament, but it increasingly corresponds to the real world. Gone are the days when defence technology always led civil technology, and military reseach was conducted primarily in barbed-wire establishments. Advances in electronics have been driven by the civil market, particularly in Japan, whose defence industry is still meagre compared with its civil economic prowess. The result has been that more and more technology can be considered dual-use, like the computer that can design a car or guide a missile. This trend has brought the Cocom regime, the controls which Western countries plus Japan put on militarily sensitive exports to Communist countries, close to collapse in recent years. And project 1992 poses a fresh problem to these export controls.

Endgame Questions

Almost obscured by the attention paid to the future of national import quotas – if and when EC internal frontier checks come down after 1992 – is the problem of what to do about the security controls on exports which EC states administer nationally. Ireland, outside NATO, does not belong to the Coordinating Committee (Cocom) in Paris where the Western allies and Japan meet to decide what products and know-how can be freely shipped East and which cannot; but Irish customs officers informally abide by Cocom's rules. The issue for the other eleven EC states is not that they should join together any more than they do at the moment in setting Cocom rules. Rather, the problem is that once a computer can be moved as easily from Birmingham to Athens as it can at present from Birmingham to Dover, the Eleven, indeed the Twelve, will have to enforce the rules in precisely the same way.

Creating a single export control regime in the Community will require mutual trust, not only among EC states but also between them and the United States, which is the EC's number one outside supplier of high-technology and number one worrier about that technology getting into hostile hands. Persistently throughout the 1980s, Washington has complained of the behaviour and capabilities of some of its Cocom partners in Europe. Italy, for instance, did not until recently even publish a control list, so that Italian businessmen could hardly be blamed for not knowing what they were not supposed to ship abroad without special licence. Portugal has no technology specialists among its customs officers to spot errant computers, while Greek officials have had the reputation of turning a blind eye to techno-banditry. Nor is the possibility of Warsaw Pact countries getting their hands on militarily-useful technology the sole, or indeed the main, concern. In 1987 the big Seven – the United States, Japan, Canada, West Germany, France, Britain and Italy – announced they were setting up a Missile Technology Control Regime (MCTR), basically to keep any rocketry that could carry nuclear warheads out of Third World hands. Efforts by countries like Iraq to acquire Western missile technology show this to be a worthwhile, if elusive, goal. If, however, the four EC participants in the MCTR no longer, after 1992, have any checks on goods passing across frontiers with their other eight EC partners, the latter will somehow have to be brought to abide by the same controls.

Agreeing on a common way of checking goods leaving the Community should be no easier, nor harder than establishing common controls on people coming in (see Chapter 6). To help customs officers of the Twelve get to know each other's problems better, the Commission has launched the Mattaeus programme (St Matthew is the patron saint of customs officers, keeping watch over the great green channel in the sky). Some member states may well take umbrage at the idea of export security rules being brought into the Community's ambit. But they will be rowing against a tide that will sweep the military and civil aspects of European integration closer, whether or not the Community ever acquires the navy, army and airforce that Euro-federalists dream of.

11

THE
RULE OF LAW

*Heroes and Haverers in the
Pursuit of Legitimacy*

"The treaty [of Rome] is like an incoming tide," said Lord Denning, the British legal sage. "It flows into the estuaries and up the rivers. It cannot be held back." Project 1992 is creating a new wave of EC law which seems, for the moment, to have irresistible political momentum in passing new directives and regulations. But will this momentum carry through into practice? Will this new European law really be written into national law and complied with? Here is where doubts arise about 1992.

In the past thirty years, the Treaty of Rome has indeed flowed up the legal estuaries and rivers of the members. The primacy of Community law over national law has been clearly established by the European Court of Justice. It is this feature of the Community, above all others, that sets it apart from any other international organisation or grouping of states. But the 1992 programme puts new strain on the rule of law in the Community, because there are so many new and, for existing vested interests, inconvenient rules to comply with. The early omens are not good. Despite all the self-congratulation about the progress on the programme laid down in the internal market White Paper, by end-1989 only 14 of the 88 directives that were meant to have been translated into national legislation had actually been so in all member states.

Even before project 1992 was embarked upon, the caseload of the European Court was mounting sharply, as the Commission started legal proceedings against members for failing to abide by what they had agreed to (see table on page 132). Italy has long held the gold medal for dragging its feet in adopting EC laws, while Greece, one of the Community's newest members, now sports the silver one.

Here is a matter in which the deadline of 1992 may harm the single market. The rush in the EC Council of Ministers is the problem. "The

131

The caseload of the Court

Year	Cases brought	Judgments delivered	Cases pending on 31 December	Average time in months to deal with cases	
				Direct action	References for a preliminary ruling
1978	268	97	265	9	6
1979[1]	230	138	245	18	9
1980	279	132	318	18	9
1981	323	128	432	12	12
1982	345	185	459	13	12
1983	297	151	486	14	12
1984	312	165	458	17	14
1985	433	211	575	20	14
1986	329	174	510	21	15
1987	395	208	527	22	18
1988	372	238	599	24	17.5

[1] Figures for 1979 have been adjusted to allow for 1,112 staff cases brought that year which were, however, divided into 10 groups of related cases and treated by the Court as only 10 cases for all purposes including judgment. The unadjusted figures are: cases brought 1,332; cases pending on 31 December 1,347.

Source: Court of Justice of the European Communities

Community's decision-making process carries within itself the seeds of bad application because good political compromises often produce bad policies," declares Professor Yves Meny, a French expert on Community legislation. A likely example of this is in taxation, where the requirement for unanimous approval will probably lead to special concessions for every member state and a fudging of the changes need-ed to create a fraud-free, unbureaucratic tax regime across a truly open market.

Uneven implementation of EC rules could distort competition across the market quite as much as having no rules at all. The setting of penal-ties for breaking EC directives is left to member states. If some states enforce EC law punctiliously, while others either fail to get EC decisions onto their statute books or pay scant attention to them, there could be a backlash from the virtuous states, leading to bureaucratic tit-for-tat, and a "single market" sliding back into an anarchy of covert protection-ism rather as the Common Market did in the 1970s.

The European Court

The task of ensuring that EC law is applied throughout the Community falls to thirteen judges dressed in red silk and velvet robes who sit on the bench of the European Court of Justice in Luxembourg. (This court is no relation to the European Court of Human Rights which sits in Strasbourg as an arm of the Council of Europe.) Each EC country nominates one judge to the European Court. There is an additional one to enable the Court to reach decisions by majority vote (though the Court's decisions are always represented to the outside world as being unanimous). In addition, there are six advocates-general who give individual "opinions", a kind of dry run at a decision which the Court then usually but not always endorses.

Acting as the Community's Supreme Court, the judges rule on disputes between the Community's institutions, between member states and those institutions, and between companies or individuals and Community institutions. They also – and this is a role of increasing importance – give preliminary rulings to national judges on how to apply Community law when an EC issue or principle of law arises in their courts. Such requests for guidance numbered 179 in 1988, compared with 144 in 1987 and 91 in 1986.

Two Heroic Principles

There was a heroic period when EC judges, armed with only scanty provisions in the Treaty of Rome, went out to do battle with the member governments, and thus claimed fresh swathes of competence for the Community. The heyday of that phase was the 1960s, when the Court established the two cardinal principles of Community law:

● **Direct Effect of EC Law** The first principle is that EC law has "direct effect". That is to say, EC law is binding – imposing obligations and confering rights – not only on member states and Community institutions, but also directly on EC citizens and companies. Established in the Van Gend en Loos case of 1963, concerning the serious matter of a 5 per cent differential tariff on glue, this "direct effect" principle may be of even greater significance in the future than it has been in the past. It establishes the general right of individuals and companies to invoke EC law in national courts. Most of the cases in which the principle can be applied involve public authorities in member states, and the judge in the national court will usually ask the European Court for a preliminary ruling. It is thus an indirect way for private individuals and companies to put national authorities in the Luxembourg dock. It further means that the task of ensuring compliance with the EC treaties does not have to be left to an overworked and understaffed Commission in Brussels. Supervision can, instead, happen throughout the Community by people or companies taking, say, their local authority or water company or telephone service to court, directly under European law. In addition, where an individual or company contests a decision by the Council of Ministers or the Commission specifically directed at him or it, the plaintiff can go directly to the European Court.

● **Primacy of EC Law** The following year, 1964, saw established, in the Costa v. ENEL case, the even more important principle that EC law overrides the national laws of member states. Falminio Costa, a shareholder in Edison Volta, objected to the nationalisation of the Italian electricity industry and refused to pay a bill for L1,925 ($2) to ENEL, the newly nationalised electricity corporation. Mr Costa contended that the nationalisation had contravened the Treaty of Rome. The Italian judge in the case asked the European Court for an opinion. Before this was given, however, Italy's Constitutional court intervened to pronounce that because the Rome Treaty was ratified in Italy in ordinary Italian law, the provisions of any later piece of Italian legislation that conflicted with the Treaty must supercede those of the Treaty. The European Court overturned this ruling, saying that EC law prevailed over the laws of member states whose acceptance of the Treaty of Rome "carries with it a permanent limitation of their sovereign rights".

So, out of a squabble about a few hundred lire a legal principle was confirmed that has not been challenged since. Although only the Netherlands has the primacy of EC law written into its constitution, neither the governments nor courts of the other eleven member states have questioned this principle. For instance, in 1989 there was a legal wrangle over a national law requiring boats fishing in British waters to be British-owned. Westminster passed this law to prevent Spanish fishermen effectively buying their way into British fishing quotas, but it clashed with EC law demanding non-discrimination between member countries. The European Court said the nationality provision had to be struck out of the UK fishing law.

The 1960s, then, was an activist period for the European Court in widening the envelope of Community law. There were parallels with what was happening at roughly the same time across the Atlantic where the US Supreme Court under Chief Justice Earl Warren took a series of fundamental civil rights decisions which expanded federal power. A perhaps more exact analogy with the United States, though, would be found in the 1930s, the era of Roosevelt's New Deal, when the US

Supreme Court asserted the principle of the supremacy of federal law over that of the hitherto potent laws of individual states.

Havering Doubts

Heroes, some critics say, have since been replaced by haverers on the bench of the European Court. Lord Mackenzie Stuart, who was plucked off the Scottish bench to become Britain's first European Court judge in 1973 and the Court's president from 1984 to 1988, disagrees. "At the beginning," he said in an interview on his retirement, "there were a number of important legal decisions to be taken, the pros and cons were simpler and perhaps more readily understood. We are now, and have been for a decade or more, into the problems of the second phase of the Community: problems which are more subtle and which by their very nature require on the part of the Court a rather more shadowed, nuanced approach. I think this approach will continue."

Another senior Court lawyer stressed that "the key function of the Court is to preserve the balance between the centre and the member states". He said "years ago the Court helped redress the balance of power towards the EC institutions. Now, arguably, it is the states who need protecting". This, benevolence could, however, change, if member states are seen to be blatantly backing away from their 1992 commitments.

Blazing the 1992 Trail

In several judgments in recent years, the Court has, perhaps without always knowing it, pushed the European Community into new realms of supranationalism which would probably have left Commission and Council deadlocked had they tried to agree such interpretations of the Rome Treaty through political negotiation. The best known, and most important, of these was the Court's 1979 Cassis de Dijon ruling, which laid down the important principle of "mutual recognition" and changed the whole definition of a "single market" (see Chapter 7) into something much more compromising than a mere free-trade area.

Other cases have shown the Commission the way forward in other fields. In the 1986 Nouvelles Frontieres case, the Court confirmed for the first time that EC competition rules could be applied to government-cartelised air transport. In the same year, it ruled that in liberalising the insurance sector, the Commission should first free the market for professionals underwriting commercial risks, and leave until later reforms affecting the man-in-the-street and his life-savings. This is precisely the order of priorities the Commission has since followed in drafting its directive for the single market in insurance. Again, in a case involving the Pronuptia wedding-dress franchise, the Court made clear which aspects of franchising – an increasingly important way of selling an idea through many European outlets – were compatible with competition rules, and which were not.

In fact the Court's role in forging the EC by progressive interpretation of the Rome Treaty is so remarkable that there are some critics who worry about it as much as they worry about the "democratic deficit" discussed in Chapter 4. A senior French diplomat and EC expert, Henri Froment-Meurice, wrote, in a paper on project 1992 for the French government, of the danger that the EC could be governed by a government of judges inadequately balanced by institutions of political power. In contrast, Sir David Hannay, the British ambassador to the EC in Brussels, has noted with satisfaction that case law is shaping the EC rather as the evolution of common law shaped Britain.

The Court itself is not subject to any higher judicial review: it is to the European Community what the Supreme Court is to the United States. Yet EC judges feel that, if anything, their tenure of renewable six-year terms is inadequate protection against political cross-winds. Lord Mackenzie Stuart argues that the European Court should model itself on Germany's Federal Constitutional Court where judges are appointed for twelve years (with no possibility of reappointment). Judicial tenure should be longer, he thinks, because some European Court cases take up to two years (see table on page 132) and, more important, because it would prevent governments playing politics with the renewal of judges' mandates.

The Court and the Commission

The Court insists that its duty is simply to interpret the EC treaties, not to help the Commission assert itself. But that is precisely what the Court is accused by its critics of doing in the matter of anti-dumping actions. This has been a source of contention ever since the Commission launched a run of big anti-dumping cases, mainly against Far Eastern producers and mainly on electronic products, in the early 1980s. All the big cases, sometimes involving hundreds of millions of dollars, have been appealed to the European Court, though the appeals have only come after the dumping duties have been made definitive by the Council of Ministers. It is a fact that, apart from the very first big dumping case, over imports of surprisingly good and cheap Japanese ball bearings in 1979, the Court has always found in favour of the Commission and against the exporting company.

One Court lawyer admits that the Luxembourg bench takes "an unduly restrictive" look at dumping cases. In his view the Court tends only to satisfy itself, in its review, that there has been no "manifest error" in the procedure followed by the Commission. It has not formed an independent view as to whether "dumping" has really been happening in a damaging way and whether the penalties are appropriate to the damage caused.

It was partly to give dumping cases more effective judicial scrutiny that, under the Single Act, it was decided to set up the Court of First Instance. (The other reason was the growing caseload of the main Court which is clogged up with employment disputes about the personnel of the EC institutions – an absurdly petty duty for a "supreme" court.) This extra court was duly set up in autumn 1989, but because of objections from two quarters – the Commission and France – it will not deal with dumping cases for at least the first two years of its life. The two objections may reflect a desire to keep a proven supporter of the Commission handling of dumping cases on the job for as long as possible. The Commission has argued that it has not got enough staff to present dumping cases twice over – to the Court of First Instance and then to the main Court on appeal. However, in putting the case to ministers in autumn 1988, Willy de Clercq, the EC's external affairs commissioner, is said to have argued: "The Japanese have all the advantages – why should they have judicial review?"

One good reason to have proper judicial review is that the Commission has so much autonomy in dumping investigations, and even more in competition cases. The Commission can instigate antitrust cases against companies, decide whether the firms are innocent or guilty and how much to fine them – all off its own bat (though it usually consults a committee of officials from member states on its verdicts). In cases about unfair state subsidies the Commission can decide on its own how much a given state aid distorts a market and whether, and how much of the money should be "recovered".

The Court has in fact imposed some limits on the Commission's power of investigation in competition cases. While it quashed IBM's attempt to block the Commission's investigation of the computer giant's affairs, in cases involving Akzo, the chemical company, and AM&S Europe, a zinc producer, the Court gave some protection to company correspondence and documents from the prying eyes of Commission "trust-busters". A favourite ruse of the latter is the "dawn raid", the surprise swoop by Commission officials, usually accompanied by officials from the relevant national anti-monopoly commission (if there is one), on firms suspected of joining together to rig markets. On only one occasion have Commission officials ever been shut out. This was in 1986 when they descended on Hoechst, the German chemicals company, only to be turned away because they had not got a warrant from a West German judge. In September 1989 the Court upheld the Commission in its action against Hoechst.

Europeans: good, bad, indifferent

The temptation will mount for member states to renege on EC commitments that multiply and become more onerous as project 1992 and its manifold directives bite more deeply into their affairs. No member has ever flatly rejected a Court ruling; to do so would be tantamount to denial of membership of the EC. But some countries get taken to the Court by the Commission for infringing EC law far more frequently than others (see table on page 140).

Some of the reasons for the malingering are understandable. One is the new tension that project 1992 is creating within federal states that are members of the Community – West Germany, Italy, Spain and Belgium. As the Community extends its tentacles into matters, such as social, environmental or cultural policy, where federal states have devolved competence to their regions or provinces, those regions become touchy. One answer is to try to involve the regions in EC decision-making. But it is unwieldy for four ministers (three regional and one national) to represent Belgium at an EC Council of education ministers. The Treaty of Rome recognises only national, central governments: it is meant to be up to them to see that EC directives are reflected in local laws, be they national or regional ones.

Some of the "legal lag" arises because EC directives do not allow enough time for national law to be changed. The crispest form of EC law is the "regulation" which enters into force the moment it is published in the Community's Official Journal – when it also has direct effect in the member states. But the overwhelming preference among the members is for "directives". These leave it to the discretion of

Leaders and laggards of 1992

Single-market directives that should have been made national law by December 31st 1989 (total=88)

Legend: Implemented | Not implemented | Commission taking action | Government has asked for waiver | Directive does not apply

Scale: 10 | 20 | 30 | 40 | 50 | 60 | 70 | 80 | 88

Denmark
United Kingdom
France
Germany, West
Netherlands
Ireland
Luxembourg
Belgium
Spain
Greece
Italy
Portugal

Source: European Commission

Commission action against the bad boys

LETTER OF COMPLAINT

	1981	1982	1983	1984	1985	1986	1987	1988
Belgium	29	27	34	55	68	56	55	52
Denmark	21	16	13	21	27	26	36	29
France	39	68	55	92	93	69	66	58
Germany, West	22	26	16	36	29	40	65	58
Greece	-	8	26	60	69	106	77	64
Ireland	28	30	16	33	33	44	46	41
Italy	64	66	69	67	70	61	73	107
Luxembourg	17	30	24	28	37	43	26	36
Netherlands	16	32	16	28	48	30	41	42
Portugal	-	-	-	-	-	2	11	18
Spain	-	-	-	-	-	22	32	31
United Kingdom	20	32	20	34	29	37	44	33
Total	256	335	289	454	503	516	572	569

FORMAL ALLEGATION

	1981	1982	1983	1984	1985	1986	1987	1988
Belgium	26	18	8	17	37	25	28	23
Denmark	6	10	3	3	4	3	6	6
France	22	33	21	29	36	30	29	27
Germany, West	14	15	8	13	17	17	17	24
Greece	-	2	4	27	30	24	28	32
Ireland	4	17	6	12	10	8	24	10
Italy	41	34	21	26	61	31	27	52
Luxembourg	19	8	2	6	16	12	10	8
Netherlands	7	16	3	5	11	9	11	12
Portugal	-	-	-	-	-	-	-	7
Spain	-	-	-	-	-	-	8	11
United Kingdom	8	4	7	10	11	5	9	15
Total	147	157	83	148	233	164	197	227

COURT CASE

	1981	1982	1983	1984	1985	1986	1987	1988
Belgium	9	8	4	4	23	15	7	10
Denmark	2	1	3	1	2	1	-	3
France	5	8	12	14	14	8	8	10
Germany, West	2	4	4	7	9	11	2	8
Greece	-	-	2	4	10	11	11	14
Ireland	3	3	1	3	9	2	3	8
Italy	20	14	12	12	31	18	21	14
Luxembourg	2	3	-	3	6	4	2	2
Netherlands	5	2	3	2	4	-	4	3
Portugal	-	-	-	-	-	-	-	-
Spain	-	-	-	-	-	-	1	1
United Kingdom	2	2	1	4	5	1	2	-
Total	50	45	42	54	113	71	61	73

Source: European Commission

member states to decide how they will incorporate the EC regime into national law.

There the true malingering starts. Italy is the worst miscreant. The willingness of its government to agree to EC proposals far outstrips the capacity and willingness of its parliament or civil service to put them into effect. Italy is not unique in this. Greece is similarly upbeat in its enthusiasm for the EC and unable to deliver compliance. In its rush to get into the Community before the election in 1981 (won by the then anti-EC Andreas Papandreou), the Karamanlis government agreed to deadlines for adopting EC law which Greece had little hope of meeting. In fact, as the table opposite shows, Greece has tended to put things right after the Commission has sent it a letter of formal notice (*lettre de mise en demeure*). Relatively fewer Commission complaints have resulted in Court action in the case of Greece than of Italy.

Italy's special problem has been that its legislative programme and timetable has been in the hands of its parliament, rather than of its government. Until 1988 a system of secret voting in the Italian parliament weakened whatever party discipline Italian politicians might have. With voting now public, and with the new grouping of EC legislation into omnibus bills before the Rome parliament, Italy may improve upon its so-far lamentable track record as an EC law-enacter.

For the moment Italy remains not only the biggest offender, but also the biggest repeat offender. On ten occasions, the Court has had to issue a second ruling, ordering a member state to comply with a first ruling. All ten of these second rulings have been directed at Italy. For instance, Rome has yet to comply with a 1987 Court ruling ordering it to comply with a 1983 ruling ordering it to comply with EC norms on the inspection of fruit and vegetables. Since 1978, Italy has been unable or unwilling to write into its national law an EC directive on conditions governing large-scale redundancies, despite formal European Court rulings against it in 1982 and 1985. Having to issue a second ruling to back a first one, highlights an inherent weakness of the Court: like the Pope, it has no army to enforce its will. Indeed, it is for just this reason that some in the European Court would prefer the Commission not to press so many suits against errant member states.

All members have dragged their feet in implementing some EC law or other. Britain, which pats itself on the back for living up to its EC commitments better than other more vociferously *communautaire* members, was taken to Court in autumn 1989 for failing to meet water purity standards it had agreed to in 1985. West Germany has paid no attention to European Court rulings against the bogus voyages that the "butter ships" of northern Germany take into international waters in order to sell goods to bogus seafarers tax free.

Laying Down the Law

There are no common sanctions for breaking EC law. Neither EC directives nor regulations prescribe penalties. This is because criminal law has not been placed within the Community's competence. Where the EC enforces its law directly – say in competition policy – the Commission imposes fines.

One of the very few detailed studies of what happens to EC regulations in the different member countries showed just how uneven their fates can be. Dr Alan Butt Philip, a British academic, studied the EC rules requiring lorries to carry tachographs – or "spies in the cab" as they are known by those who detest them – to monitor the hours and speeds of drivers. He discovered what sanctions member governments took against those found to be breaking the rules. The penalties varied widely. Four countries allowed a prison sentence for extreme and systematic offenders, but only Britain has ever in fact jailed anybody for tacho-abuse. Other states imposed fines, often very light, and in France generally less than a trifling FFr160. No country has seen fit to combine stiff sanctions and stiff enforcement. Germany, with its tradition of tight regulation of road transport, took enforcement seriously, but slapped offenders on the wrist with fines of between DM20 and DM500.

The upshot, Dr Butt Philip says, is that this particular set of EC rules has achieved few of its aims. It has led to only slight improvement in road safety; it has failed to "level the playing field" for road hauliers in different member states; and it has done little to redress the balance between road and rail freight – one of the tachograph campaign's ulterior motives.

What, then, is the answer? Coercion is out of the question. A form of this is provided for in Article 88 of the Treaty of Paris, which established the European Coal and Steel Community. (In this, as in other respects, the Paris Treaty, a product of an earlier and more Euro-idealist time, closer to the horror of the war, was more supranational than the subsequent Treaty of Rome.) It says that if a member has not complied with a decision within a time-limit laid down by the High Authority (the ECSC's equivalent of the Commission), the High Authority with a two-thirds majority of member states may suspend budget payments to the offending state. This is nice for Euro-connoisseurs to roll off the tongue; but unused and unusable.

The Way Ahead

The Commission could be still more vigilant. In 1988 it uncovered, by itself, over 300 suspected infractions of EC law by members. But there is a limit to what the Commission can do. Nearly four times that number of infractions (1,137) were reported by European citizens. Public opinion is important. A big reason why the tachograph campaign proved so rubbery was public resistance: people sympathised with drivers being spied upon by machines. In contrast, the well-publicised wanderings in 1988 of the freighter, *Karin B*, looking for somewhere to dump a load of Italian chemical waste prompted even the Italian government to adopt EC rules on the international transport of dangerous waste.

The "direct effect" of Community law, giving European rights and obligations directly to European individuals and enterprises, means that the citizenry can do their own policing. This is already happening in competition policy – most Commission investigations stem from companies complaining of rigged markets. Perhaps the same grassroots approach will spread to enforcement of internal-market legislation. This is what some Commission lawyers hope. And it is probably true that the flesh will be put on the bare bones of 1992 only by countless individuals finding out what they can get away with across the European market under Europe's changing law.

This will be a long haul however: managements usually have better things to do than pursue foreign public authorities through foreign courts citing foreign laws that foreign judges haven't heard of. If project 1992 is going to take off in practice as fast as it has taken off in theory, the member governments that really want to see Europe "open for business" will have to put more pressure on those who like the sound of 1992 but not the reality.

12

COMPETITION POLICY

Touching the Nerve of Sovereignty

No one, surely, can tell a sovereign government how to spend its own money on its own companies on its own soil? Wrong. Brussels can, and does. With increasing regularity the European Commission is forcing EC members to scale back the cash they give their companies, even to the extent of ordering governments to recover their subsidies from corporate treasuries. And the Commission has now realised an old dream. From September 1990 it will have the power to vet, and if need be, block all mergers with a combined worth of more than 5 billion ecus.

Subsidies and mergers: one might think that these would offer Brussels sufficient scope to promote vigorous competition. But the Commission is pressing still deeper into traditionally sovereign economic territory — into the government-run restrictive practices that shape such businesses as telecommunications, energy and air transport. Europe's governments, which have watched with equanimity as the Commission's trust-busters have set to work on private cartels (fining several of them a record total of 80 million ecus in 1988), have taken a more jaded view as the Commission has turned on them and the sectors that they hold dear.

France, for instance, has taken the Commission to the European Court. It is challenging the Commission's decision to dust off a little-used weapon: Article 90 of the Treaty of Rome, which gives the Commission the right, in matters concerning state-dominated businesses, to issue a directive without getting the Council of Ministers' approval in the normal way. The Commission wants to use this power to open up the market for telecommunications terminal equipment in Europe.

But even though the French government and several others feel the Commission has marched a directive too far in this matter, there is a surprisingly wide consensus that anti-subsidy and anti-trust policies are essential to the success of project 1992. Of course, governments and companies remain quick to spot the crimes of others while turning a blind-eye to their own. Thus, Mrs Thatcher's government was happy to award Rover double the amount of state aid that the Commission eventually let her give, in order to find this problem-child of the British car industry a new home with foster parent British Aerospace. At the same time, the British prime minister made "a strengthened Community competition policy" a key condition of her support for the internal-market programme, and indeed any step towards closer economic and monetary cooperation.

Irresistible Arguments and Wishful Thinking

There are various reasons to want the deregulation of project 1992 to be policed with a tough competition policy. Paolo Cecchini and his team of Commission economists, whose voluminous study on 1992 became the main sales brochure for the internal market, estimated that opening up the European market could add as much as 200 billion ecus, or 4.5 per cent of current GDP, to the wealth-creation of the Community by the late 1990s. But only a small part of this gain would stem from measures in Lord Cockfield's 1985 White Paper – that is to say removing non-tariff barriers like frontier red-tape, closed public procurement markets and differing product standards. The big benefits – and here the Cecchini report's econometrics came close to guesswork – will supposedly flow from "a new and pervasive competitive climate". In this climate businesses will cut their costs as they expand unhindered to meet Europe-wide demand, new entrants will make their mark upon each market, and innovation will blossom.

Where the Cecchini study is less questionable is in predicting the dangers: "In this new and blustery climate, there is a good chance that some of the economy's players will seek various forms of shelter from competitive reinvigoration." Such "shelter" might take the form of companies sharing markets and/or shutting out new entrants, or getting their governments to do the dirty work for them.

It is in this respect that competition policy could well decide whether project 1992 succeeds or fails. Peter Sutherland, the Irishman who put new steel into EC competition policy in the years between 1985 and 1988 when he was in charge of the dossier in Brussels, certainly believed so: "If you remove national trade barriers, and if you also leave the capacity of governments to interfere with trade by supporting unfairly one industry against another, or allow companies to carve up markets and fix distribution, you would have the same effect of destroying 1992 as if the barriers were left untouched." His successor as commissioner for competition policy, Sir Leon Brittan, has repeatedly worried aloud that as 1992 – both the date and the programme – advances, there will be a mounting temptation for governments to resort to state-aid to industry as more traditional forms of protectionism or non-tariff barriers fade away.

So companies must look to the Commission to deliver on the promise of undistorted competition – happily if they feel hobbled at the moment, gloomily, if they have a nice little fix going for them. Sutherland, a rugby-playing Irishman, defined such competition as "a level playing field where individual talent, effort and comparative advantage lead to victory, rather than an inclined pitch with moving goalposts, a biased referee and an opposing team full of steroids".

Aid under Fire

Article 92 of the Treaty of Rome bans "any aid granted by a member state or through resources in any form whatsoever which distorts or threatens to distort competition by favouring certain undertakings or the production of certain goods". The principle is clear, though the article allows the Commission discretion to allow such aid on certain (mainly social) grounds. Here is an aspect of competition policy that is almost unknown at the national level. State aid is not something with which the anti-trust division of the US Justice Department, or the West German Federal Cartel Office, or the British Monopolies and Mergers Commission concern themselves. Among states belonging to the Organisation for Economic Cooperation and Development (OECD) and to the General Agreement on Tariffs and Trade (GATT), attempts have been made to regulate state subsidies for exports. But nothing negotiated in those organisations compares with the Commission's armoury of weapons against state aid inside the Community – the requirement that member governments notify Brussels for prior clearance of state aid, and the power of Brussels to suspend, to reduce, or even to order repayment of such aid.

Much of Brussels' new ferocity about state aid has been kindled by its new awareness of how extensive state aid is. Government subsidies should be intrinsically easier to track than business cartels; ministers often like to take public credit with voters for the state aid they have bestowed, while companies are invariably publicity-shy about their restrictive practices. Time has obscured from view many earlier subsidies, which like archeological strata have been overlaid by later state aid; yet public money still flows through such earlier schemes. In 1985 Peter Sutherland decided he wanted to know more. He set his competition officials the task of trying to compile a complete inventory of the state-aid superstore.

Quantifying the Aid Plague

They dug for four years. What they unearthed astonished them, and even some of the governments that their findings implicated. The Brussels diggers found that during 1981–86 the ten EC states (Spain and Portugal had yet to join the EC) spent an annual average of 82 billion ecus, or 3 per cent of their collective GNP, in aid (see table below). Nearly half of that went to agriculture, transport and coal — sectors which for social reasons are likely to go on getting state subsidies without too much hindrance from the Commission. But aid to manufacturing industry still amounted to around 5,000 ecus per worker each year.

The other striking fact unearthed was the divergence between the biggest aid-givers. Through the 1980s, the trend has been downward in Britain, stable in France, slowly upward in West Germany and sharply upward in Italy. As a result of these trends, Italy was by 1986 doling out to its industry three times as much in absolute terms as Germany, four times as much as France, and eight times as much as Britain. A year

The state aid-givers league, 1981–86

	In billion ecus	As % of GNP	Per Worker
Italy	27.7	5.7	1,357
Germany, West	19.1	2.5	761
France	16.7	2.7	792
Britain	9.4	1.8	396
Belgium	4.0	4.1	1,113
Netherlands	2.2	1.5	444
Ireland	1.1	5.3	1,036
Greece	1.0	2.5	278
Denmark	0.9	1.3	353
Luxembourg*	0.2	6.0	1,562

* Luxembourg has one large steel company, Arbed, which has received almost all the duchy's state aid.

Source: European Commission

147

later, the Italian industry minister himself, Adolfo Battaglia, was complaining that aid intended for special cases had become "generalised or broadened in application, with a notable effect on public finances".

The attitude of Italian officialdom to Brussels always seems to be: "make us chaste, but not just yet". For instance, during the first half of the 1980s, Finsider, the Italian state-owned steelmaker, had swallowed the largest chunk of aid going to any EC steelmaker. Yet in 1988 Mr Battaglia was back in Brussels proposing to give another huge dollop of national aid (L5,198 billion or £2.4 billion) to this insatiable aid-guzzler. In theory this would be an end of the guzzling, because the profitable bits of Finsider would be transferred to a new company called Ilva, and the rest closed or sold. A year later, the aid had still not been agreed by Italy's EC partners – a new and stringent feature of the European steel business is that, since the Commission wound up its official production-sharing cartel in mid-1988, unanimous approval of all the member states is needed for any one of them to give any further aid to its steel industry.

States have subtler ways of giving aid than simple cash grants. France and the Netherlands, for instance, have been known to let their largesse take the form of subsidised energy prices. More pervasive are the practices of governments in increasing companies' share capital, writing off their debts, subsidising interest rates on their loans, or granting them specially tailored tax relief. Debt write-offs, for example, were the form in which the British government gave aid to carmaker Rover and to the Belfast aircraftmaker Shorts; Brussels approved the aid (or a portion of what was proposed) in both cases because the companies were being returned to the disciplines of the private sector. In countries like Italy, Spain and France with much bigger state sectors, the problem is correspondingly larger and compounded by the way state-owned companies like Renault in France, Enasa in Spain and IRI, Finmeccanica and ENI in Italy tend to be regarded as national champions.

Public and Private Concerns

EC officials in Brussels insist that the impression that they particularly pick upon the public sector in cracking down on government aid is wrong. On the contrary, they say, EC action against state aid to private companies is, if anything, more frequent, because the flow of such aid is easier to spot than murky transactions between the state as aid-provider and the state as aid-receiver. One of the trickiest forms of state behaviour for Brussels to evaluate arises when governments inject equity capital into a company. The Treaty of Rome is supposed to be impartial between private or public share-ownership. The key criterion, in the eyes of EC officials, is the element of risk in the state's investment. In other words, if prospects for the company concerned are reasonable, then the state is judged to be behaving like any other investor and no aid is deemed to have changed hands. If, on the other hand, a government is investing in a company which no sane private investor would touch, then for equity read aid.

Cases of this sort are not too frequent at a time when privatisation is more in fashion than nationalisation. In 1988 Brussels approved the Dutch government purchase of 49 per cent in Fokker, the aircraft company which had made big losses the year before; the rationale for the approval – that the Dutch government was behaving as a reasonable private investor might – was, luckily for the Commission, justified by the fact that Fokker has since returned to profit. But the issue highlights an awkward paradox for EC competition policy: it is all right for a government to help a firm that does not need help, but not one which does.

This, in turn, highlights the "popularity problem" for EC competition commissioners. They all feel it. Frans Andriessen, now in charge of the Community's external relations but in 1981–84 responsible for competition policy, admitted in late 1984: "You get tired of being seen as a policeman, always prohibiting and handing out fines." The Dutchman's successor, Peter Sutherland, seemed less bothered by this, even to the point of relishing his sobriquet (coined by Jacques Delors) of "the little sheriff". But even he stressed the "positive" ends to which governments could put their money rather than fruitlessly subsidising their industries. His successor, Sir Leon Brittan, too, has sought to accentuate the positive side of his job: making sure that the benefits of project 1992 and greater competitiveness are passed to consumers, not hoarded by companies as windfall profits.

The Commission Cracks the Whip

For all his distaste of the policeman image, it was Frans Andriessen who took the first significant step in the campaign against state aid. In September 1983 he got his Commission colleagues to issue a formal warning that henceforth Brussels would order repayment of all state aid. That it could legally do so had been affirmed in a European Court ruling ten years earlier, but this was never followed up. Andriessen was prompted to act by complaints from Bonn that its predominantly private steel companies were being put at an unfair disadvantage by other governments subsidising their largely state-owned steelmakers. (Ironically, Bonn is an inveterate state-aider of other sectors, such as the car industry).

That warning in 1983 largely evaporated into thin air. It fell to Peter Sutherland to re-open the battle and get the next Commission to reaffirm the 1983 decision by pledging itself to systematic repayment of illegally-dispensed aid. He fought again and won the battle against a reluctant Jacques Delors. The Commission president was worried that this toughness might give the Commission a negative image, even though by that time the French government was talking of scaling back the subsidies that had burgeoned in the early 1980s.

But Jacques Delors expressed more than mere concern when the following year Mr Sutherland wanted to order the French government to recover aid it had given the ailing Boussac textile group – a company Delors himself had decided, as finance minister, to help. However, arguing that the 1983 and 1986 decisions would mean nothing if the Commission ducked the Boussac case, Sutherland prevailed. In July 1987, with Delors and the other French commissioner, Claude Cheysson abstaining, the Commission ordered Paris to reclaim FFr338 million of the total FFr600 million aid that had gone to Boussac. The other half of the aid was considered irrecoverable, because it had covered closure costs of bankrupt Boussac subsidiaries.

At roughly the same time, the Commission jumped an important legal hurdle to its aid-recovery campaign. Some recipients of state aid baulked at paying money back on the not unreasonable ground that they had received it in good faith – that the rules were being changed retroactively. One such company was Deufil, a German synthetic fibre producer, which used the "good faith" argument in the European Court to contest repayment of money to Bonn. The Court overruled it in March 1987. Commission lawyers claim that the 1983 public warning effectively nullified the "good faith" argument, and they take as proof the increasing tendency for potential recipients of state aid to check with Brussels before banking any money given them by their national government.

The Commission has cracked down on state aid to the car industry with special severity. It has argued that as the market in a particular business becomes more pan-European the distortions of competition created by giving some companies aid are felt ever more keenly by those who get none. The car industry received an estimated 11 billion ecus-worth of state aid in 1981–86, and is still receiving substantial amounts, despite the record sales and profitability it has enjoyed since 1986.

One swingeing measure which the Commission took in December 1988 was to require every grant of aid worth 12 million ecus or more to get prior clearance in Brussels. Two governments have not accepted this. West Germany claims that its aid to the car industry does not affect intra-Community trade and is a vital part of its regional policy, while Spain argues that Brussels should also come up with an EC-wide sectoral strategy for cars. The Commission disputes both arguments, and has started legal proceedings against Bonn and Madrid.

Three Big Ones

The most spectacular state-aid cases have involved Britain, Italy and France.

● In 1988 the Thatcher government wrote off £800 million of Rover's debt as a "sweetener" to induce British Aerospace (BAe) to take the car company off the state's hands for £150 million. London contended this was a justified way of ending the £3.8 billion-worth of state aid Rover had swallowed since 1976. The weakness of its case was that it had negotiated exclusively with BAe, had not sought competitive bids and had not seriously investigated whether any other company would take Rover for a higher price or with a lower debt write-off. Therefore, when the Commission said it could approve the British government wiping out only £469 million of the debt – and BAe, after only twenty-four hours of prevarication, said it would still buy Rover – the British government looked decidedly silly. The Commission, by contrast, had saved the British taxpayer £331 million. It later transpired that even this level of largesse was not all that the British government had dispensed. In late 1989 the UK National Audit Office exposed a further £38 million in "sweeteners" that had secretly been given to BAe to take the car firm off the government's hands.

● In Italy there was controversy over the 1986 sale of Alfa-Romeo to Fiat, partly because a rival non-Italian bidder, Ford, had offered more than Fiat. But Commission investigators found no fault with the price Fiat paid for Alfa. Its complaint was with Finmeccanica, which is part of the IRI state holding company and which owned Alfa-Romeo until 1986. Finmeccanica had injected L615 billion (£269 million) into Alfa

151

in 1985–86 without demanding any restructuring and despite the fact that the car company was operating at only 40 per cent of capacity and losing money heavily. (Once more the paradox: state aid is OK as long as it's not needed.) In 1989 the Commission ordered Finmeccanica to repay the L615 billion to its ultimate owner, the state.

● High financial and political stakes ride on the outcome of the third major case – Renault. In March 1988, just before the French general election, the Commission reached a conditional deal with the Chirac government. It gave approval to FFr12 billion in aid for Renault provided the state-owned company did two things. One was to stick to a plan closing down a quarter of its capacity between 1984 and 1990; the other was to change its stature from that of a government "regie" to that of a publicly-owned limited company subject to the normal harsh commercial realities such as the possibility of going bankrupt. The deal became shaky, if not unstuck, when the Rocard Socialist government took over. It said that because of Socialist-Communist opposition in the French parliament it could not change Renault's status by legislation, though it eventually did so by government decree. Brussels argued that such a decree was too reversible and did not fulfil the March 1988 conditions. It also complained that Renault reneged on the 25 per cent capacity cut.

Bucking the Market

As is clear from some of these cases, the Commission has room for manoeuvre in cracking down on state aid, and uses it. As Manfred Caspari, the dapper German who was director general for competition policy for most of the 1980s, likes to put it: "You can always negotiate with us; you can't negotiate with the market." In other words, sensible levels of state aid which do not distort competition can be agreed with Brussels, but market realities will always in the end catch up with companies propped up by state aid.

Though Sir Leon Brittan claims he is pulling down the "No Trespassing" signs, certain areas remain off-limits to Brussels investigators. Aid to the defence sector is still a national prerogative, since the Treaty of Rome excludes defence. A benevolent (and protectionist) eye is generally turned on aerospace (hence Commission approval in 1989 of the large amount of German state aid in the proposed takeover of MBB by Daimler-Benz), and on electronics and computers, because the competition is largely from outside rather from within the Community.

Industries where there has been little competition across member states' borders, such as that making railway equipment, have not been scrutinised closely.

However, this may change as markets open up. Sir Leon Brittan has waved his investigators forward into two important new areas of exploration – subsidies for exports and aid incentives for inward investment. Both are prized instruments of national policy, and if Brussels treads too heavily on them, the shouts of pain from member states will be heard across the Community. Taking it a step further, the Commission is concerned that helping companies export outside the Community incidentally gives them an indirect advantage in intra-EC trade (longer production runs, lower unit costs). The other worry is that investment aid should help genuinely poorer regions (in other words, the Paris basin should not be given the same level of investment "allure" as Scotland's Highlands and Islands). In fact, the canny Japanese appear to have decided to sidestep any impending row over investment aid. In some of their recent decisions to locate plants outside assisted areas in Britain, the Japanese have tended to eschew aid.

Merger Control: Recognising reality.

Merger control by Brussels can stamp on national sovereignty just as heavily as control of state aid. While ostensibly for the protection of competition, merger control is often used by governments for political or nationalistic ends. It is therefore all the more surprising that member states have agreed to put into the Commission's hands a formal power to vet large-scale company mergers. This is yet another instance in which we see project 1992 carrying the Community beyond what was envisaged in the Cockfield White Paper.

But the Commission, with the crucial backing of European industry, won the argument that the single market requires one, not twelve, referees of big mergers. Or, as Peter Sutherland liked to call it, a "one-stop shop" for merger clearance. The merger regulation, agreed in December 1989 to come into effect nine months later, provides for:

● Commission vetting of mergers with a combined turnover of at least 5 billion ecus world-wide, of which at least 250 million ecus must be within the Community. If, however, each of the companies derives two-thirds of their business from one and the same EC state, then the merger is left to the scrutiny of that country's anti-trust authorities.

● The yardstick by which Brussels is to judge mergers (which could include tightly-knit joint ventures as well as outright takeovers) is whether the newly combined business would impede competition in the Community market. The decision to stress competition as the criterion for judging mergers was a relief to Britain and West Germany which opposed the desire of southern EC states, and of France to some extent, for Brussels to take social, regional and industrial policy factors into account in its decisions.

The 1952 Treaty of Paris establishing the European Coal and Steel Community gave the High Authority (as the fledgling Commission was once grandly styled) some formal control over mergers. It had historical reason to do so. Coal and steel were then still thought to be the crucial elements in a nation's war-making capacity, and no one wanted to see a military-industrial complex like the Krupp empire re-created.

But five years later the writers of the Rome Treaty did not think to put in a word about mergers in other sectors of the European economy. They confined themselves to bans on competition-restricting agreements (Article 85) and abuses of dominant market positions (Article 86). If anyone in the 1950s thought about mergers, they probably considered them wholly helpful to the rebuilding of Europe rather than potentially problematic. And this still remains the attitude of all those parts of the Commission which are trying to promote cross-border mergers or cooperation, by financing joint R&D, evolving a common framework of European company law, broking marriages between smaller firms and so on.

It was not until the 1960s that individual states began to develop proper merger controls on a national basis, which in turn set the Commission thinking about what it should do at a Community level. But the first catalyst for action did not come until 1973, with the European Court ruling in a case involving Continental Can, the US packaging company. The Court upheld the principle that Article 86 of

Mergers and acquisitions involving EEC-based companies

Years ending June	National	Community	International	Total
1984	101	29	25	155
1985	146	44	18	208
1986	145	52	30	227
1987	211	75	17	303
1988	214	111	58	383

Note: In the first nine months of 1989, the number of deals totalled 377.

Source: European Commission

the Rome Treaty could be used to block mergers which so strengthened a company's dominant position "that the only undertakings left in the market are those which are dependent on the dominant undertaking with regard to their market behaviour". The fact that the Commission lost the case, because the Court ruled it had failed to justify its narrow definition of Continental Can's market, did not really matter to Brussels. It could henceforth hold over the heads of governments and companies the threat of using Article 86 against mergers.

Adding Strength to Article 86

At the same time, however, the Commission remained aware of the limitations of Article 86: it was and is a very blunt instrument which imposes no requirement for mergers to be notified to Brussels in advance; and effectively required that for the Commission to intervene in a merger, one of the companies involved had to have a dominant (more than 50 per cent, as a rule-of-the-thumb) market position. So in 1973 the Commission put a proposal for pre-emptive merger control on the table of the Council of Ministers. And there it stayed for fifteen years, with the Commission occasionally making an amendment or two to it but the Council taking little notice.

It might have gone on gathering dust, had not three things happened in 1987–88. First, Peter Sutherland felt moved to give the cause of merger control a fresh push. Second, the European Court ruled in November 1987 in a case involving the tobacco giant, Philip Morris. It held that Article 85 could prohibit changes in ownership (such as mergers/takeovers) if these resulted from an agreement between companies, whereby one company acquired control or decisive influence in another in such a way as to distort competition. With the Continental Can and Philip Morris precedents under its belt, Peter Sutherland claimed that the Commission had a form of merger control at its disposal. This control was less clear-cut than European industry wished it to be. So – the third factor – the big industrial lobbies, like UNICE, the European federation of employers, began to see merit in the EC removing this uncertainty and giving the Commission a clearer mandate to control mergers.

Dawn Comes ...

The truth began to dawn that the Commission could, as Sutherland claimed, use Articles 85 and 86 to unscramble mergers once they had happened. This led British Airways, no sooner than the ink was dry on its takeover of British Caledonian, to start negotiations over the deal with Brussels. In March 1988 BA agreed to Sutherland's demands that it shed some of the routes and flight slots at Gatwick airport which it would otherwise have gained as a result of merging with B-Cal. In the summer of that year, Sutherland showed what the "luck of the Irish" means. His stroke of luck related to his own country – to a consortium bid by three British and Irish food-and-drink companies for Irish Distillers. The consortium, made up of Grand Metropolitan, Allied-Lyons, and Guinness had unwisely announced beforehand how they would share out Irish Distillers' products if they got hold of the company. This, said the Commission, smacked of illegal market-sharing, while the very nature of a consortium bid, a decision by the three companies not to bid against each other, was a restraint on competition. The consortium bid was dropped in the face of the Commission's displeasure.

... Bringing Questions

However, it was one thing to agree on the need for a European merger-control authority, quite another to agree on its precise form. This took two years of first Sutherland, and then Brittan, pounding away at member state's various objections. The December 1989 regulation has by no means dispelled all concerns. These are of three kinds. Can the Commission cope? A 5 billion ecus threshold is likely to bring Brussels about fifty mergers a year for vetting; yet the Commission wants the threshold lowered to 2 billion ecus by 1994. At the same time, it has a tight timetable to stick to – within a month of being notified of a merger it must decide whether to start a formal investigation which it then has four months to complete. Will the Commission really be tough and apolitical enough to make the effect on competition the guiding light of its decisions? Northern states have residual doubts here; the southern states residual hopes. Won't the "one-stop shop" for merger approval be illusory in many cases? For, the dividing line between Brussels vetting all mergers above 5 billion ecus and member states dealing with everything below this level of combined turnover is far from clean. National authorities can block a merger to which Brussels has given the green light (not the other way round, though) where sensitive sectors like defence or the media are involved, and where a particular problem of market dominance might arise in one state. This last "let-in" for national scrutiny was demanded by West Germany for its Federal Cartel Office, and provides plenty of scope for argument.

Cracking Down On Cartels

In a sense, private (as distinct from government) cartels or market-rigging agreements are the easy ones for the Commission to cope with. Not that they are easy to track down: being private, they are more easily kept secret, although banned under Article 85. Most investigations of such market-fixing stem from complaints and tip-offs from rival companies, which can in turn lead to "dawn raids" on the offices of suspected cartel members. In 1989, for instance, such swoops were made on producers of cement and chemical soda ash. Sometimes, Commission inspectors are lucky, finding in one of their probes of rigging of the plastics market a file of cartel documents that an ICI executive had considerately left on his window-sill.

If there is proof, which the Commission feels could be sustained in any appeal to the European Court, then the remedy is simple and increasingly draconian: a fine of up to 10 per cent of a company's annual turnover. (Such a maximum fine would thus wipe out most companies' yearly profit). In 1988, a bumper year, fines for illicit cartels totalled 80 million ecus – including 13.4 million ecus imposed on Italian flat-glass manufacturers and 60.5 million ecus levied on virtually all the big EC chemical companies for trying to fix prices in two plastic cartels. In the previous year total fines had run to only 7 million ecus, but in the 1986 fines had amounted to 66 million ecus, with chemical companies paying a record 57 million ecus for misbehaviour in plastics.

However, the cartels that are the most difficult for the Commission to crack down are the out-in-the-open market dividing-and-sharing arrangements cooked up between governments. Governments are tougher to take on than companies. But, as the common market takes shape and competition policy with it, it has becoming increasingly clear to Brussels that most of the remaining big distortions to free trade lie in businesses where states are habitually involved as regulators and where there is little or no competition.

The Commission has some weapons under the Rome Treaty. It has wielded, for instance, Article 37, which requires member states to "progressively adjust any state monopolies of a commercial character" restricting imports, against state monopolies in tobacco in Greece and in oil in Spain. It can also turn to a controversial reserve power in Article

90. This allows the Commission to issue directives or decisions purely on its own authority to ensure that "public undertakings and undertakings to which member states grant special or exclusive rights" do not thwart free competition but operate in the general Community interest.

Targeted Sectors

The Commission has decided to focus its Article 90 fire on telecommunications, given the entrenched government regulation in this area, the rapidity of change in the business of world telecommunications and the importance to the single EC market of matching this change in Europe. In 1988 Brussels issued an Article 90 directive freeing up the market in telecommunications terminal equipment, and was promptly challenged in the European Court by the French government. In mid-1989 it threatened to use the same weapon to end state monopolies on such new telecommunications services as videotext, electronic mail, facsimile communication, and banking and shopping by computer. This time the threat worked; in the dying days of 1989 ministers agreed that these so-called value added services, but not the basic telecommunications networks, will be gradually opened up to competition from 1990 onwards. This prospect amounts to a minor revolution in all member states except Britain, where British Telecom no longer has the total telecommunications monopoly of the old British Post Office.

Two other areas of government-sponsored regulation which Brussels has lined up in its sights are energy and air transport. Creation of a single market in energy has started late – it was deliberately excluded from the Cockfield White Paper – and will take time to achieve because of the massive financial and political investment in the present national set-ups. In contrast, moves to shake up air transport are well under way. In 1987 the Commission got member states to agree to a first stage of liberalisation, involving more flexibility in the setting of fares, more capacity-sharing between existing airlines and more liberal market access for new ones. The results have so far been modest – a fall of perhaps 15 per cent in fares on routes plied by the most aggressive carriers. At the close of 1989 ministers agreed to a second phase in freeing the airways by 1993.

For the sake of Europe's single market, such action was overdue. No industry except farming has flown more in the face of free market sense than air transport.And nothing will bring home to European people the benefits of project 1992 like cuts in the excessive prices that they still pay to fly across the great market.

13

MACRO-MONEY

Towards Economic and Monetary Union

The hitherto flightless EMU is once more on the runway, and this time it might just take off. Nothing, short of a straight leap to political union and a United States of Europe, could be more ambitious than the idea of the Twelve committing themselves to Economic and Monetary Union – a single money and monetary policy run by a single central bank (albeit federal), and with centralised control over key aspects of national economic and budgetary policies. Nothing, too, could be more contentious. Not only for Britain whose prime minister has said it would be "the biggest transfer of sovereignty we have ever known", but also for West Germany which is deeply worried about losing its post-war monetary stability.

Monetary union, says Jacques Delors, would "put a second tiger in Europe's tank" (the first being the single-market programme). Maybe, but it could prove a hard tiger to handle. If the Twelve were to fail to agree at the end of a protracted conference, or if EMU were to come apart, or if the German Bundestag were sometime in the early 1990s to vote against an EMU painfully agreed between governments, it would set back discussion of monetary union as decisively as France's failure to ratify the European Defence Community in 1954 deferred moves towards European defence for a generation.

Yet in the final month of 1990, amid the Roman fireworks of another Italian-hosted summit, the Twelve are to open an intergovernmental conference (IGC) to thrash out the terms of EMU. The real negotiation will start in early 1991, and continue at weekly meetings of diplomats and monthly reviews by foreign and finance ministers. They may come to a head by the December 1991 summit to be held in the Netherlands. Laid before the governments at the start of this process will be the Delors plan, a three-stage progress to an eventual European System of Central Banks (ESCB), "the irrevocable locking of exchange rate parities" and macro-économic policy coordination, including "binding rules" for budgetary policies. Try as she might – and she has already tried with an alternative British plan – Mrs Thatcher has not managed to push the Delors plan from centre stage. For the Delors plan, unlike previous EMU initiatives, has behind it the weight of the Community's twelve central bank governors who were on the EMU study-committee chaired by the Commission president.

It is now for the politicians to weigh in. And weigh in they surely will, against the most contested and contestable points of the Delors plan – the requirement for rules binding the hands of national budget-fixers; the question of how poorer EC members will compete in a monetary union without adequate transfers of money from a relatively puny EC budget; and the question of democratic accountability (who will guard the guardians?) of any new system.

Treaty revision will take time. This may be a good thing, for time here could prove a teacher, if not a healer. Its lesson will be the experience of life under the first of Delors's three stages. All members, including Britain, have agreed on an initial move towards greater economic and monetary cooperation, to start no later than July 1st 1990. Indeed Britain now says it is positively enthusiastic about stage one, because it should include removal of all trade barriers, free flows of money and financial services, and because London reckons it is ahead of its partners in this area. Stage one is also to involve more intense policy discussions between finance ministers and central bank governors of the Twelve, of a kind the British can live with. More dramatically – for the British rather than for anyone else – stage one is supposed to be the occasion for the august entry of the pound sterling into the exchange rate mechanism of the European Monetary System. But the entry will not be august: it will be the scrambled entry of someone throwing themselves onto a train already steaming towards a terminus called EMU.

The German anchor

What has built up its head of steam? What is wrong with the current functioning of the much-vaunted EMS, with its remarkable record, proven over ten years, in getting the other full participants in the system to bring their inflation down to West German levels? The paradoxical answer is that, in political terms, it has been almost too successful in achieving that goal. Most of Europe been turned into a Deutschmark zone. The Bundesbank in Frankfurt has become Europe's de facto central bank. Other EMS participants have to ape a German monetary policy in which they have no formal say. If they are lucky, they will get advance warning from the Bundesbank that it is about to raise or lower its interest rates. As often as not, and partly because of internal wrangles inside the Bundesbank council which is composed of state (*länder*) banks and which takes collective decisions, they will get only a few minutes notice from Frankfurt before they must scramble to adjust their rates to German ones.

No one, least of all the Bundesbank, foresaw this when the EMS was created in 1979, out of a classic Franco-German political fix. Helmut Schmidt, the West German chancellor, had to overrule the Bundesbank, which feared others would tamper with its anti-inflationary policies, in order to get the EMS off the ground. A row over its impact on farm prices delayed its start for eleven weeks. Britain refused to join its exchange rate mechanism (ERM), and more recent EC entrants similarly declined, though Spain finally put its peseta into the ERM in June 1989. During its first four years the system suffered seven of its eleven parity realignments to date. But gradually the Deutschmark and West Germany began to pull the monies and monetary policies of other EMS members towards them, helped greatly by France's 1983 change towards sound money and by the way in which the ERM works (see explanation on page 162).

The one-sided manner in which the ERM functions makes it easy to see how all of the relatively weaker currencies have been dictated to by the virtuous Deutschmark. The EMS's designers tried to make sure that it would not work as lop-sidedly as this. They provided for a "divergence indicator", which measures how far out of step a currency is from the average of all other currencies in the system and sets limits on how far it should diverge. This indicator was meant to point the finger firmly at excessive virtue. But the Deutschmark has several times blithely approached, if not crossed its divergence threshold, without the Bundesbank intervening to stem its rise. Other member states have not cried foul because the accusation of being too tough against inflation is such a feeble one. However, it is clear from this why some of Germany's partners complain the EMS is "asymmetrical", in that the burden of adjustment always falls on the weak, not the strong. This feature of "asymmetry" shows first why the EMS has worked in bringing inflation rates down to the German norm, and second why some of Germany's partners fret at their powerlessness in the system.

The fretters gained some satisfaction from technical tinkering with

The ERM Explained

There are three basic elements in the way the exchange rate mechanism operates:

● A basket of defined amounts of each of the member states' currencies, depending on the state's relative economic weight, make up the European Currency Unit (the ecu), giving it its current value of just over one dollar (see chart on page 165). Vis-a-vis the concocted monetary unit each currency has a "central rate", which can be changed by a commonly agreed realignment. (For technical reasons, every EC currency has a central rate, even those which like the British pound, the Greek drachma and the Portuguese escudo do not participate in the ERM.) From these central rates flow a series of bilateral rates – the Dutch guilder against the French franc, the Deutschmark against the Danish krone and so on. The bilateral rates form the cat's cradle known as the ERM parity grid. This is the operational part of the EMS, because the rule for most currencies is that they may not depart by more than 2.25 per cent from their bilateral central rate with another ERM-participating currency. The only exception is Spanish peseta which is allowed to fluctuate by up to 6 per cent against other ERM currencies; in January 1990 the Italian lira joined the narrow-band currencies.

● Intervention is compulsory whenever one currency hits its outer margin of fluctuation, relative to another. In theory, the central banks of both currencies are supposed to intervene to keep their currencies within 2.25 (or 6) per cent of each other. Typically, this should be done by the strong currency's central bank buying the weak currency, and dishing out its own in exchange, and the weak currency's central bank selling the strong currency (if necessary by first borrowing it directly from the issuing central bank, under various credit arrangements).

● But because there is a presumption of virtue about strong currencies (strong, because of lower inflation or trade surpluses), it is left, in practice, to the authorities of the weak currency (weak, because of higher inflation or trade deficits) to take action. The latter have no choice but to use up their foreign-currency reserves, then borrow until hitting their borrowing limit, and also to raise interest rates to entice people to hold their currency again, to squeeze inflation and to cramp import demand.

the EMS in September 1987. Meeting in the Danish seaside resort of Nyborg, EC finance ministers agreed on measures, mainly aimed at strengthening the EMS in advance of lifting all capital controls, but which also slightly eased the burden carried by weaker currency countries. The measures created a presumption, but not a right, that the weak could borrow foreign currency from the strong to intervene on the foreign-exchange markets before (not only after), their currencies hit their ERM limits; that they could have slightly longer in which to repay this money; and that they could settle rather more of their debts with the convenient currency cocktail of the ecu. These changes were prompted by the botched coordination between France and Germany that led to the January 1987 EMS realignment – an adjustment that was widely regarded as unnecessary. The agreements proved their worth in keeping the EMS stable when the dollar plummeted after the October 1987 stock-market crash. But the Nyborg changes also had the perverse effect of convincing several of West Germany's partners that they had gone as far as they technically could in creating a "fairer" EMS, and that something much more radical was needed.

Other factors, too, were working for change. With all the publicity about project 1992, many business people began to hanker after a single money to go with the single market. Opinion polls show a large majority of Europe's business community, unbothered by notions of sovereignty, even in Britain, would like the Community to have one currency, instead of eleven (Belgium and Luxembourg share their franc). It would make the planning of long-term investment easier, and cut out conversion costs. A feeling that Europeans were being swindled by the money changers was supported by consumer surveys showing that a traveller visiting every country in the Community and changing his money at each frontier could lose £47 out of every £100 in exchange commissions.

The hankering after a common currency has been partially met by the ecu. Though created by the central bankers for their own EMS bookkeeping purposes, the ecu has been adopted by the private markets as a convenient, risk-spreading unit of money in which to denominate bonds, loans, treasury bills, even personal accounts (including cheques and credit cards). Some 200 billion ecus-worth of financial assets are now held worldwide. But neither the man-in-the-street nor central bankers have taken enthusiastically to the idea of the ecu circulating in parallel with national monies. The shopper remains a bit bamboozled when he sees prices set in ecus, as became evident when Luxembourg tried to get all its shops, hotels and restaurants to set their prices in ecus during November 1989.

The Bundesbank is particularly loath to see a soft composite like the ecu (soft, because it has components other than the Deutschmark) being officially encouraged to compete with a hard national currency. It worries about banks creating ecu – which they will do each time they accept an ecu deposit and make an ecu loan – and thus, in effect, creating Deutschmarks, which form part of the ecu basket. This Bundesbank bias against the ecu as a parallel currency was reflected in the Delors report. The symbolism of the ecu, however, should not be underrated in the story of European monetary union. If the Community ever gets a single currency, it will almost certainly be called the ecu. The "eeck-you"? How much better if it could be called the Monnet.

Driven Towards One Currency

"Who ever heard of a single market with eleven currencies?" complained ex-Chancellor Helmut Schmidt, as did fellow EMS founder, Giscard d'Estaing, a tireless propagandist for monetary union. One decision, above all others in the 1992 programme, convinced many European politicians of the need for radical change. This was the commitment by the eight richer member states in June 1988 to lift all their remaining exchange controls by July 1st 1990, with Spain and Ireland following suit two years later and Greece and Portugal getting a further grace period until 1994–95.

This decision, which France has already reinforced by lifting its remaining exchange controls prematurely, will be without doubt the single most important 1992 directive, because of the way it has driven forward the monetary debate, and because it fills the most glaring gap in the first thirty years of Community integration. The Community started well in the matter of money. For instance, by the early 1960s companies were free to move money from one EC member state when they wanted to invest directly in another, and individuals in one member state were free to buy shares in another. But the sorry 1970s put an end to much of this. The barriers went up again, so that by the mid-1980s only four members – West Germany, Britain, Belgium and Luxembourg – had no capital controls. A fifth state, the Netherlands, had some controls but honoured its Community obligations. The rest had all slid backwards. Chief among the backsliders were France and Italy. These two countries chose the exchange rate discipline of the

What is in an ecu

One ecu comprises defined percentages of national currencies. The pie chart shows the composition of the ecu (including for the first time the peseta and escudo) agreed by EC finance ministers in June 1989 and effective from September 21st 1989.

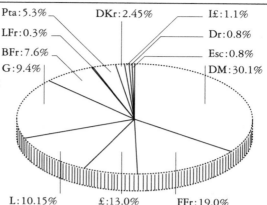

Pta:5.3% DKr:2.45% I£:1.1%
LFr:0.3% Dr:0.8%
BFr:7.6% Esc:0.8%
G:9.4% DM:30.1%

L:10.15% £:13.0% FFr:19.0%

The ecu is equal to the sum of defined amounts of national currencies. The values opposite were calculated on the basis of the percentages in the pie chart and the exchange rates recorded in the European markets at 2.15pm on September 20th 1989.

Germany, West	DM	0.6242
France	FFr	1.332
United Kingdom	£	0.08784
Italy	L	151.8
Netherlands	G	0.2198
Belgium	BFr	3.301
Luxembourg	LFr	0.130
Spain	Pta	6.885
Denmark	DKr	0.1976
Ireland	I£	0.008552
Greece	Dr	1.440
Portugal	Esc	1.393

The central rates of national currencies against the ecu are for the purpose of maintaining the money-market rates of the currencies within an agreed range. The rates opposite entered into force on January 12th 1987 and were still in force when the composition of the ecu was revised in September 1989. The rates for sterling, the drachma and escudo are theoretical because the UK, Greece and Portugal were not part of the Exchange Rate Mechanism

Germany, West	DM	2.05853
France	FFr	6.90403
United Kingdom	£	0.739615
Italy	L	1483.58
Netherlands	G	2.31943
Belgium	BFr	42.4582
Luxembourg	LFr	42.4582
Spain	Pta	133.804
Denmark	DKr	7.85212
Ireland	I£	0.768411
Greece	Dr	150.792
Portugal	Esc	172.085

EMS, but funked the discipline of allowing free capital movements. Britain did the reverse; it took the plunge of lifting all exchange controls in 1979, but funked the challenge of joining the EMS. Only West Germany managed to do everything at the same time; it kept free movement of money, joined the EMS and (because of its dominance) retained a largely independent monetary policy.

Knowing full well the enormous implications of capital liberalisation, the Commission adopted a "softly-softly" approach when it came up with its proposed directive in autumn 1987. Certainly, it told the member states, there was a risk that liberalisation might lead to quicker, sharper jumps in EMS rates, once short-term speculative money was free to slosh around Europe. But the Nyborg agreements provided adequate defence against this risk. However, the wider ramifications of setting free Europe's money had already been made clear in the Commission's Padoa-Schioppa report of 1986. There was an "inconsistent triangle", said the report. In their triple quest for free capital movements, fixed exchange rates and independent monetary policies, EC member states could have two of these – any two – but not all three. If the casualty was not going to be the fixed exchange rates of the vaunted EMS, and if it was not going to be capital freedom (without which the single market would remain forever incomplete), the casualty would have to be independence in monetary policy.

By 1988, therefore, a number of things had dawned upon a number of European governments. They felt that they had reached the limit of technical tinkering with the EMS. They surmised that the imminent freeing of Europe's capital might force big changes on governments and central banks. And they saw that the prospect was for an even more extreme version of what had gone before – a rigorous existence in the grip of the sound money of the Bundesbank. France spoke up first. Edouard Balladur, finance minister in the Chirac government, circulated a paper around his EC counterparts. It was a litany of complaints about the "asymmetry" of the workings of the EMS which shoved the burden of intervention and adjustment on to weak currency countries, regardless of whether they were to "blame" for imbalances, and said that "no country should be, a priori, exempted from rectifying its policy when the latter departs from commonly-agreed goals, no matter whether this policy is excessively expansive or excessively restrictive". The sting was in the tail. The Balladur paper concluded by suggesting a study of a European central bank replacing the EMS. The idea was hardly new, but for the first time in many years it was beginning to get official backing.

Italy then weighed in with a paper by Giuliano Amato, its finance minister. He was still more explicit in his criticism of the EMS and the German role in it. There was, said Mr Amato, a fundamental problem with the EMS because, far from containing "an engine of growth", it was downright deflationary. "Not only is the pivot currency of the system fundamentally undervalued, but the growth of domestic demand in Germany is lower than the average." The result was that Germany had structural surpluses in relation to the rest of the EC. These surpluses, both commercial and current, both induced tension in the exchange system, pushing up the Deutschmark, particularly when the dollar was weak, and removed growth potential from the other nations. Battle was joined, when Mr Amato concluded by preferring "an agreed loss of autonomy" through a European central bank, in which all would have a say, to the unilateral loss of autonomy that Germany had imposed on its partners.

Ironically, just as France and Italy were complaining about the EMS's shackles, the German economy was picking up steam, with growth reaching 3.4 per cent in 1988 and with subsequent events in Eastern Europe steadily brightening the prospects for West German expansion. Indeed the Community economy as a whole bounced along very nicely at or above 3 per cent average growth through 1989, whether because of a 1992-induced investment boom (as the Berlaymont propagandists insisted) or because of low oil prices and the continued strength of the US economy, or a combination of such things. But the Franco-Italian desire for structural change in Europe's monetary arrangements lost none of its force, even though France (alone of Germany's partners) had less to complain about because it had by this time set up a Franco-German economic council. To the pique of the Bundesbank, which was not consulted on its setting up, this body inferred that France would have a privileged hand on the German steering wheel.

It is still, however, possible that the Franco-Italian initiative might have gathered dust but for Hans-Dietrich Genscher, West Germany's free-wheeling veteran foreign minister. Mr Genscher's precise motives, like much about the man, are a mystery. But in line with his long record of support for Western European integration, he responded quickly to the stirrings in Paris and Rome. Within a week of the Amato paper, he had issued a memorandum the first words of which were: "The creation of a single European monetary zone, with a European central bank, constitutes the economically indispensable centrepiece of a European internal market."

In fact, in subsequent weeks, Mr Genscher sang the same tune as the Bundesbank and the Bonn finance ministry to the rest of the EC: if you want to join us in the driving seat, the Euro-bank will have to be a vehicle of German design and, like the Bundesbank, legally committed to price stability, and independent of governments. But, unlike his fellow German politicians, Mr Genscher felt that the central bank deserved study. As foreign minister effectively running Germany's presidency of the EC Council of Ministers during the first half of 1988, he was well placed to do something about it. He persuaded Chancellor Kohl to put the idea of a bank study on to the agenda of the Hanover summit in late June. The summiteers, albeit very reluctantly in the case of Mrs Thatcher, gave it their blessing.

Powerful support for the idea came just before Hanover. On June 13th EC finance ministers agreed in Luxembourg that all but the poorest and newest member states would lift every remaining capital control by July 1st 1990. Inside the dreary Council building on the Kirschberg Plateau, there was some huffing and puffing from France and, to a lesser degree, from Italy. They were, and still are, afraid that tax-shy money would bolt out of France and Italy the minute citizens were allowed to have bank accounts abroad. But their worries were assuaged when the Council instructed the Commission to come up with proposals for an EC-wide withholding tax on interest income, or other ways of stopping tax leakage. (The plan died a year later.) This was enough to get unanimity in Luxembourg, though in fact only a majority was required of the 1992 programme's most important financial directive because it did not directly concern tax.

The Delors report

By midnight on the first day of the Hanover summit, Jacques Delors was over the moon. Passionately interested in money since his lowly days at the Banque de France, aware of its significance since his time as finance minister, he had been put in charge of a committee with the task of "studying and proposing concrete stages leading towards economic and monetary union". In other words, he was charged with rewriting the monetary map of Europe. The Commission president was both elated and nervous about the composition of his seventeen-member study committee, numerically dominated by the governors of the twelve national banks set against Delors himself, another commissioner, Frans

Andriessen, and three outside experts. Elated, because at long last the Commission was in the monetary driving seat and among the real experts, the central bankers. Nervous, because such hard-headed practitioners were just the people to see pitfalls, rather than possibilities, on the road to EMU. But, if that was precisely the reason why several government leaders wanted the central bank governors on the committee, it proved a serious miscalculation.

The traditional Community ploy would have been to appoint a group of wise men – Euro-enthusiasts, detached from practical or political responsibility, whose views would carry relatively little weight and whose report should be just one more addition to the Brussels archives. A Committee of Five Wise Men was what Mr Genscher had proposed in the run-up to Hanover. In putting the central bankers on the committee, the government leaders had selected a group that was unusually predisposed both to cooperate with each other, and to take a European, rather than national, view.

Take, for instance, the single most revealing sentence in the final report, which describes the post-1992 effects of capital freedom and European financial services on the central bankers themselves. "Once every banking institution in the Community is free to accept deposits from, and grant loans to, any customer in the Community and in any of the national currencies, the large degree of territorial coincidence between a national central bank's area of jurisdiction, the area in which its currency is used and the area in which its banking system operates will be lost." The blurring of the lines separating national money policies could not have been better described. Such uncomfortable logic makes it easier to understand why even Sir Robin Leigh-Pemberton, the governor of the Bank of England, signed up to the report, thus ensuring that when he appeared before the House of Commons he was virtually accused of high treason by backwoods Tory MPs muttering about Agincourt being fought in vain.

The committee held eight sessions in Basle from September 1988 to April 1989. At the outset it agreed not to repeat the mistake of setting a deadline for EMU as the Werner report of 1970 had done (within ten years) and as the EMS founders had done (calling for a European Monetary Fund within two years). EMU was not, like the single market, a long-desired goal which needed a mind-concentrating timetable to achieve. The committee also agreed quickly that the final stage of EMU must be clearly defined and that the path to it would have to consist of parallel economic and monetary tracks. No one wanted a repeat of the religious wars of the 1970s between "the economists" (Germany plus allies who believed monetary union could only follow close economic convergence) and "the monetarists" (France plus allies who held that leaping into the strait-jacket of a new monetary institution could force economic policies together).

But something of this division reappeared between the committee's two main protagonists. In the "economists" corner was Karl Otto Pöhl, the smooth Bundesbank president. Wearing the "monetarists" colours was Jacques de Larosière, the dry Banque de France governor and former managing director of the International Monetary Fund. One prominent question on which they sparred was: could substantial advance be made towards EMU without institutional changes that would need revisions to the Rome Treaty, or must treaty revision be squarely faced at the outset? It was here that de Larosière made a "monetarist" power play. At the third meeting the French bank governor slapped onto the table a proposal that even in the first stage, a European Reserve Fund (ERF) should be set up, without any treaty change. This embryo Euro-bank would manage some pooled reserves, carry out some intervention on the foreign-exchange markets, and generally learn by doing. This slippery-slopemanship was resolutely opposed by Pöhl, who thought that represented a dash towards a Euro-bank without facing up to the thorny issue of parallel economic convergence. The ERF is the only item on which the Delors report acknowledged division. Its importance was that it highlighted the French interest in fast movement towards EMU.

Karl-Otto Pöhl was central to the way the other main arguments were resolved in the committee's one genuinely stormy session, in March 1989. Early on it had been decided that parallel economic and monetary progress to union would mean that states would have to agree to constraints on their budgetary deficits, though this point caused Sir Robin Leigh-Pemberton of the Bank of England, and some others, much disquiet. But at the penultimate session, in March, Pöhl weighed in very strongly to insist on *binding* budgetary rules. Indeed, some around the table felt that in his heavy-handedness Pöhl was reflecting the concerns of his Bundesbank council rather than his own. He also insisted that the report blathered on less about how desirable EMU was and why it flowed naturally and logically from the single market. In this, he had an ally in Pierre Jaans, head of the Institut Monetaire Luxembourgeois – not surprisingly, because Jaans had spent several years working in the Bundesbank.

Smarting a bit at Mr Pöhl's excision of some of his purpler prose, Delors nonetheless got what he most wanted – the unanimous backing of committee members for the report. Proudly, a month later, on April 17th, Delors unveiled it to EC finance ministers, an occasion marred for him only by the fact that it had already leaked in the *Financial Times* that morning. The bare bones of its provisions were these:

● **Stage One** Starting July 1st 1990. Greater economic convergence using existing institutions. All currencies inside the EMS. Realignments still possible but with main reliance on other adjustment mechanisms. EC central bank governors committee gets formal right of proposal to Council of Ministers. Committee divided on creation, in this stage, of ERF as precursor to European System of Central Banks (ESCB).

● **Stage Two** No date set for start. Transition period: more collective decision-taking, but ultimate responsibility for economic and monetary policy still with national authorities. EC Council sets guidelines (not yet binding) for national budget deficits and their financing. ESCB set up to subsume all existing EC monetary policy bodies. Realignments of exchange rates become adjustment mechanism of last resort.

● **Stage Three** No date. Exchange rates irrevocably fixed between the Twelve; a single currency preferred. EC Council imposes constraints on national budgets to prevent stability-threatening imbalances. ESCB acquires and manages official reserves of the Twelve and decides exchange market intervention in third currencies.

● **Requirement** Change in the EC Treaty.

The Ball Starts Rolling

Reaction was predictable. Open praise from France, Italy and a few smaller countries, mixed signals from West Germany and open hostility from Britain. What particularly stuck in the British craw was the report's insistence that creating EMU must be "a single process". The contentious paragraph 39 said: "Although this process is set out in stages which guide the progressive movement to the final objective, the decision to enter upon the first stage should be a decision to embark on the entire process". In other words, taking the first bite committed the diner to swallow the entire meal. The whole subsequent UK government strategy has been aimed at detaching the first from the second and third stages.

British tactics shifted however. Nigel Lawson, UK chancellor of the exchequer, was damning EMU, even before he knew the Delors version of it, as "incompatible with independent sovereign states with control over their own fiscal and monetary policies". The day the report came out, he said full EMU meant "political union, a united states of Europe, which is not on the agenda". While Britain was interested in closer monetary cooperation, he could not give "a political commitment to the entire process, because it represents a concept that the UK, and others, do not share". But the emphasis shortly began to change, as it became clear that no other country was joining Britain in out-and-out opposition and as, for domestic policy reasons, Mr Lawson came to view with increasing favour one element of stage one of the Delors report – the entry of sterling into the ERM.

Indeed, the Thatcher government's attitude to the Delors report was powerfully shaped by the long-simmering dispute within her cabinet over exchange rate policy. This dispute burst into the open with Nigel Lawson's resignation in October 1989. Mr Lawson had long been a closet supporter of full EMS membership, and for some time put sterling on a course of shadowing the Deutschmark. A desire to keep sterling's external value stable was one of the reasons why he was, by his own later account, too slow to raise interest rates to choke off the surge in inflation that occurred in spring 1988. This mistake only reinforced Mrs Thatcher's instinctive dislike of exchange-rate pegging. But by summer 1989, other events combined to weaken her hand against those of her ministers like Mr Lawson and Sir Geoffrey Howe, her foreign secretary, who sought a less confrontational attitude towards Brussels, and who argued that pledging early participation in the ERM was the right signal to send Britain's EC partners. The main such event was the June 1989 elections to the European Parliament. The British Labour Party trounced the Tories, and returned to Strasbourg with forty-five seats, the largest delegation of one party from a single country in the new Parliament.

In the run-up to the Madrid summit, and under the indirect pressure of example from Spain which in mid-June put the peseta into the ERM, Mrs Thatcher began to change her stance. By the time she got to Madrid, she said that Britain would slot sterling into the ERM grid, when it got its (then still rising) inflation down, and when the Community had made real progress towards its single-market goal. The other eleven leaders did not exactly fling their arms around her in gratitude. They had no real cause to, since they believed that Britain would be doing itself a favour by coming into the ERM. But the effect of her gesture on others, notably on Helmut Kohl, was to make them back away from any ill-considered rush towards EMU. There was just such an attempt at ill-considered rush by President Mitterrand, who tried to insist that the summiteers commit themselves there and then to hold a treaty-changing conference in the second half of 1990. The French leader made the counter-productive threat that unless countries like the UK were ready to go fully down the road to monetary union, "we would be obliged to reconsider our position" in lifting exchange controls in mid-1990.

The French president had said the wrong thing, too late. He had to back down in the face of a consensus (which included Mrs Thatcher) for:
● Stage one to begin on July 1st 1990, as recommended in the Delors report.
● Stages two and three to be negotiated at an intergovernmental conference, which "would meet once the first stage had begun and would be preceded by full and adequate preparation".

For Mrs Thatcher's name to be on this historic agreement was pretty remarkable. Even the other Frenchman at the summit, Jacques Delors, desperately anxious lest his report be picked to pieces and keen as Dijon mustard for an intergovernmental conference, acknowledged the achievement of brokers like Felipe Gonzalez, the summit host, and of Helmut Kohl in getting agreement. For her part, Mrs Thatcher, railed against the Delorian final vision of EMU; claimed that passing national budget decisions up to the EC level "would be the biggest transfer of sovereignty we've ever had"; and insisted that "there was nothing automatic about going beyond stage one" of the Delors report. But in a frank admission – which appalled her entourage – of her relative helplessness, she said: "I have not the slightest shadow of a doubt that I will vote against (convening the intergovernmental conference); I have not the slightest shadow of a doubt that I will be in a minority." She had thus learnt the bruising lesson from Milan four years earlier (see Chapter 2) that, given that a treaty-revising conference could be called (but not concluded) on a simple majority, the best she could do was to postpone the fateful vote.

From then on, delay and diversion became the British tactic. Mrs Thatcher signalled her intention to come up with some form of alternative British plan as early as the end of the Madrid summit, when she spoke approvingly of an article in that week's edition of *The Economist* pointing out that monetary union did not have to go hand in hand with economic/political union. The UK Treasury was set to work on an alternative. But more than two months later Nigel Lawson still did not have a prepared paper to set in front of his fellow EC finance ministers when they gathered in Antibes on September 9th for one of their half-yearly "informals". These meetings are one of the few Community occasions for genuine debate by ministers unpressed by time or the need to take tricky decisions. But all that Mr Lawson did was to talk, half-convinced and unconvincingly, of the desirability of letting national monies and monetary policies compete to produce a market-driven convergence towards EMU. If, however, procrastination was the name of the British game, there was no point in rushing the British alternative to have it seriously debated and perhaps discarded before the year was out. In any case, it was November before Britain, under a new chancellor, John Major, produced its "Evolutionary Approach to Economic and Monetary Union".

Essentially, this was a dressed-up version of the Delors report's stage one. Despite its title, it virtually ignored the issue of economic union, as Mrs Thatcher had hinted she would. Focusing on monetary union, it set three objectives. The first was price and currency stability. This goal, it said, could be met under the EMS, if (as foreseen in stage one) all participants lifted exchange controls and were thus subject to the full pressure of the market to adjust their "inflation performance in line with the best in the Community". Greater mobility of labour and capital, created by the single-market programme, would also give governments "an incentive to minimise inflation" to attract investment. The second and third aims of monetary union, said the British paper, were to reduce the costs of financial transactions and to allow everyone to borrow, lend and invest in whatever Community currency they choose. This was where the British paper claimed to break new ground. It said that stage one of the Delors report and the 1992 programme would still leave certain transaction costs and investment restrictions in place. So, it proposed going further to reduce "restrictions on the currency and geographical location of the assets of long-term savings institutions" (such as Germany's requirement that its pension funds invest mainly in Deutschmark assets). It also proposed further simplification of cheque-clearing and electronic payments systems across borders.

This was a chilly alternative vision. It essentially said: "what we like about the ERM is precisely the Bundesbank-driven rigour that has made all the Euro-softies seek a more inflationary alternative." And it had the gall to say this from outside. It lauded the "asymmetries" that loaded all the pressure for adjustment on weak currencies, rather than strong. This was a volte-face even for Mrs Thatcher, who had herself said she would never belong to a "deflationary" system like the ERM. The British paper was clearly pitched at getting German support. For that reason, it failed to provide an answer to the "sovereignty" issue posed by West Germany's occupancy of the EMS driving seat. Might not an ERM-participating Britain one day come to fret at German control just as other countries have done? This was not a question that British ministers and officials, one step behind the rest for having stayed outside the ERM for so long, were ready to answer.

At the end of the December 1989 Strasbourg summit, at which hers was the sole voice against an intergovernmental conference, Mrs Thatcher showed the ambiguity of her position. The main reason for joining the ERM, she said, was "the rigid and valuable discipline" of the Bundesbank. But "the moment you go from that discipline ... to mixing it up with other disciplines, other views, the 'let us have a bit of inflation here or there' of other economies, you lose the very thing which leads you to want to join an exchange rate mechanism which is getting inflation down". The irony is that Britain is one of those "other" economies which always tends to have a bit of inflation here and there.

The Unanswered Questions

Is EMU desirable? The Delors report never gave a straight answer to this, partly because Karl-Otto Pöhl did not want it to be turned into a Commission propaganda sheet, partly because the committee had not been asked to take a view on the matter, only to describe EMU and map out a possible path to it, if governments decided that they wanted it. The responsible answer must be: yes, if the aim is to give the single market a single currency; no, if the real aim is to make monetary conditions in the EC a little less Germanic and a little bit more inflationary. Monetary union (whether by eleven currencies locked together or formally melted into one – the difference would be cosmetic) must help a true single market emerge by reducing money-conversion costs to zero, by eliminating the risk of doing business in one currency to pay salaries and dividends in another, and by making prices in different countries directly comparable, where today differences are camouflaged by rates, mental arithmetic and unknown conversion costs. These conditions point firmly towards an independent, central central-bank charged with the unblinking task of keeping the value of the ecu or the Monnet constant. Nothing less would be acceptable to the West Germans, but in

Britain Mrs Thatcher turned down a suggestion by Nigel Lawson that the Bank of England be given a degree of independence from government control.

Should EMU be achieved by gradual evolution or in one shot, and should it be by treaty? There is a legal answer to this. The Single European Act says any "institutional modification" in the monetary field requires treaty revision by unanimity; this creates the irony that if the Community were now trying to set up the EMS, they could only do so by treaty amendment. As for "one shot" versus "evolution": it depends upon your point of view. Countries like France and Italy might, shorn of their exchange controls, have a rough ride during stage one. Dangerous, say the EMU enthusiasts, they must have treaty-assurance that they will regain, via the ESCB in a later stage, some of the monetary policy-making power they have lost. Not at all, the realists (and we) would say, these countries must show that they can take the political rigours of a non-inflationary, open financial market, before a non-inflationary one-currency system is bolted into place.

The real political need for a treaty-based plan is that West Germany will never give up what it currently has until it sees what it is going to get. Some assurances have already been given. As part of the ground-laying for stage one of EMU, the finance minsters have given the EC Central Bank Governors' Committee a new mandate with a promise of "adequate institutional autonomy" and a commitment to "price stability". But the German government and its parliament will want to see the cold print of a treaty before agreeing to change the Bundesbank's statutes.

Must monetary union be backed by binding budgetary rules? The Delors Committee reply was: yes. There are a number of reasons to fear that the fiscally-lax south European countries – Italy, Greece and Portugal – could exploit and/or upset an EMU. No longer having the responsibility of a separate exchange rate to manage, they might embark upon a borrowing spree, playing on the implicit backing of the rich or more financially orthodox members. This could drive up interest rates around the Community, leading to pressure for a more accommodating monetary policy (generating inflation) and for a depreciation of the Community currency against the outside world (importing inflation).

Yet in most federations around the world, with the exception of Australia, individual states can, and do, retain independence in borrowing, spending and taxing. The capital markets from which they borrow differentiate between the virtuous and the less virtuous parts of such federations and vary their lending rates to them accordingly. However, the history of federal states (the United States, Canada, West Germany, Switzerland) may not be a very good guide because they tend to be more similar than the EC nations, and to have state budgets that are small relative to that of central government. In the EC, Brussels accounts for about one-thirtieth of European public spending. Nor was the Delors Committee very sanguine about the free market's consistency in deciding which countries were creditworthy. It remembered that the markets went on shovelling money out to, say, New York City in the mid-1970s and to Latin America in the early 1980s, and were then panicked into cutting off all credit. Ah yes, the non-binders retort, and is government always wiser than the market? And the case of New York City showed that part of a monetary union can borrow its way into bankruptcy without compromising the union.

What would binding budget rules mean in practice? Suppose that Italy's EC partners feel that the time has come to tell Rome that it has to stop living beyond its means. Will they really order Italy to take decisions that might mean closing schools or hospitals? The scenario is not far-fetched. Even in preparation for the universally-approved Delors report's stage one, EC finance ministers agreed in late 1989 that, where member states were thought to be rocking the "economic stability and cohesion" of the Community, the Council could "formulate specific recommendations to one or several member states with a view to encouraging the necessary economic policy corrections". Henning Christophersen, the EC commissioner for economic and financial affairs, said he hoped this kind of peer group pressure among finance ministers would produce "relaxed, highly political" discussions within the Council of Ministers. Deficit cutting? Relaxed? Tell that to the International Monetary Fund.

Would EMU make the poor poorer? In an EMU, Ireland, Portugal and Greece have all made clear they would want more money than they are to get even after the doubling of structural economic aid over the 1988-93 period. Denied the freedom, as a first or last resort, to devalue their currencies against the currencies of their richer, more productive EC brethren, they fear losing competitiveness and becoming depressed areas on the Community rim. One painful form of adjustment would be emigration, already high in Ireland's case. Another form would be wage cuts or restraints. This would be painful, too. On the other hand, the poorer peripheral countries cannot afford to have a certain labour flexibility denied them by Community social policies. This is why some of them were nervous about the European Social Charter, until it became clear that key elements like pay were to be left to individual states to set. The stage is set for a major argument, because most of the richer states are dead set against a further big increase in aid to the poorer.

Who calls the tune? If EMU leads to centralised control of fiscal policy it will inevitably require an improvement in the democratic steering of that control. Both those for and against EMU agree on this; though those against cite this as an anti-EMU argument rather than as a reason for improving pan-EC democracy. Decisions over taxing and spending are the life-blood of national legislatures, and some of these decisions would pass to the Community level. The most logical forum for controlling them would be the European Parliament, which in the Delors plan would be the body to which the ESCB would report, just as the US Federal Reserve reports to the Congress.

All this is highly fraught. Mr Pöhl has warned that the loss of national sovereignty (involved in EMU) would be "so serious that it would probably be bearable only in the context of extremely close and irrevocable political integration". Claiming that states have tended to get together politically before they get together monetarily, he cites his own country where Bismarck's unification of Germany in 1871 preceded creation of the Reichsbank in 1875. History may well look back at Karl-Otto Pöhl and marvel at the way he fended off EMU – not taking brickbats for Thatcherite contrariness but by being a perfectionist and selective European.

Yet Mr Pöhl's history is selective. Over the forty years prior to the creation of the Reichsbank, the German states had traded together in the Zollverein, set up in 1834. Pöhl omits to point out that the reason why the Zollverein worked was that after only four years, in 1838, the two main currencies used in the customs union locked their exchange rates together and threw away the key. Of binding rules on budget deficits, there was no sign.

14

THE IDEOLOGY OF
1992 AND BEYOND

A Tangled Web of Politics and Nationalism

"We have not successfully rolled back the frontiers of the state in Britain only to see them reimposed at a European level with a European super-state exercising a new dominance from Brussels." Thus spake Margaret Thatcher in her September 1988 speech in Bruges, the strongest coun-terblast by a national leader against the Community since Charles de Gaulle took France, briefly, out of the EC Council of Ministers a quarter century earlier. The most striking thing about her cry was that it was not a complaint only about the rights of sovereign nations in the Community, but also about the role of government.

Ideology and the evolution of the European Community have inevitably become entangled. It is impossible to envisage moves towards an "ever closer union" without developing a European view of the role of the state in that union. This question has lurked, unasked and unanswered, in everything this book has discussed. The European Commission likes to use the word "subsidiarity" to soothe national sen-sitivities about the EC. This means, broadly, doing from the centre only what needs to be done from the centre. Subsidiarity is an india-rubber word because it immediately begs the question of what really needs to be done centrally, just as the neat idea behind the mutual recognition of laws – that only "essential" standards need to be decided and upheld at the centre – begs the question of what is essential. West Germans and Austrians regard it as natural that consumers should be protected by the state from cheap-and-cheerful beer or chocolate. Others would say that the consumer should have the right to choose. The fact that beaches in some European countries may be dirtier than *plages* in others will be seen by some Europeans as part of the rich tapestry of European life, by others as a failure of Brussels to do its job.

Wherever Brussels incontestably must have the last word, the prob-lem of ideology is unduckable. An open single market requires a central view of protectionism, of state subsidy and of competition policy. During the particular decade of the 1980s, Europe has been relaunched upon a wave of liberal thinking. Normally Euro-sceptical but newly-liberal Britain was made more European by the prospect of championing an open European market. Normally protectionist and interventionist France was going through a free-market phase of its own that made this pragmatic, deregulatory route to European Union acceptable to it. Free-trading but normally rule-bound West Germany accepted a dilution of its rules in the same cause. It is an irony that this liberal consensus served to deepen the EC's supranationalism irrevocably.

Whether it continues to set the tone of that supranationalism is open to doubt: already at the close of the decade there were signs of a leftward drift in the national politics of the member states, reflected in the results of elections to the European Parliament. But for the moment the rallying points for Europe's beleaguered interventionists are the "social dimension" of the Community – the call for central rules for the rights of workers; and, hovering over the debate about monetary union, the question of the duties of a European central bank and of the so-called "structural funds" – flows of money from Brussels to the EC's poorer countries.

Ingrained attitudes

History, geography, even religion condition the differing attitudes of the Twelve to the evolution of the EC. Catholic christendom imbued Europe, including part of what is now called Eastern Europe, with a feeling of unity until the end of the Middle Ages. The earliest pan-European sentiment arose out of reaction to a common enemy with an alien religion – the Muslim Ottoman empire. Today, the same sentiment fuels the objection of many in the EC to the would-be membership of nominally secular but predominantly Muslim Turkey. The fact that all members of the EC have Christian values in common, coupled with presumptions that democracy and free markets are the least bad ways of organising society, are basic to their willingness to accept subservience to some common European law.

But despite the instincts that Christians have in common, religion is also divisive within the EC. Largely-Protestant Danes, for instance, tend to think of the Community as "those Catholics down there", while the British Tories find it impossible to link up with the Christian

Democratic group in the European Parliament partly because of the latter's Catholic overtones. Broadly speaking, Catholicism seems to have bred an acceptance of *dirigisme*. Protestantism tends towards self-reliance.

The concept of the nation-state developed at different times and with varying intensity across Europe. These differences still show, too. Britain and France, whose sense of nationhood developed early and strongly, and where "nation" has long been closely identified with "state", have found it hard to adjust to sovereignty-sharing in the Community. The adjustment has been easier for Italy and Germany, which were more recently unified into nations and which subsequently went through the traumas of Mussolini and Hitler.

The catastrophe wrought by the latter made West Germany a unique case. It was only through integration into the Community (and into NATO) that the Federal Republic refound its sovereignty. Acceptance into the Community was not a question only of political acceptance and kudos for ostracised Germans, but also a recovery of self-control. Severe restrictions on the production of coal and steel in the Ruhr were relaxed by Germany's occupying Western powers only on condition that West Germany joined the European Coal and Steel Community in 1952. Little wonder, therefore, that there should be fears today that the revolution in East Germany may distract West Germany from the EC. Reunification now provides West Germans with the national goal, for which the Community was long a surrogate. The Belgians, in contrast, are unlikely to undergo such a distraction. Bisected into French and Dutch speakers, they identify as much with co-linguists as with co-citizens, and would therefore weep little if their nation were subsumed into a larger Europe.

The Community inevitably draws some of its character from its core – six adjacent countries, largely sharing Catholicism and law based upon the Napoleonic code. Commission polls consistently show that the Britons, Danes, Irish, Portuguese and the Dutch are less prone to think of themselves as "Europeans" than the seven other Community nations. If the Dutch come as a surprise in this list of lukewarm Europeans, Greece – shaped for so long by Turkish rule – is surprising in its enthusiasm. Money can help to buy love, and Greece gets a fair amount of it in the form of Integrated Mediterranean Programmes, set up in the mid-1980s ostensibly to benefit all Mediterranean countries, but in reality aimed at persuading ex-Prime Minister Andreas Papandreou out of his anti-Community mood. But more important,

Greece, Spain and Portugal all feel that being in the EC confirms their place in the line-up of modern, democratic nations.

Nevertheless the phase of economic liberalism in the northern and core countries of the EC that bred the 1992 campaign, before rolling with stunning effect into Eastern Europe, has created unease in Italy and the EC's poorer southern countries. Italy's adjustment to the 1992 programme has been much more faltering than, say, that of France. Italy has great difficulty in contemplating the cut-off of the flow of government money to its sprawling state-owned industries, and has faced up to the lifting of its exchange controls in mid-1990 with some trepidation.

Rome's delaying tactics have so far eased the pain. Clever Italian officials have, for instance, endlessly spun out objections to demands by the Commission and the other eleven EC member states for the closure of a state-subsidised steel plant at Bagnoli near Naples. Unassiduous Italian politicians have a long record of failing to translate EC directives into domestic law. Spain, Portugal and Greece all fear, in varying degrees, their home markets being swamped by products from the more competitive north. For the Iberians, however, entry into the Community and project 1992 have coincided with a remarkable surge of inward investment, balancing their trade deficits; and for all the poorer countries – Ireland included – the doubling of Community structural economic aid over the 1988–92 period has had a powerful mollifying effect.

The same sort of north-south divide has shown itself in the closely related matter of external trade. A simple rule of thumb is that the greater the share of trade that an EC member state does outside the Community the more likely it is to be a free-trader, and vice versa (see the chart on page 183). This helps to explain why, in the matter of trade, France is still more likely than not to line up with the southern protectionists, and why Germany, so equivocal in its attitudes to EC internal business deregulation, is a loyal member of the free-trade club.

The southern countries' desire to shield themselves from imports from outside the Community comes as no surprise when one considers that a country like Portugal is dependent for more than a quarter of its exports on relatively low value-added textiles and shoes, which are under great pressure from Asian or Third World producers. The north-south divergence is visible in the two issues regarded as the main tests of the Community's trading intentions – banking reciprocity and Japanese cars. In both cases, France, the one country to straddle the Community's north-south divide, has sided with the south.

Direction of trade* (%)

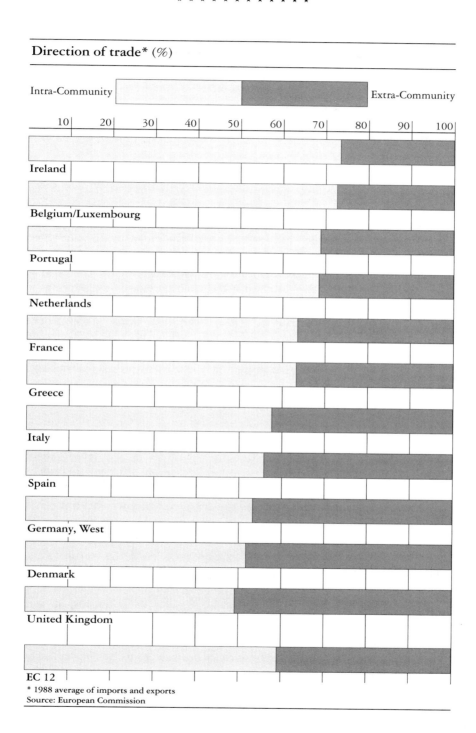

Intra-Community | Extra-Community

Ireland

Belgium/Luxembourg

Portugal

Netherlands

France

Greece

Italy

Spain

Germany, West

Denmark

United Kingdom

EC 12

* 1988 average of imports and exports
Source: European Commission

The Business of Workers' Rights

There is one area, however, where the free-market bias of project 1992 has provoked a northern reaction, and that is in the "social dimension" of the EC, and, in particular, the Social Charter of workers' rights. EC leaders, with the exception of Mrs Thatcher, adopted this charter as a "solemn declaration" at their summit in December 1989. Not until it becomes clear what social law ultimately flows from this Charter will the final impact of the 1992 project on the competitiveness of European business be known. Mrs Thatcher's eleven-to-one isolation on the Charter may have made the issue seem just another example of typical British recalcitrance. It is, in fact, the current battleground of Euro-ideology: where the British government sees the clearest signs of near-Marxist bogeymen hiding in the Berlaymont in Brussels; and where continental Socialists see some reassurance that traces of social obligation can still be found floating on the free-market tide.

Jacques Delors started talking about the need for a social charter (socle, or pedestal, he called it) in 1988 as the single-market plan began to make progress. He argued that if no grand gesture were made towards the EC's workers, they would feel threatened by the new world of tougher cross-border competition. They might turn against the single-market plan, with damaging effect. Many employers counter that these days trade unions are a paper tiger, and that the Commission is trying to con them into paying an unnecessary price for union support. Unions are no longer such a power in a Europe where the only growth in membership is in Scandinaniva (largely out of the EC), where in three countries (France, Spain, Portugal) well below one-third of the workforce carry union cards, and where in a previously strong union country like the Netherlands, organised labour's share of the workforce has dropped ten percentage points in five years to 30 per cent. Nor should the state of the job market be exactly conducive to worker disaffection. The 1988–89 period saw a net increase of some five to six million jobs, with average Community unemployment falling nearly one percentage point in a year to 8.9 per cent in November 1989.

So far, therefore, the Berlaymont economists seem to have been confounded in their predictions. These were that, though project 1992 might in the medium and long term create somewhere between two to five million new jobs net, a "J-curve" would develop, with job losses outweighing gains in the short term. But the real trendline may be more like a wobbly W, as 1992-style deregulation hits at different times different sectors like financial services (note recent job losses in the City of London), air and road transport, and industries serving previously captive public markets. The Berlaymont pollsters, for their part, have detected a consistent trend in their opinion surveys for those who consider themselves "working class" to be more negative or apathetic than the average towards the single market. Politically, too, the Social Charter worked wonders for Delors with the British left, enticing the Trades Union Congress (TUC) and the Labour Party out of their anti-EC bunker. Delors went to Bournemouth in late 1989 to address the TUC annual conference, and was rousingly greeted as "Frère Jacques" in a way that set Mrs Thatcher's teeth on edge.

But Delors has other, more philosophical reasons to give the Community a social dimension. He has a vision of a Europe able to take on the United States or the Far East in open competition, but caring more for its workers, and spreading the benefits of growth more than a Taiwan or a United States. He vaunts a "European model" of society quite different from the " American neo-radicalism" espoused by Mrs Thatcher. He feels that the Community has to be given more "soul" than a mere single market. As the break-up of the old order in Eastern Europe has gathered pace, an additional argument for the Social Charter has been bandied about: it would help make the Community's "pole of attraction" for the East that much more magnetic, by showing East Europeans that there was a civilised half-way house between communism and Thatcherite capitalism.

The other key champion of EC social legislation has been Ernst Breit, who doubles as head of the Deutsche Gewerkschaftsbund (DGB), the German trade union federation, and of the European Trade Union Confederation (ETUC). He and other union leaders, especially from the richer northern EC states, very successfully sounded the alarm bells about something dubbed "social dumping". Like dumping in trade, this refers to an undercutting of price, but in this case the price of labour. The (predominantly northern) fear here is that the great market will lead to competitive devaluation in wages and labour standards, to attract or keep investment and jobs.

So far this social dumping is more fear than reality. Investment has indeed flooded into Iberia (much of it from outside the Community) but not because Spanish and Portuguese unions have been giving foreign companies sweetheart deals. West German managers in sectors like cars and microchip manufacture have been warning their unions that they might have to work weekends in order to stay competitive with southern Europe. Yet West Germany is still making cars and microchips, and not at weekends, because its high unit labour costs are earned with higher skills, greater efficiency and snappier distribution. However, the German unions have realised that if they are to continue to push for still better conditions – such as the 35-hour week which German metalworkers are demanding – it would be safer to do it in a Europe with Charter-boosted pay and labour standards.

Britain is not among this group. It is not a high-wage economy (on the German or Danish level), though it has a remarkable tendency towards wage inflation. One of the achievements which the Thatcher government is proudest of is breaking the power of the unions. When Mrs Thatcher talks of "rolling back the frontiers of the state", near-total deregulation of the UK labour market is at the forefront of her mind. Equally significant is the ideological difference between the Thatcher brand of conservatism and continental centre-right Christian Democracy. This Christian Democracy is a swing factor in many countries, equally able to ally itself in coalition with Socialists as with right-wing liberals. It also has links with trade unions; in Belgium the largest union federation is Christian Democrat with the Socialist federation in second place.

Heavy on Symbolism

All this means that for continental Christian Democrats there are votes to be lost, not won, in union-bashing. It explains the solid backing for the Social Charter across the political spectrum in northern continental countries, including some pretty staunch centre-right conservatives like Helmut Kohl. But, if it is all a northern plot, has the south let itself be duped? And if so why?

First, the Charter is symbolic. It is not legally binding, and would not have been so even had it been adopted by all twelve states. Its political effect is to put on record the support of the overwhelming majority of states for some broad principles of social policy. But only Commission legislative proposals, such as contained in the Commission's "social action programme", can give these principles actual effect, and the way these legislative proposals will be fought out (by majority or unanimous vote) is unaffected by the Charter.

Second, there is little specific in the Charter's twelve categories of "fundamental social rights". They cover freedom of movement; employment and pay; improvement of working conditions; social protection (ie unemployment benefit); freedom to form unions, bargain collectively and to strike; training; equal treatment between the sexes; information, consultation and participation for workers; health and safety at work; protection of the young; pensions; job help for the disabled. Most of these rights are stated in vague "motherhood and apple pie" terms. The only specific detail is a minimum work age of fifteen years. Almost all the rights exist in national legislation of the Twelve. Perhaps the only exception is the right to strike, which exists explicitly or implicitly in the constitutions of nine states. In Denmark the right to strike is written into various sectoral agreements between employers and unions, while British and Irish strikers have to rely on a system of immunity from legal prosecution if they follow certain rules when they strike.

Third, some southern countries have been clear-headed in getting the Charter amended to suit them. For instance, Portugal insisted that the Charter should still leave it free to exploit its competitive advantage of having the lowest wages in the Community. Specifically, contractors in the richer north should not have to make high local social security payments for every Portuguese worker they bring in on subcontract. Equally, Ireland managed to get modified the threat it saw in the Social Charter's right to strike provision to the specially sweet deals Irish unions offer foreign (mainly US) investors.

In the light of all this, no southern country felt its national interest strongly enough endangered by the Social Charter to want to ally itself with Mrs Thatcher's ideological opposition to the document. Such a stance would have been unthinkable anyway for the socialist leaders of the southern and quasi-southern countries of Spain and France. In fact, by the time the Charter was adopted in late 1989, the tension had temporarily gone out of the ideological dispute. Both sides – Britain on the one hand and its eleven partners on the other – seemed almost happy to agree to disagree, knowing that the Charter was only the phoney war and that the real ding-dong struggle will take place on the Commission's social action programme.

Even this contains far less Community action than European socialists and trade unionists wish. Brussels is proposing to take no action to push for what the Charter says about collective bargaining and non-discrimination. It intends to leave unemployment and social security benefits and the all-important issue of minimum pay to member countries. At the EC level, it plans to come up with measures in 1990 that would set health and safety guidelines for working hours, overtime and rest periods; that would prevent employers using workers on "atypical" (part-time, temporary) contracts to undercut their competition; that would widen previous Brussels proposals requiring managers of multi-national companies to keep their workers informed and consulted. All past proposals for worker participation have stirred an ideological hornets' nest, and got almost nowhere. The main reason is that workers' participation is the sacred cow of German governments, but the *bête noire* of British (Tory) governments. There is idiocy in both positions. A degree of worker participation (and now share-owning) is considered standard practice among good British managements. Bonn vaunts the merits of its *mitbestimmung* (co-determination) system, but knows full well that German management would love to escape from the system's rigours; it therefore wants to block any bolt hole for German management by insisting on worker participation in any measure relating to European company law, including the European Company Statute.

This might seem enough social legislation for EC governments to chew on. But it is too feeble and slow a start to please the left-wing constellation (Socialists, Communists, Greens) which since June 1989 has a majority in the European Parliament. This "progressive" majority may not carry out its threat to censure the Commission formally, but it will, for the lifetime of the current Parliament (until 1994), seek to goad the maximum in social policy measures out of Brussels.

A Single Labour Market?

Despite the melting of frontiers, and some prospect of a single European currency, the idea of an American-style single market for European labour will be slow to evolve: it is incompatible with the robust differences between the EC's member states. A single wage rate for the Community is a non-starter where different pay rates are needed to offset the productivity of, say, Germany over Portugal. Social security payments among the twelve countries range twice as widely as those among individual states in America. Any attempt at common pay or social security rates across the EC would spell economic death to those member states, mainly in the south or on the rim, with lower productivity. Enormous legal, as well as economic, differences exist among the Twelve. It is not just the difference between having lots of labour rules like Germany and few labour rules like Britain. France (with weak unions) orders its labour market by statute; Denmark leaves it entirely to its employers and unions to sort out in a typically Scandinavian consensus. These differences must be the stuff of which the famous "subsidiarity" principle is made.

But some things can and should be done. Anything that encourages the mobility of labour, such as the ability to take social security and state/private pension rights from one EC state to another, deserves welcome. Some countries have labour surpluses, others labour shortages, and the two never match up because people don't move towards jobs (for reasons of culture and language) in the way they do in America. Only some 4.8 million EC citizens live in an EC state other than their own; at 1.5 per cent of the total population, this is a far lower degree of internal migration that in the USA. Most foreigners in the EC – around 8 million – come from non-Community countries, especially Turkey, Yugoslavia and North Africa. If an Economic and Monetary Union (EMU) with fixed exchange rates ever materialises, it will require people from poorer peripheral regions to be more prepared to move towards jobs in richer places.

The large intra-EC migratory flows of guest workers of the 1960s and 1970s, when southern Italians flooded north to find work, are considered history. 1992 policies to promote cross-border cooperation and competition are likely to encourage only relatively small ripples of international job offers and requests. It is not clear what will happen when remaining restrictions on Iberian workers moving to the other ten EC states are lifted in January 1993, with the ending of transition arrangements for Spain and Portugal. While the booming Spanish economy has kept most Spanish workers at home, no one is betting this will be the case for poorer and less dynamic Portugal. But the likely post-1992 trend is, according to the Commission, "fluid exchanges of skilled people moving about all over the Community without any particularly significant net migratory movement". Perhaps. But so far such exchanges have been pretty slender. This is partly because the EC's labour exchange system is creaky in the extreme. Although national labour authorities telex in to Brussels their vacancies every ten days, the information is often incomplete and inaccurate, and barely a thousand people a year find jobs this way. A more important reason for stickiness in the EC labour market is the difficulty that EC states have in agreeing on what constitutes minimum training for a particular profession and therefore in recognising each other's diplomas and professional qualifications. Painfully and slowly, doctors, dentists, midwives, chemists and so on have acquired the right not automatically to have to repeat their training when they move from one EC state to another. But the resulting movements of labour have been minuscule. France, for instance, has since 1958 received only 763 doctors who qualified elsewhere in the

Community even though the total number of EC doctors exceeds 700,000. More impressive results may follow on the agreement by EC governments to recognise the validity of each other's higher-education diplomas and degrees.

Far and away, the biggest obstacle to Europeans moving or doing business across frontiers is language. This is why the UK government was so short-sighted to object, on the ideological ground that the Community is legally incompetent to meddle in education, to the Lingua programme to promote foreign-language training in schools. There is also sense in the Community promoting job, as well as language, training – by payments from the EC Social Fund, by encouraging discussion between employers and unions at Community level, and even (as stated in the Social Charter) by giving EC citizens a minimum right to on-the-job training. Many EC countries, including Britain by the Thatcher government's own admission, suffer from a woeful lack of skilled labour power. Compared to Far Eastern countries, Europeans are extremely badly trained relative to their level of wealth. Economic liberals have a strong self-interest in seeing improved job skills in all parts of the Community; the more regions like Portugal, or even parts of northern England remain dependent on low-skilled industry for their livelihood, the more such regions will continue to clamour for trade protection against equally low-skilled, but even lower-cost competition from the Third World.

The ideological dispute about Europe's "social dimension" started out with an argument over how the fruits of the single market should be spread, and over the role of government – in this case the European Community – in spreading them. In the end, the only way to close the argument is to recognise that the single market is aimed at improving the lot of the consumer –not of the business person nor of the worker – and that we're all consumers now.

15

TRADE WITH THE WORLD BEYOND

Fear of a Fortress

"And beyond the Wild Wood?" asks the Mole, in *The Wind in the Willows*. "Beyond the Wild Wood comes the Wide World," the Rat replies, "and that's something that doesn't matter, either to you or me. Don't ever refer to it again, please." 1992 was conceived to solve an internal European problem, so there was a touch of such xenophobia in Lord Cockfield's White Paper of June 1985. It said barely a word about the EC's attitude to trade with the world outside, for its 280 measures already contained quite enough to give vested interests within the EC the shivers, without adding fear of unchecked foreign competition to the picture. Even by 1988, more than two years into the project, officials of the Commission had still to admit that external trade was an unopened book.

It could not remain so for long. First, a common external trade policy was inescapably implied by the pledge to demolish Europe's internal frontier controls (see Chapter 5). Second, the rest of the world became more and more agitated as word of the success of Europe's relaunch spread. In 1987 the United States and Canada had signed their wearisomely negotiated free-trade agreement. This pact had already revived fears that the world was being divided into trading blocks. These would give countries in Europe, North America and perhaps East Asia privileged access to each other, while trade between the blocks would become tenser, and those outside the blocks would become more isolated. Wasn't Europe's 1992 project, legal though it might be under GATT rules, a dramatic lurch in the same direction?

In 1988 a notion that the EC was constructing a "fortress Europe" took hold abroad. Foreign watchers, and *The Economist*, too, saw fresh evidence of modern protectionism – a toughening of the EC's rules against dumping, a tightening of "rules of origin" to stop convicted dumpers side-stepping those rules, and an uncompromising demand for "reciprocity" abroad in the draft regime for pan-European banking. They also noted the pleas for protection by European industrialists, such as Umberto Agnelli of Fiat.

Declarations of Openness

The Community's first formal statement of how the opening of the great market would affect its trade policy came in the communiqué of the European summit in Hanover in June 1988. This promised openness, certainly, but the promise was posed in decidedly cagey terms. "The Community must be open to third countries and must negotiate with these countries where necessary to ensure access to their market for Community exports. It will seek to preserve the balance of advantages accorded, while respecting the identity of the internal market of the Community."

It was a reflection of the mounting worry about "fortress Europe" that Margaret Thatcher made trade policy a cardinal point of the celebrated critique of the Community that she delivered in the Belgian town of Bruges in September 1988. "My fourth guiding principle is that Europe should not be protectionist," she said. "It would be a betrayal if, while breaking down constraints on trade to create the single market, the Community were to erect greater external protection. We must make sure that our approach to world trade is consistent with the liberalisation we preach at home."

This speech marked a breaking of the facade of unity with which the twelve members were building their great market. And in the matter of trade, it left outsiders with a stronger impression of an argument to be won than of a principle firmly enshrined. Indeed, the "liberalisation which we preach at home" was a very British gloss on sentiment within Europe. Countries outside the Community are all too aware that there is no "government" of the EC to impose a philosophy of trade. There is a continuous tug of war between members, and between Brussels commissioners, with protectionist inclinations and those with liberal leanings. In such circumstances the only sensible policy for outsiders is to complain incessantly to give the free-traders as much psychological support in the tussle as possible.

After autumn 1988, Brussels' protectionist image improved. In late October that year the Commission published a much more detailed statement of the EC's trading intentions. It stressed how much the EC has to lose in a protectionist world: its external exports (that is, the

EEC trade ($ billion)

Exports to:
Imports from:

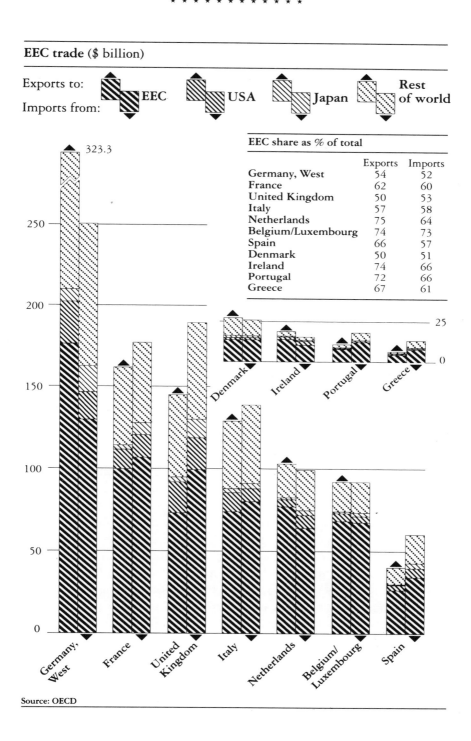

| EEC | USA | Japan | Rest of world |

EEC share as % of total		
	Exports	Imports
Germany, West	54	52
France	62	60
United Kingdom	50	53
Italy	57	58
Netherlands	75	64
Belgium/Luxembourg	74	73
Spain	66	57
Denmark	50	51
Ireland	74	66
Portugal	72	66
Greece	67	61

Source: OECD

exports of its members to countries outside the EC) are 20 per cent of world exports, against the United States' 15 per cent and Japan's 9 per cent. Those external exports are equivalent to 9 per cent of its own GDP, comparable with Japan's 9.3 per cent and greater than the USA's 6.7 per cent. (The Japanese economy is often imagined to be much more export-dependent than it really is.) The Commission promised loyalty to the GATT's rules for multilateral trade. As for the types of trade not covered by the GATT (in services, say) it defined in broadly unfrightening terms the kind of reciprocal access to other countries that it might be pushing for. It conceded that it might, in certain cases, replace national protection (which the planned opening of internal frontiers would make unworkable) with Community-wide protection: but it vowed that the overall level of protection would not go up. The leitmotiv was: "not fortress Europe, but partnership Europe".

The Commission Takes a Liberal Turn

So far, so fine-sounding. A more tangible promise of a liberal Europe was a new line-up of commissioners in Brussels with great influence on the EC's trade policies. When the Delors Commission started its second four-year term, Frans Andriessen, a cool and economically liberal Dutchman, became commissioner for external relations and trade policy, replacing a colourful Belgian, Willy de Clercq, who had said one or two rash things that outsiders had seized upon as evidence of Euro-protectionism.

Out went Lord Cockfield, pulled home by Mrs Thatcher because his Brussels zeal had proved too much for her. This was a sad put-down for someone who had done much to give Britain the pragmatic Europe it wanted. But it seemed by then that, like the Sydney opera house, it would take one sort of genius to design 1992 and another to make it stand up. In came one of West Germany's economic liberals, Martin Bangemann, as commissioner for the internal market and for industrial affairs. In, too, came Sir Leon Brittan, from Britain, as commissioner for competition policy, where he continued the liberal campaign conducted by his forthright Irish predecessor, Peter Sutherland. Sir Leon was also put in charge of financial institutions – a portfolio particularly neuralgic for foreign trade officials.

This trio of newcomers formed, and still forms, a powerful block within the Commission, pushing for a more open Europe. The president, Jacques Delors, does not, as a French socialist, side naturally with their point of view. But there is a hard-headed economic realism in Jacques Delors, as he showed in the early 1980s when he got France back onto the straight-and-narrow, and set it off on a course of very unGallic deregulation. He has not yet tried to quash the new Commission's free-market tendencies. Instead, he has sought to compensate for them by championing Europe's "social dimension" and by projecting with great vigour a vision of Europe that stretches way beyond the completion of an open market.

American Fears

Both the United States and Europe are currently trying to shape up to a daunting economic challenge from Asia. The USA ponders the need for industrial strategies, self-refereed "fair" trade, and government-funded project development. Books that justify such ploys – showing that the Japanese are not "normal" commercial competitors – sell well in the United States at the moment. Europe pushes for the economies of scale, bracing competition and the foreign-investment lure of its great market. Each professes a sustained faith in open, multilateral trade. Each notes actions by the other that belie such faith. Facing the same challenge they jostle each other and eye each other warily.

Awareness of 1992 impinged across the Atlantic only in early 1988, spreading from the corporate world, through the Washington bureaucracy to Congress and the Administration. By the spring of 1989 it had become a temporary obsession which persisted until it was overshadowed by the great upsets in Eastern Europe. The Community's agricultural policy has long been a thorny trade problem in the United States, and rows over this at the Uruguay session of the GATT in 1988 and over the sale in Europe of US hormone-enhanced beef made 1988 a bad year for the USA to be cheerful about the early external vagueness of the 1992 project. The assumption in Washington was that the EC would be bound to cushion the pain of European industry's adjustment to a more open internal market, and would do this with external protectionism.

By the spring of 1989 the worst suspicions were ebbing away. Carla Hills, President Bush's trade representative, said that her frame of mind was "optimism tempered with vigilance". The vigilance was focused upon three main areas:

● **Standards** The United States fears that as Europe develops its "new approach" to regulations and standards the rules will be drafted in obscurity and in a way that hurts US exports. Officials in Washington

195

EEC exports ($ billion)

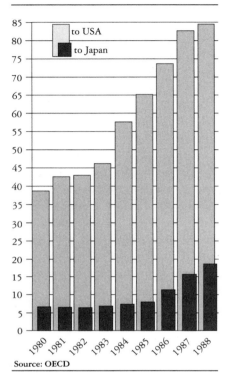

Source: OECD

EEC trade balance ($ billion)

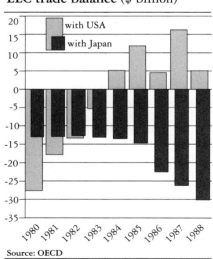

Source: OECD

US direct investment in the EEC ($ billion)

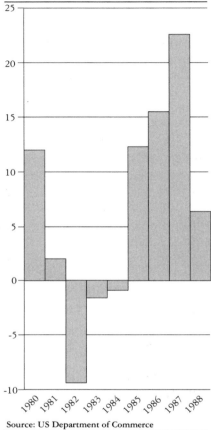

Source: US Department of Commerce

Japanese investment in the EEC ($ billion)

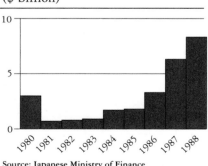

Source: Japanese Ministry of Finance

say that they have been denied observer status at CEN and CENELEC – the European standards-setting bodies – and that talking with them is like "trying to grab jelly". The American National Standards Institute is, they claim, open to its European counterparts. Washington also wants US laboratories to certify the Euro-worthiness of American exports. The EC has said yes in principle, but it could take many years for US laboratories to qualify.

● **Rules of origin** The United States does not want to be forced to set up plants in Europe in order to sell there. It wants access for US exports. Senator Lloyd Bentsen, the Democratic chairman of the Senate finance committee, has said darkly of 1992 that he is "senator for all Americans, not just multinational companies". The European "diffusion rule" under which integrated circuits must be "diffused" in Europe was viewed as a clear ploy to force American semi-conductor manufacturers to set up in Europe. The USA is understandably sensitive, too, to Brussels officials deciding whether a Japanese product made in America is really made there or not: this was the issue in a recent case about Ricoh photocopiers made/assembled in California. Washington was particularly upset in late 1989 by the EC rule that more than 50 per cent of the programming of European television channels should "where practicable" be sourced in Europe. It saw this, rightly, as a clear swipe at one of America's fortes. Happily, the rule is unenforceably vague.

● **Reciprocity** In 1988 it seemed likely that the EC would ask for more than "national treatment" for European banks in the United States as its price for admitting new US banks into Europe. This prompted a stiff reaction from the US treasury, which feels that this reaction was one reason why the EC toned down its reciprocity formula. There may be a replay of this argument in the matter of public procurement.

Japan, the Would-be European

The Japanese have followed the Americans through a period of exaggerated fear about 1992 to one of rather more cautious optimism. They have greater reason to be worried. They know that the single-market project is partly aimed at them. They are formidable in exactly those industries that European governments are most likely to protect – cars and electronics. And the clearest signs of pan-European protectionism – more determined use of the anti-dumping weapon – have been aimed mainly against them.

Cars remain the great test-case of the post-1992 Community's free-trading resolve. Five EC countries have negotiated more-or-less voluntary quotas limiting the inflow of Japanese cars to a share of their car market, or to a fixed quantity: France (3 per cent), Britain (11 per cent), Italy (3,200 cars a year), Spain (2,000 cars a year), Portugal (10,000 cars a year). The battle over whether and how to replace these restrictions with a pan-European car regime has swung to and fro. In late 1988 some people in the Commission put forward quite restrictive proposals. These would have insisted that Japanese imports into Europe stayed proportional to sales of European cars in Japan – the worst sort of quantitative reciprocity. They would have laid down a minimum amount of local content for Japanese cars made in the EC. And they would have placed controls on the amount of national development aid going to Japanese motor industry plants in Europe.

This proposal then appeared to be quashed by the liberal troika of commissioners mentioned earlier. By June 1989, Martin Bangemann, vice-president of the Commission and responsible for the industrial dossier, was singing a very different song. Existing national restrictions would be abolished, use of rules on local content to justify trade restrictions within the Community would not be allowed. The EC members would "jointly monitor" the trend in Japanese imports for a "transitional period": tradespeak for an overall voluntary export restraint exercised by Japan. But at the time of writing, the final outcome of the argument was still unclear because EC governments had yet to have their say.

The Japanese have tried to influence such debates within the Community in a way different to the Americans. First, the threat of a world divided into trading blocks has converted them to devotees of the multilateral trading system refereed by the GATT. Until recently Japan was shy of playing the GATT card because its own trade practices, particularly in agriculture, made it hard for Japan to appeal to the GATT with a straight face. But Japan now sees the GATT as a good defence against being singled out by Europe and the United States for particularly tough treatment.

Second, the Japanese are less anxious than the Americans to preserve Japan's right to export to Europe and to fight off pressures to make its companies invest there. The Japanese see themselves as natural foreign investors: the strength of their currency dictates it, protectionism encourages it and the prospect of a less fragmented European market demands it. The Japanese investment diaspora is not seen, as it has come to be in the USA, as causing a loss of jobs at home. It is the next phase of the rise and rise of Japan as an economic power – just as the United States felt in the 1930s. So Japan's most powerful business figures – men like Soichiro Toyoda, head of the Toyota car company – talk constantly of being "good corporate Europeans".

What worries the Japanese is that the EC will distort their foreign investment plans with rules demanding a lot of local content. They want to preserve the quality of their products, which can become harder to do the higher the proportion of locally-made parts grows. They do not want such rules to bar them, effectively, from countries such as Spain or Portugal where labour may be cheap and willing but local industry is simply not up to supplying parts of adequate quality. The nub of the Japanese concern is not free trade but access. The Japanese have no conceptual problem with a "fortress Europe": they are dab-hands at fortress-building themselves. They do not argue furiously against "voluntary" import restraint agreements. Such agreements are an excellent way to ensure that Japanese exports are profitable. The important thing for Japan is that , when and if Europe's walls go up, Japan's global companies should qualify as insiders.

No Truck with Dumpers

The single most damning piece of evidence in favour of the claim that the EC is constructing a "fortress Europe" has been the evolution of its anti-dumping policy – that is, its use of sanctions against importers said to be selling at unfairly low prices. The temptation for the Community to use anti-dumping actions as a form of protectionism is great. Here is a weapon whose use is legal under the GATT, yet which can be aimed, contrary to GATT principles of multilateral trade, at a particular country or company. Here is a weapon, too, which the Commission can fire without initially needing the approval of the member states (which must, however, approve any final imposition of dumping duties) and which is so complex that few critics will ever understand it.

If the Commission can show that a European company is being injured by Asian competition – and show, too, that the Asian competitor is selling his wares in Europe at below the price he is charging at home, or at less than the cost of production plus a "reasonable" profit, it can under GATT rules force him to pay import duties or to raise his prices in Europe. The EC and the United States have few grounds to insult each other about use of anti-dumping actions; each is adept in making use of them against communist or Asian countries. Their

Anti-dumping actions initiated by:*

	EC	USA
1981	36	13
1982	57	25
1983	46	38
1984	43	44
1985	56	61
1986	19	65
1987	28	40
1988 est	38	38

* Including those against non-members
Source: GATT

mounting problem is that as the trend towards international direct investment in factories continues, they find themselves firing at plants in each other's territory.

Project 1992 has not directly affected the number of anti-dumping actions being launched by the Commission. The table above shows a slight decline, but it is also true that the weapon is being pointed less at the United States and the communist countries, and more at Japan and the newly industrialised countries. Some recent changes in the way that the EC has used the weapon have given an impression of a new zeal that the numbers do not convey.

● Since 1987 the EC has cracked down on Asian companies, notably Japanese producers of office equipment, supposedly dodging existing anti-dumping duties on completed products by setting up "screwdriver plants" to complete them in Europe. It can now impose anti-dumping duties on the parts coming to such factories from their home country unless at least 40 per cent of them (by value) come from Europe or other countries outside the dumper's own. Japan has challenged this rule in the GATT – a sign of its new willingness to play the GATT card.

● The EC has extended this technique to dumpers' plants in the United States, forcing Ricoh of Japan to add more value to its photocopiers in the USA if the EC is to regard them as being of American origin. Two worries here: first, it is a recipe for trade tension if the EC starts telling other countries whether their own certificates of origin are valid or not; second, the EC criteria for origin are, as is explained later, becoming increasingly subjective and specific to the product in question.

● The EC has extended its use of the anti-dumping weapon into services by challenging the pricing of Hyundai Merchant Marine of South Korea.

● The EC is increasingly prepared to pile additional duties on convicted dumpers whose prices in Europe do not move after being hit with a first round of duties. (Its remorseless logic is that absorption of anti-dumping duties merely makes the earlier degree of dumping worse.)

● The EC has launched eight anti-dumping actions against Hong Kong since the start of 1988. These have been contentious because of the openness (and smallness) of the Hong Kong economy and the lack of financial clout of many of its firms, and suspect because Hong Kong is particularly reluctant to bow to protectionist pressure with voluntary restraint of its own exports.

There has been much debate, of late, about the way in which the Commission works out whether or not an import is being dumped. The argument is intensely complicated: put simply, it is about the scope for massaging upward the reported price of the product in the producer's own country, and downwards in Europe, with the net effect that dumping is more likely to be found. It appears that the GATT's anti-dumping code was designed for commodity-type products and is defeated by trade that involves complex marketing of complicated products which are being constantly superseded by new models, all in a world of volatile exchange rates. Within GATT rules the creative dumping-inquisitor can demonstrate just about anything.

Proof, or no proof, the Commission has been put on guard by recent scrutiny. In a typical year it receives a hundred complaints of dumping from hard-pressed sections of European industry. It investigates roughly fifty of them and, in these cases, finds dumping in roughly thirty. It imposes duties in about fifteen cases and insists on price rises in the rest. In the first nine months of 1989 it launched no new anti-dumping inquiry into any important type of consumer good.

In the spring of 1989 an inquisitive team of British officials, spurred into action by a campaign against excessive anti-dumping zeal in the *Financial Times*, left Brussels broadly satisfied that the Commission was not using dumping as a systematic form of protection. Nevertheless, malice is not a criterion for misuse of the anti-dumping weapon. It sits there, available, when industries feel competitive discomfort. Its use seems justified by the reasonable instinct that fairness in trade is desirable, for a capitalist system cannot allocate resources properly if it must cope with variously subsidised competition. But it can fire broadsides which would be considered laughable if fired within the Community or even across the Atlantic – against the price at which British cars are sold in Belgium or the United States, relative to their price in Britain, for instance; or against the price at which continental food producers sell into Britain when confronted with a hard-bargainer like Sainsbury's, the supermarket giant. The anti-dumping code, used in the modern world, confuses what is methodically cross-subsidised with what is horribly competitive.

Rules of Origin

So long as an unrefined anti-dumping weapon is available under the GATT, importers into the EC will want to know what criteria they must satisfy to be outside its line of fire. This need leads straight into the complicated matter of "rules of origin" and "local-content regulations": one of the most insidious means of persuading non-European manufacturers that they would do better to set up within Europe.

Rules of origin are the handmaidens of trade distortion. Wherever a degree of preference or a non-tariff barrier creeps into trade, a rule of origin is needed to decide to whom the preference or the barrier should apply. If there is a quota or an anti-dumping duty on a product from Japan, there has to be a definition of what makes that product Japanese. If the EC wishes to preserve "Community preference" in its more open, post-1992 market in government purchasing, it must define what goods or services qualify as having EC origin. This is inescapable.

The EC's basic definition of origin remains the one that was internationally accepted in 1968: goods originate where they undergo their "last substantial transformation". But in time the EC has overlaid this simple definition with a mounting number of more precise ones, many of which involve stipulations of local content. Rules of local content are thus one way of writing a rule of origin.

Among the rules of origin that abound are:

● For the purposes of protectionism practised by particular EC countries (under Article 115) radios, televisions and ball-bearings are deemed by the Commission to be European when 35–45 per cent of their value is added in the EC. A similar rule for video-cassette recorders is being considered.

● To qualify for low-tariff access as products from EFTA, cars must have 60 per cent EFTA content.

● Whenever a product from a particular country has been found to be dumped, the same product made in the dumper's plants elsewhere in the world must have at least 40 per cent of its value added outside the dumping country, though only if the plants were set up after 1987 (when the EC introduced its "screwdriver" rule) or if production inside the Community was subsequently expanded.

● Integrated circuits must be diffused (that is, etched onto blank silicon wafers) in Europe to be regarded as European. This was a pre-emptive answer to an unresolved anti-dumping complaint against Japanese memory chips and also part of the EC's armoury against anti-dumping dodging through the use of "screwdriver plants". Got that?

● Definitions as to what comprises a dumped photocopier have been tightened. Once it was enough that the optical system be made outside the dumping country. Now it no longer is.

● There has been much talk, subsequently rejected by the Commission, about what degree of local content would constitute a European car built by Japanese companies in Europe. Figures as high as 90 per cent have been bandied about. The Nissan cars produced in Britain were the main cause of this dispute.

In the matter of rules of origin the EC can paradoxically become more liberal and more protectionist at the same time. It can become more liberal in that the pan-European market will offer more opportunities to foreign traders than the patchwork of national regimes did before. Yet the EC can simultaneously seem more protectionist because the mere creation of a single European market throws up a need to define what is European and what isn't that did not exist before. The stakes for outsiders become higher because the consequences of being accepted into, or debarred from, a market become more important the bigger the market gets. This fear of greater "relative discrimination" (of, say, a US company feeling less well placed to beat a German competitor on the French market than it did before) plays its part in the worries of EFTA that are described in Chapter 16.

The Heart of the Matter

Relative discrimination also goes to the heart of 1992's relationship with the GATT and the multilateral order (ie, one in which all countries are treated equally) that it has championed since it was set up in 1947. There are those who argue that any free-trade area distorts the law of comparative advantage that should drive an efficient world economy. The logical extension of this argument is that the United States should be broken up so that oranges from Florida could compete on equal terms in New York City with oranges from Brazil. It is to side-step such perfectionism that the GATT allows countries to form free-trade areas provided that their external frontiers are not more protectionist than before.

The more serious potential problem is that the emergence of free-trading blocks could supplant the GATT's efforts, in its 1986–90 Uruguay round of negotiations, to keep its regime relevant to the modern world. This is a world in which the rich countries can no longer go on arguing that national security and pressing social problems demand that they protect their agriculture at the expense of less developed ones. It is a world in which trade in goods is blocked not by tariffs or border controls but by legal barriers within (see Chapter 7). It is a world in which a fast-mounting share of world trade is made up of services, which the GATT has no rules for, and one in which recognised rights of intellectual property become steadily more necessary. The risk is that in all these matters the hoped-for world order will not be a GATT order at all but a web of bilateral deals between blocks and powerful countries. Hence the need for all to sit down and negotiate the Uruguay Round.

Agriculture is the most immediate area in which the evolutions of the EC and of the GATT can conflict. The future of Europe's agricultural policy is crucial to the fate of the GATT's Uruguay session. But the 1992 project and the CAP are divergent, not mutually reinforcing undertakings: an open market is actually going to make today's compartmentalised CAP that much harder to sustain (see Chapter 9).

Farming aside, the completion of Europe's market and the evolution of the GATT affect each other in two ways. In its emerging "internal" rules the EC is acting as a pioneer in the quest for an international regime against non-tariff barriers, or for trade in services, or for respect of intellectual property. In all these matters abuses cease to be matters of quotas, recalcitrant border officials, paperwork or frontier payments. The protection comes from the laws of sovereign states: standards for exhaust gases or for beer purity, rules for the proper behaviour of banks, state favouritism that gives contracts to local firms. So the referee of the trading system suddenly begins to need powers to adjudicate over such national laws, either to "harmonise" them – the discredited route that the EC tried for so many years – or to allow them to infect each other, provided that essential standards are set at the centre – the EC's "new approach". This is the contentious new dimension of the single market in Europe – the onward march of supranationalism.

How far down this supranational road can and must the GATT go? The fate of project 1992 will help determine the answers. The emerging rules for trade within the Community in new activities such as financial services, intellectual property, and government procurement provide examples to the GATT of how trade in such things can work given a set of common rules that sovereign states accept as binding. In fixing their rules for trade in intellectual property (patents, copyrights, computer software), for example, the EC and the GATT have already fed upon each other most usefully. More daunting is the notion that to find a workable alternative to the GATT's elastic anti-dumping code the world will have to work out something akin to the EC's highly-intrusive competition policy.

In the meantime the EC is negotiating how such modern forms of trade might be ordered given no GATT rules, or given GATT rules that involve a lesser surrender of sovereignty than the EC's new internal regime. Here there is a chance that bilateral deals will establish the principles of a new multilateral regime. There is also a risk that such deals may sap the international will to agree such a regime. In these non-GATT-regulated areas, the (supposedly) temporary substitute is being woven out of deals on "reciprocity".

The most powerful and topical example involves trade in financial services. The internal EC regime, a model for a truly interdependent world order, has a potent impact on law-making sovereignty. The external regime for financial services – pending completion of the Uruguay round of GATT negotiations – has been exploring what is feasible given a lesser surrender of sovereignty. And the critical question here is this: given that the real protectionism in financial services consists of the toughness of local rules – such as the South Korean rule limiting the number of insurance companies, or the US rule that divides banking into commercial banking and investment banking – how much breaking-down of local rules should trade in financial services involve?

The initial EC attitude was to ask for a lot, in line with the freedoms it was creating within. It wanted "reciprocal treatment" of European institutions abroad as the price for allowing foreign banks to participate in a newly liberalised and opened European banking market. The Americans responded angrily, insisting that the Europeans ask for no more than "national treatment" – in other words, "when in America do as the Americans do". This might not be too bad a fate in the United States (although its financial system is still hamstrung with quaint laws). But it would be highly unsatisfying in Taiwan. In the end the Commission settled for a compromise "national treatment that gives effective access". This implies a mild bending of local rules to get foreigners into rule-bound markets. And it happens to tie in well with

GATT guidelines, agreed in Montreal in the winter of 1988/1989, for the current negotiations on trade in services.

Fortress: Yes or No?

Drawing these strands together, the verdict on "fortress Europe" can still only be tentative. So many examples of national import restraint have yet to be avowedly removed, let alone abandoned in practice and the results accepted. The car import regime, above all, is the one to watch. But many other tough problem-areas remain — textiles, consumer electronics, shoes, bananas, sheepmeat. And use of the anti-dumping weapon, backed up by a raft of local-content rules, definitely encourages foreign suppliers to secure a physical presence within the EC.

The positive gloss is that there is no grand protectionist plan afoot, nor European industrial policy lurking: the current Commission is too liberal for that. The great market remains an exercise in economic liberalism — in creating an unfettered market — and has not so far seen this approach badly undermined. Equally, the laborious process of negotiating openness between twelve modern economies is proving a valuable test-bed for a more up-to-date regime for world trade. On balance, it is still fair to say that Europe is building a more open internal market without becoming more protectionist to the world outside.

16

THE OTHER EUROPEANS

Around the Honeypot

The European Community's relaunch happened just in time. It re-established the credibility of the EC shortly before the post-war order in Europe went through its astonishing spasm of 1989 – the accelerating collapse of communist regimes in Eastern Europe. Many outside countries were sufficiently impressed by the EC's new momentum to seize upon the Community as a fixed star when the rest of the European firmament began to shift and dissolve in the autumn of that year.

America – turning gradually in on itself during the late 1980s – saw project 1992 as a timely psychological benchmark in European history. Already in June 1989, before the rush of events in Eastern Europe, Raymond Seitz, who now leads the US State Department's bureau for European affairs, said he regarded Europe's 1992 programme as "pivotal" to the West's reaction to the changes there. He argued that a strong EC economy would help East European countries towards the wealth that communism had failed to deliver, and that a strong EC political identity would help make sure that the German lurch towards some form of reunification happened under conditions in which the "old instabilities do not arise again".

Where ten years ago, America preferred divide-and-rule in Europe, in order to be the big NATO chief among fourteen smaller indians, it is now happy to see the EC build itself into a European pillar of the Western alliance – not least because this would allow it to save itself some of the expense of maintaining the security of Europe. It has thus rediscovered enthusiasm for what it avuncularly urged straight after the war – a united Europe, strong enough to ween itself off military dependence upon the United States.

In July 1989, the Group of Seven industrial countries signalled a global acknowledgment of the EC's place in the world order. At their summit in Paris in July 1989 they said that the Brussels Commission should coordinate the aid of twenty-four Western aid donors to Poland and Hungary, the two Warsaw Pact countries which had at that time moved towards democracy. Thereafter the potential scope of this role expanded as East Germany, Yugoslavia, Bulgaria, Czechoslovakia and Romania each moved in their own significant ways towards democracy and market-driven economies.

The members of the other Western European club, the European Free Trade Association, had their attitude towards the EC transformed by the 1992 relaunch. As late as the beginning of 1989 the six EFTA members – Austria, Finland, Iceland, Sweden, Switzerland and Norway – were in disarray about their reaction to the 1992 programme. They talked of a "third way" between being "marginalised" outside the EC and accepting the mounting obligations of membership. But the third way seemed likely to be a series of individual, bilateral deals between the EFTA members and the EC; for what were these countries outside the EC for but to preserve their individuality? By the autumn of 1989, as events in Eastern Europe rolled on, and the strength of the EC as a fixed star waxed, the appeal of being in a united second-tier, with some concerted influence over the policies of the EC countries grew too. A new EFTA-EC regime now has much more chance of emerging.

Finally, within Comecon itself, project 1992 and perestroika fed upon each other powerfully. Comecon (the Council for Mutual Economic Assistance, as it should properly be called) and the Community had snubbed one another frostily since 1957, each refusing to accept the right of the other to speak for its members. It was not until 1985 that Mikhail Gorbachev, moving his own country towards economic reform, hinted that Comecon might allow its members to sign individual trade agreements with the EC; and not until 1988 that a joint Comecon-EC pact was struck that allowed such individual deals to go ahead. Since then the Community has established diplomatic relations, and has either signed or is negotiating trade agreements, with all seven European members of Comecon.

Take all these shifts in sentiment together, and the post-war clubs of Europe – unlovely in their twentieth century acronyms, Comecon, EC and EFTA – seem to be falling into a sort of popularity-based pecking-order. The relaunch of the EC has challenged the wealthy countries of EFTA to rethink their relationships with it. The prospect of the economic reconstruction of the Warsaw Pact countries has been an added incentive for those EFTA countries not to be marginalised out of some potentially rich business opportunities. And the wealthy combination of the EC and EFTA are, in turn, a powerful lure to the reforming, capital-hungry and skills-short countries of Comecon.

So, without any Yalta-style summit to ordain it, a ground-plan of what Mr Gorbachev called the "common European house" is now emerging. Stonehenge-like, it consists of concentric circles, with the EC at the centre, the EFTA countries in the second ring, and the Comecon countries in the third ring. And these rings broadly but inexactly consist of NATO alliance countries in the first, neutral countries in the second, and Warsaw Pact countries in the third.

All too neat? All so much Brussels wishful-thinking? Certainly, when in the autumn of 1989 the iron curtain began to come down along the Austria-Hungary border, and young East Germans started to pour across into the West, it seemed possible that the crumbling of the EC's unpleasant but conveniently definite Eastern boundary would tear apart the consensus on which the Single European Act and the relaunch of the Community had been based. For that consensus had been built upon a comfortable vagueness: the goal of ever-closer European union allowed ardent Europeans to believe in a federal Europe, while doubtful Europeans could kid themselves that the EEC's development was based, in the words of Mrs Thatcher, on "willing and active cooperation between sovereign states". Neutral Austria's application for membership posed choices that might expose this non-meeting of minds, but that problem was neatly shelved by an agreement between all the governments of the Twelve that there should be no further increase in the EC's membership until the 1992 programme was complete.

Suddenly, the growing flood of East Germans into the West posed another, similar challenge, but one which EC leaders could not delay. There was the prospect of German reunification through people-power – of a cornerstone of Comecon and the Warsaw Pact merging uncontrollably with a cornerstone of the European Community and NATO. The possibility of such a reunification had for years kept Germans wistful and other Europeans titillated – but it was never taken seriously. The underlying assumption was that the EC would take its final shape before greater Germany regained its old one. Suddenly, in the autumn of 1989, the prospect of a reunited Germany began to threaten to mould the future of EC, rather than vice-versa.

The West Germans were well aware of this prospect, and of the deep-seated fear in France of an over-mighty, reunited Germany. They insisted, in the always Delphic words of Hans-Dietrich Genscher, the West German foreign minister, that Germans must "embed our national interest in the European interest". But Genscher said in October 1989, before correcting himself later, that the European Union should steer clear of defence and security matters and concentrate on matters economic, technological, cultural and environmental. In that way the EC could remain open to neutral states such as Austria and Sweden and to central European ones that reformed themselves enough to join. Security and defence would remain the preserve of another, rather more comatose, European club – the Western European Union.

So the scope for an argument whether the EC should be "broadened" or "deepened" became clear. There were those like the French, or Jacques Delors, who wanted to speed up the progress of Europe towards federalism in order to bind West Germany in. There were those, like the British or the Danes, who were anxious not to be bounced into such a move and who were inclined to say that the EC must remain open to all European democracies. The West Germans meanwhile seemed to want it both ways: anxious both to develop their links with East Germany, but also to be reassuringly "good Europeans". It is understandable for them to want both, but difficult to explain how the integrity of the Warsaw Pact will be combined with an open German-German frontier, or how the integrity of the EC could be upheld with an open frontier to what might still be a non-market economic system.

That argument, and that ambivalence, are very much alive today. West Germany was anxious to reassert its commitment to European union by forging ahead with the Schengen agreement to have totally open frontiers with France and the Benelux countries – though not, of course, at the price of erecting any obstacles to East Germans coming across (see chapter 6). Where was the new Eastern frontier of the EC? A week after the Berlin Wall was punctured, the Twelve heads of state came together for a discussion of the right reaction from the EC: they were all agreed that democracy must be the precondition for aid to Eastern Europe, that they should not aggravate Mr Gorbachev's parlous predicament, and that the disposition of opposing forces in Europe should not be disturbed. Sincere words, but not long afterwards the Czechs, Poles and Hungarians were asking their guests from the Soviet army to return home.

EFTA Gets Thrilling

Only six days after that impromptu EC dinner-summit at the Elysée on November 18th 1989, the Commission announced that ambitious negotiations for a new deal between the EC and EFTA could start in 1990. That announcement was another historic moment for the EC's emergence as the centrepiece of a new European order. From its start in 1960 the EFTA – which today embraces Austria, Finland, Iceland, Sweden, Switzerland and Norway – symbolised a rival view of the European Community, one that eschewed supranational institutions where the EC from the start embraced them. That rival view progressively lost out. EFTA's members defected to the EC: first Britain, then Denmark and Ireland, then almost Norway but not quite because its people said "No" in a referendum, and most recently Portugal.

Nevertheless, during the 1970s, EFTA membership could boast various rival attractions to the EC. It allowed its geopolitically neutral members (Sweden, Austria, Finland and Switzerland) to remain uncompromised. It could count on the support of helpful EFTA "old boys" within the EC. Its members still had work to do in removing the remaining tariffs and restrictions on trade with the Community. It could watch the EC going through a dispiriting phase in the wake of the oil crisis, and count itself lucky to be out of the squabbles about EC farm-prices and budget contributions.

From the mid-1980s onwards those comforts ebbed away. The ex-EFTA members became less supportive. The comfortable assumption that the EC would develop haltingly became rapidly less tenable. By 1984 the EFTA-EC tariff-free zone had been created, posing the question how EFTA could evolve further. In Luxembourg that year, the French foreign minister, Claude Cheysson, speaking as president of the EC Council of Ministers, gave an answer. He suggested that the EFTA and the EC work towards a "European Economic Space" – a vaporous concept said to embrace, among other things, a truly free internal market. But within a year, Mr Delors had launched the EC's own project for a proper internal market, whose regime made it plain what an un-EFTA-like pooling of sovereignty and supranationalism a truly free internal market must entail.

Suddenly the EFTA countries found EC club-membership both harder to do without and harder to contemplate. Some 65 per cent of EFTA's non-mutual trade goes to the EC, equivalent to about 14 per cent of EFTA gross national products. As project 1992 and the changes wrought by the Single European Act gained momentum, the EFTA countries worried on three scores:

● They feared relative discrimination. Where, to take random examples, Sweden and West Germany are now equally well-placed to sell widgets to France, once a genuinely open internal market in widgets is created West Germany will have the inside track there. A big Swedish telecom-munications-equipment company, Ericsson, fears being discriminated against in the EC's supposedly open procurement market. Nestlé, the Swiss foods giant, is buying heavily in Europe to make sure that it is firmly established as a Community company. The newly formed Swiss-Swedish power-generation combine, Asea Brown Boveri, which has half of its 140,000 European employees within the EC, feels a compulsion to site new plants within the EC – it does not want to be discriminated against on grounds of not being truly European.

● EFTA countries would be in the grip of EC regimes, rules and stan-dards without being able to affect their framing – not by statute but just as a fact of business life. There would also be constant pressure on EFTA countries to reciprocate in letting goods meeting EC standards into their markets as a quid pro quo for letting EFTA goods into the EC.

● The two EFTA countries which are members of NATO, and Norway in particular, would be frustrated not to be involved in the forming of European foreign and security policy, whose outcome might effect them deeply. But even the neutral states would feel left out if the EC's rela-tionship with, say, Eastern European countries and Russia, evolved importantly.

All these were good reasons for the EFTA countries to join the EC quickly. But Austria, Sweden, Switzerland and Finland also knew that the growing foreign-policy cooperation between EC members was becoming ever less compatible with their neutrality. And many EFTA countries had, in any case, strong cultural reasons for not surrendering their sovereignty lightly.

At this moment of heightened ambivalence, the EC began to play harder-to-get. The Commission stated expressly that "internal develop-ment takes a priority over enlargement" (admitting new members). Anxious that the EC's relaunch should not be stifled by an influx of Vikings, Jacques Delors offered the EFTA countries, in January 1989, an alternative road to satisfaction. He proposed "a new and more struc-tured partnership with common decision-making and institutions ... to highlight the political dimension of our cooperation".

At a summit in Oslo in March the EFTA Six nervously agreed in a joint declaration to forge such a partnership. But even as they announced it, Austria made it clear that it really wanted to join the EC and Switzerland stressed its opposition to any sort of EFTA supra-nationalism. It seemed that EFTA would not find the collective will to negotiate a joint regime with the EC. But the next few months of discussion in EFTA surprised the sceptics. The Nordic countries were very keen to take up the Delors offer. Austria, having got over the shall-we-shan't-we of applying for full membership, threw itself into the framing of an EFTA deal: it knew it was in for a long sit in the EC's waiting room. Even Switzerland, which houses EFTA's headquarters in Geneva, was swept up in this enthusiasm, amid much earnest discussion of whether neutrality really existed in the modern world.

By December 1989 officials of EFTA and the EC were able to announce that they had forged a joint agreement laying down a framework for the creation of an European Economic Space. And both sides professed themselves confident that ministerial talks could lead to agreement on such a treaty within a year.

Now Bring It Down to Earth

The underlying breakthrough was acceptance of the EFTA members that they would accept the EC laws which govern the "four freedoms" – of movement of goods, services, capital and people – and accept them as taking preference over their own laws. These EC laws include rules, for instance, on the single banking passport, the harmonisation of industrial standards and open public procurement. Exceptions will be negotiated for things that EFTA considers to be of deep national interest: Iceland is very anxious not to have its waters over-fished; Switzerland is very worried about immigration. The EC also accepts that EFTA should not have to swallow the common agricultural policy, or its trade policy (including anti-dumping measures). Consistent with this, the complete removal of frontier controls between EFTA and the EC is not envisaged.

EFTA also agreed to bow to EC regimes that flow from the existence of the four freedoms – such as the need for uniform policies on competition, state aids, procurement and environmental policy. EFTA countries will also take part in the Community's research and development programmes, and help aid the EC's backward regions.

There is still much scope for argument over the detail of these broad commitments – for instance, EFTA wants to be able to apply stricter industrial standards than the EC. The Community, true to its principle of "mutual recognition" says that of course EFTA may do this, provided that the stricter standards do not prevent the sale in EFTA of products that are on sale in the EC. Here, popping up again, is that child of 1992, the "optional standard". It seems improbable that EFTA will buy it.

But the real battle will be over the institutional arrangements to govern the European Economic Space (yes, the EES). The metaphors used by the two sides to describe the way forward are menacingly mixed. There will be "two pillars" linked "by osmosis" and equipped with a "common organ". This biped will apparently thrive on much discussion to help minds meet on new laws; a powerful committee representing the Commission and EFTA at the highest level; and a special court, including EFTA judges, which will ensure compliance with EES law. The crucial point, already mentioned, is that this law would have primacy over national law, so the EES will be pulling the EFTA countries clearly in the direction of supranationalism.

But the EC insists that EFTA should take part only in the shaping of EES decisions, not in actually taking them. Thus "Eftans" could help draft new laws, but would be excluded from the EC working parties and ministerial meetings that finally pass them. If the EES osmosis fails to osmose, Eftans would find themselves having to implement Community decisions that they did not like. EFTA will not accept this loss of sovereignty. It wants joint decision-taking, and says that if a consensus cannot be reached on a given EES measure, it should not apply. Finland, one of EFTA's four neutral members, insists that unless EFTA could block EES decisions, Finland's neutrality would be sullied.

The Community replies that joint decision-making would mean changing its own constitution, which it will not do. Frans Andriessen, the commissioner for foreign affairs, admitted in December 1989 that the EC plan is "perhaps a bit uneven. But that is the unevenness of life." He says that you cannot give everyone the privileges of club membership, or there is no point in having a club.

Squaring this circle has long been the nub of the EFTA-EC problem. This book is thick with examples of the way in which the simple desire for an open trading regime leads inescapably to a sharing of political power. The complex system that EFTA and the EC envisage somehow to reach a consensus on a market regime, without either actually having the power to impose one on the other, has echoes of the EC itself as it struggled to build an open market through unanimity. And the workings of the "joint organ" to make EES law also threatens to create a style of EC government that is still more opaque and unaccountable to the EC's voters.

The search will go on for a joint EFTA-EC regime, which will, in wondrous fashion, create joint rules without compromising sovereignty and without, in the words of the Commission, "compromising the autonomy of the Community in terms of its decision-taking or its institutional system". But despite the professed new will to deliver such a regime within a year, there is still a good chance that this quest will falter when the talks tackle matters where the difference between control and non-control cannot be fudged. If that happens, the prospect will be of more defections from EFTA to the EC; for once countries such as Sweden and Switzerland have resigned themselves to some supranational dilution of their sovereignty, the point of principle is conceded and the question becomes only: "What do I gain and what do I lose from being only a half-member of the Community?"

Eastward Ho!

No global warming has melted ice-caps faster than the one that has warmed the links between the Community and the communist countries of Eastern Europe. The commercial links between the two blocs were pitiful: in 1987 the EC's exports to the whole of Comecon, with its 390 million people, were 19 billion ecus, while those to Switzerland alone were 33 billion ecus. It was only in 1988 that the EC and Comecon ended thirty years of studied mutual indifference by establishing official relations. They thus paved the way for a proliferation of bilateral deals between the Comecon countries and the European Community. As the excitement of political reform ushered in the prospect of transitional economic chaos and hardship in Eastern Europe, the reforming countries tumbled over one another to secure the Community's attention.

Given the job, at the Group of Seven summit in July 1989, of coordinating Western aid to the Eastern block, the Commission soon found itself in a hotter seat than it had expected. Jacques Delors planned a trip to Hungary in November 1989 but realised that the Community had not a single person on the spot to work out his schedule or rent his limo. Eurocrats have thus been uprooted and sent east at unaccustomed speed. But the sudden rush of events did wonders for the *amour propre* of the Commission's previously rather moribund external relations directorate and its commissioner, Frans Andriessen. He found himself in a hectic diplomatic round, taking very political decisions as to how fast and on what terms the Community should proffer aid to Comecon.

At their Paris dinner-summit in November 1989 the leaders of the Twelve discussed a mixture of possible measures to help Eastern Europe. These amounted to a sort of European Marshall plan, offering trade concessions, financial aid, economic advice and technical know-how to each country according to the degree of political and economic liberalisation attained. Moreover, the summit agreed that the Cocom rules controlling the export of Western technology to the communist block would have to be revised. It would be pointless to pledge help with East Europe's infrastructure, and yet to continue to refuse to sell these countries modern telephone exchanges.

The two pioneer liberalisers, Poland and Hungary, were the earliest beneficiaries: they must have received over 700 billion ecus from the twelve members, either together or individually, during 1989 in the form of food shipments and grants for the environment, for agriculture, for training and for infrastructure. The European Investment Bank, a Luxembourg-based institution which lends for infrastructure projects, mainly within the EC, was authorised to make 1 billion ecus in project loans to the two countries over the next three years. The dinner-summit endorsed a $1 billion stabilisation fund for Poland and a bridging loan of the same amount for Hungary – both conditional on the countries reaching agreement over appropriate economic reshaping with the International Monetary Fund. It also agreed to study of a possible East European development bank, modelled on the Asian, Latin American and African ones, which would raise its 10 billion ecus capital from a spread of Western nations. President Mitterrand is particularly keen on this project.

The coordination of this aid is inevitably propelling the Brussels Commission into political involvement in the affairs of Comecon countries. In Hungary, where a weak caretaker communist government is manoeuvring against a variety of non-communist parties in advance of 1990's planned elections, Mr Delors has found himself trying to persuade all sides to take negotiations on an IMF austerity programme out of the political debate – a forlorn hope. In Warsaw he urged the government to go for a "big bang" monetary reform, similar to the one West Germany carried out after the Second World War, to create a new convertible zloty. Any such scheme inevitably involves effective confiscation and redistribution of savings, and is thus politically explosive. On a January 1990 swing around the Balkans, Andriessen found himself urging non/anti-communist groups in Romania and Bulgaria to pull themselves together into properly organised political parties and – to give them more time to do so – suggesting to interim governments in Sofia and Bucharest that free elections should be slightly delayed.

After speedy negotiations, Edward Shevardnadze came to Brussels on

December 18th, 1989 to sign his country's first agreement with the EC on trade and economic cooperation – barely a year after Moscow had finally recognised the Community. Dr Leonid Abalkin, the Soviet deputy premier and one of the main architects of economic reform, talks of "mutually beneficial, unrestrained cooperation" with the EC, where only two years ago such a Soviet official would have been grumbling that West Berlin was not part of the EC. Now he offers to put secret Soviet technology into the cooperative pot. The bulk of Russian exports to the EC are fossil fuels that bear few tariffs and quotas. Thus, Moscow will not benefit so much from an opening of EC markets as by enticing European companies to invest in Russian joint ventures and to transfer management skills to Russia. Here, any number of agreements signed with Mr Andriessen will make less difference than tangible evidence that the Soviet Union is changing its bureaucratic ways.

Governments and regimes are evolving at such a pace in Eastern Europe that it would be worthless to spell out what agreements the EC has recently struck with each country: they are so quickly outdated. The deal with Poland, for instance, has changed continuously over the course of 1989. The Community is tailoring its "cooperation" agreements to the virtues of the regime concerned. The basic ingredient of a cooperation agreement is access to the EC market, without this access necessarily being reciprocated. The pecking-order of access starts with tariff concessions limited to a few sectors, moves on to broader-based tariff breaks, then on to reduction or removal of quantitative restrictions (quotas), then on to "commercial cooperation", which means the right conditions for joint-projects in the country in question, and finally to "economic cooperation" which means talking-shops and aid.

Once Eastern Europe has been blanketed with such deals there will be barely a country in the European part of the world that is not formally cooperating with or associated with the Community. All the countries on the Mediterranean shores already have such deals except for Albania and Libya. Turkey, Cyprus and Malta all have "association agreements": their perk is that these state that customs union (ie, common external tariffs) is their ultimate aim, and, in the case of Turkey, membership of the EC. Andriessen wants to create a standardised association agreement which could be dangled in front of reformist East European countries – in effect a "third ring", beyond the EFTA ring.

It seems unlikely that such association agreements will make any mention of membership. Turkey's expectation of, and application for, membership is a source of embarrassment within the Twelve, and the

Commission gave it a polite brush-off in December 1989. The argument that Turkey is a bulwark of NATO (which it is), gets less compelling as the threat of communist expansionism recedes. The argument that Turkey is a non-European, Muslim culture gets stronger with every reminder that the next threat to Western security might be a religious not ideological one. The entire 1992 relaunch of the Community is founded upon an assumption of shared values — it is basic to mutual recognition of rules — be they on the environment, cruelty to animals, human rights, or the secular basis of the law. Turkey's instincts don't fit in, and its huge and unpoliceable Asian border makes its inclusion in an area without internal frontiers hard to envisage. "Never say never" is the EC's current approach to Turkey. "Never say ever" (while certainly not ruling it out) would be a wise approach in all future association agreements.

Divided Germany

But not to the agreement with East Germany (if there is one) because it would fly in the face of reality. East Germany is the reason why it is going to be difficult to replace the EC's tidy and inhumane Eastern boundary with a tidy and humane one. The latter would ideally be a permeable, administrative frontier between a capitalist system and a reforming socialist one, and between the NATO alliance and the Warsaw Pact — the point where commerce was controlled for reasons of security or to preserve the integrity of different economic regimes. But Germany straddles that line. The basic law of West Germany gives all East Germans the right to a West German passport. The same basic law calls upon the entire German people to achieve unity in self-determination.

The German government has uttered many well-meaning assurances — that it wishes to embed German unity in European unity (Hans-Dietrich Genscher), that "the future structure of Germany must fit into the architecture of Europe as a whole" (Helmut Kohl). The dinner-meeting of the heads of state of the Twelve in November 1989 could agree forlornly that reunification was "not on the agenda". Mr Gorbachev said initially that East German reform must not mean German unity. But no one (except through a return of repression) can stop the East Germans deciding whether they want that line to exist or not. And very soon after the momentous wall-breaking days of November 1989, Helmut Kohl found that West German political pressures forced him to come up with his ten- point "plan" for the two Germanies to move via "confederative structures" to a full federation. The Community came up with its general response a month later at the Strasbourg summit: to wit, that reunification was thinkable, in the context of EC integration and provided security alliances and the 1975 Helsinki Final Act sanctioning post-war borders were respected. Within weeks the formula was looking outdated.

The frontier between East and West Germany has long been an anomaly in the frontier of the EC with Comecon. West Germany has always insisted that flows of East German goods into West Germany were a "family affair"; but because of the shortcomings of the East German economy these flows were never large enough to be disruptive. It was only under special circumstances, like the phobia of Comecon foodstuffs in the direct aftermath of the Chernobyl nuclear disaster, that the East German exception became conspicuous. There is every prospect that this anomaly will become harder to handle from now on. East Germany will be transformed by the culture, capital and skills of the West German *wirtschaftswunder*. There may well be a transitional phase that will explore whether it is really possible to have an open frontier between two competing military alliances, and whether it is really possible to have revitalised East German industrial *Kombinate* selling into a European market that is supposed to be purged of unfair government subsidies.

These problems will not stop the transition happening. But transition to what? Surely not "one country, two systems" as Communist China hopes to play it with Hong Kong and Taiwan. That game won't work without sea or fences between the two systems. Perhaps, if the Soviet Union gets very tough about the withdrawal of its troops, a neutral Germany that bows out of NATO. So, a Germany wholly concerned with German interests? That would be a perverse thing for Russian pressure to achieve. The most probable outcome (though Moscow will hate it) is a Germany that has both its halves – whether fully merged or with separate character preserved – fully in the EC, if not within the Western alliance. After sampling both systems for forty years Germans *en bloc* will opt for the Western one.

This outcome may give France and Britain, not to say the Soviet Union, the shivers, for Germany-in-the-Community will be like a big man at the tiller of a dinghy. German GNP, if East German productivity came up to West German scratch, would be $1.5 trillion, or more than one-quarter of the expanded Community's. It would have 660,000 men under arms – roughly twice Britain's armed forces. But it would be some consolation for the other Western Europeans to know that this greater Germany's foreign and trade policy was embedded in Community ones, that its potential monopolists were under surveillance from Brussels, that its monetary affairs were embedded in the European Monetary System, or Union, that it could be outvoted by a combination of France and Britain in the EC Council of Ministers.

All Germany in the Community would be quite a culmination to the relaunch of Europe. It would make the EC unassailable as the centrepiece of the new European order described at the start of this chapter. A neutral Germany would undo the work that began with the Messina Conference that preceded the Treaty of Rome. It would return Europe to the old instabilities, in which nervous Western Europeans and Eastern Europeans wonder, like a warship with a loose cannon aboard, which way the mighty weight of Germany is going to rumble next.

17

INTO THE 1990s

By the end of 1989, Europe's relaunch had acquired a historic dimension. The complex, protracted business of building a single market out of twelve national ones was overshadowed by an awe-inspiring series of demolitions going on beyond the once-iron curtain. Overshadowed, complicated but, remarkably, not demoralised. The revolution in the East had the surprising effect of reinforcing the collective resolve of the twelve to come more closely together. Straight after the crumbling of the Berlin Wall, five of the original six members of the EC – West Germany, France and the Benelux countries – raced to sign an agreement scrapping all their mutual border controls, not just the economic ones. Much prior negotiation on this Schengen agreement had shown just what a surrender of national sovereignty a frontier-free regime would entail. No matter: the governments overruled their worried officials, precisely to show that such a pact could be struck despite Eastern distractions. Within weeks, they were regretting this gesture. They had, in the heat of the moment, forgotten the concrete problems still involved, and above all the new problem of the East German frontier – was it the frontier of "Schengenland" or not? There could have been no clearer symbol of a will to push on with the development of the EC, faced with the fact that Europe stretches beyond the iron curtain.

As a token of its resolve, soon afterwards the French presidency of the EC masterminded sudden progress towards less nationalistic European regimes in road-haulage and air-transport, by offering French concessions in both businesses. This set the tone for the EC summit in early December in Strasbourg. The West German chancellor, Helmut Kohl, was clearly of a mind to delay the calling of the conference that would determine the next steps towards economic and monetary union (EMU). Mr Kohl's political antennae told him that West German voters were not happy to mess around with a Deutschmark issuing machine that had served their economy well. But the mounting prospect of German reunification, plus France's anxious conceding and cajoling, made the EMU gesture one that Mr Kohl could not be seen to withhold. Despite the objections of Margaret Thatcher, the conference was set for the end of 1990, and, what was more, the French inferred that the EMU treaty-amendments might even be ratified by the end of 1992.

So will that famously hyped date now mark not only the "completion of the internal market" but also agreement upon a European Fed and European currency? It seems inconceivable that Britain and West Germany will be so quickly won round. But the inconceivable has become commonplace in the Europe of the late 1980s.

The relaunch of Western Europe has continually embarrassed the sceptics. *The Economist*'s "smiling mouse" of a Single European Act turned out to pack a mighty squeak. The agreement to do away with exchange controls seemed bound to come unstuck – but it didn't. The tax problem for open frontiers was bound to prove insuperable – it is being fudged, inadequately but in the right direction. The single European market was bound to be protectionist – it was if anything less protectionist than the divided one. With much huffing and puffing the twelve governments have managed to prune thickets of national vested interest into some sort of European topiary.

By the end of 1989, 60 per cent of the 280 market-building measures required in Lord Cockfield's White Paper of June 1985 had either been adopted by the twelve or had achieved the essential prerequisite of a "common position" among the governments. The essential rules on safety of machinery had taken little over a year to work out, whereas in the bad old days seventy months had been needed to agree on one European rule governing lawnmower noise. Free movement of capital took less than a year to agree, and the mutual recognition of university diplomas less than three years. Previously, it had taken eighteen years to secure the rights of qualified architects to set up offices anywhere in the EC.

Set against the ecstatic faces surging through the Berlin Wall, breakthroughs on lawnmowers, architects and machinery seem grey indeed. But they represent something quietly remarkable nonetheless: twelve unrepressed, prosperous peoples are in the process of conceding that a purely national pattern of government is no longer in their best interest. And inspired by the pace at which they have been able to do this, they are pushing on towards a particularly demanding and political approach to monetary union.

This book has examined the many different fragments of this change. It is time to step back and see the mosaic as a whole, first by looking at what sort of "common market" businessmen are going to find themselves selling in and how they might adapt to it; then – a further step back – by describing what sort of political entity the EC is becoming, and by sketching out our best guess at how this entity will fit into the architecture of Europe as a whole at the end of this century.

The American Model

What sort of market for business people? The United States acted as an inspiration for the great European market. Part of the fear of "Eurosclerosis" was prompted by the apparent strength of America's unified and deregulated economy in the early part of the 1980s. America can thus serve as a reference-object in judging how integrated the European market has become. Jacques Pelkmans, professor of economics at the European Institute of Public Administration in Mastricht, Holland, did the basic research for this when he analysed the American market as part of the Commission's Cecchini research into the costs of "non-Europe".

The first point that emerges from his study is that the American market is founded upon the *presumption* of all Americans that America is a great market. This presumption overwhelms many economic peculiarities in American states that resemble the barriers to trade that are being tackled in project 1992. The American anomalies are legion. More than twenty states still have state preference in public procurement. Interstate bank branching is still largely illegal. Insurance companies are state controlled; often with price-fixing. Road-haulage is still not open to all-comers in many states. Excise duties vary too widely between states to survive open frontiers: they are protected by a federal anti-bootlegging regime. Professional qualifications differ absurdly from state to state.

These state differences are reminiscent of some of the obstacles being fought over in Europe; yet they are not regarded in America as evidence of a divided market. The presumption is the thing. Many European businessmen – particularly those running big or multinational companies – insist that 1992 is merely a state of mind that they, in their multinational wisdom, have long since attained. How can that state of mind be encouraged to take hold more widely?

In America, it is based upon the interstate commerce clause of the constitution: "the congress shall have the power ... to regulate commerce ... among the several states." This clause is the equivalent of Article 30 in the Treaty of Rome, on which much case law, including the much-cited "Cassis de Dijon", has been built: "quantitative restrictions on imports and all measures having equivalent effect shall be prohibited between member states." But the less precise American version has been powerfully interpreted over two hundred years to mean freedom for the flow across state lines of just about everything alive, inert, tangible or intangible that could conceivably cross them. For instance, under European law, product-safety remains a valid national reason for blocking the import of goods; in America state product-safety rules may not be framed that interfere with the free movement of goods. The one-market presumption is also massively helped there by America's single language and single currency.

In short, American state anomalies are wrinkles on the face of America's economic unity. In Europe, the national wrinkles are the starting point that define most businessmen's expectations. There is no single currency. There is no single language: English is gradually proliferating but still has decades to go before it becomes a *lingua franca*. So wrinkle-removal is central to presumption-building, as is the slightly misleading propaganda about "Europe without frontiers".

The signs are that the propaganda, businessmen's natural inclinations, the wrinkle-removal and some new Euro-vistas – such as EMU – are working powerfully. Businessman after businessman has told the authors that the one-market presumption is taking hold. Take one example: Derwent Valley Food, a smallish British company, founded in 1982 among the ashes of a redundant steelworks to make expensive cocktail snacks under the brandname, Phileas Fogg. Already, with just £400,000 in exports out of sales of £17 million, it has developed a pan-European marketing strategy, based upon some careful market research. It has found that it must vary its product country by country, and seek joint ventures across Europe because national distribution systems are too complex to be tackled single handed.

Or take another: 3M, the American multinational that makes, among a myriad other things, "Post-it" stickers and "Scotchbrite" pan-cleaners. This company has not assumed that 1992 means nothing to multinational man. It is planning to cut its European inventory by one-third, because European distribution will be cheaper and quicker. It is asking each national subsidiary to take charge of the pan-European strategy for one 3M product – in other words to operate, for that product, as a European company.

The point, for sceptical European businessmen, is that the importance of the single market may well lie less in this or that directive than in the new mind-set of competitors at home and abroad. The American businessman in Kansas has no doubt that he must deal with competition from Illinois, and that to beat it he must take the battle to Illinois as well as fight it on his home patch. On the other hand, the American still lacks the presumption that modern competition comes from outside the great American market, and that to fight it he ought to meet that competition abroad. Crudely speaking, the European businessman's presumptions are the other way round – he is aware that "imports" are a problem and that "exports" are the answer, but may be unaware that selling across Europe is becoming more of a home-market affair.

Procurement – the buying of government or state-controlled monopolies – is another area where 1992 is having potent effect. The American model is of value here – both in what it shows and what it doesn't show. First, the way that the tax regimes of American states must be sustained despite unpoliced state frontiers, by keeping mobile populations happy with their blend of tax and services, means that value-for-money in procurement has a head start in America.

Second, the American experience shows that no amount of fair-procurement law will stop human nature dishing out contracts to golfing-partners: the Euro-procurement directives will not mean that European businessmen will no longer need to get on with people. Third, heavy-weight American procurement is supposedly "fair" (ie neutral between individual states) across the great market because it is the hands of the federal government. In Europe the heavy-weight procurement is in the hands of the national governments: the Commission is barely a buyer. Fourth, the fact that so many utilities in America are in private hands means that a blend of pan-American value-for-money and the working of the old-buddy network already applies to what is often state procurement in Europe.

The upshot of all this for the European businessman is that the procurement market is going to get a lot tougher. The new Brussels procurement rules will psychologically constrain those state procurers. Value-for-money consciousness will rise. Privatisation will make more procurers more commercial. The mandatory use of European standards in inviting tenders will make cross-border tenders simpler. There is much pain in the offing here. The Cecchini report showed how the number of European companies in big procurement-driven businesses such as defence, electricity generation, and telecommunications equipment was much greater than the number in America. The prospect of a more open, more uncomfortable marketplace has been the spur for some of 1992's most spectacular mergers. The envisaged link-up between Siemens, GEC and Plessey is an example in telecommunications; ditto that between Alsthom of France and GEC of Britain in power equipment. Equally, outsiders have been driven to acquire stakes within the European market: AT&T has bought into Italtel of Italy; Northern Telecom has bought into STC in Britain.

In two other areas – product regulations, and the mobility of labour – the American market is still well ahead of its European rival. The American states do impose state product regulations, but they are almost always couched in terms of national standards; and if they begin to impede trade significantly they are liable to be challenged under the interstate commerce clause. Except in the celebrated case of the motor car exhaust standards applied by California after 1966, which were specifically exempted under the federal Clean Air Act, regulations and standards within the USA do much to reinforce the presumption of a single market.

American labour mobility does the same. The absolute right under the constitution of American workers to move to, seek work in, and have social security protection in other states greatly helps America work as a single-currency area. But in line with the state barriers that exist in banking and insurance, the professions in America are swathed in state qualifications: it is in the service economy that the new European market is best set up to make America look old-fashioned.

So Tell Me What To Do

1992 is a process, not a red-letter day. No new system of trading will swing into action at the end of that year. No new rule-book will suddenly apply to businessmen. Europe will remain a series of national markets, distinguished by different languages, different tastes, different habits and different media. But these national markets will become steadily more accessible. The cost of transport relative to the cost of manufacture will come down. If there is any area in which governments will be under pressure to honour the expectations they have generated about 1992, it will be in trimming commercial frontier delays and fiscal bureaucracy to a minimum. The road-haulage business will lower its prices. Europe's airlines will be under sustained pressure to cut theirs. Shortage of infrastructure – particularly roads and runways – and environmental restraints will become the limiting factors. Railways, revitalised by France's initiative with very fast trains, will enjoy a renaissance. The tunnel under the English channel will be a vast economic success, even if it proves a speculative catastrophe for its original shareholders.

So businessmen will find themselves under mounting pressure to concentrate their production in fewer plants, made flexible enough, through automation, to serve Europe's variable tastes. Unilever, for example, will make all its dishwasher powders for Europe at one site in Lyons and all its toilet soap at one plant in Port Sunlight.

The European marketing study of the small and successful British snack foods company mentioned earlier, Derwent Valley Food, precisely echoed the consensus that is gradually emerging about the European consumer market in the mid-1990s. Derwent found that lifestyles across Europe were converging, but that tastes were not. In other words the concept behind a product (eg, we think there is a market for expensive, packaged cocktail food) is increasingly likely to be valid Europewide. But the precise taste or look of a product has to be adapted carefully to each national market. Derwent found that transport costs were low enough, even for bulky products like crisps, to make centralised production competitive right across Europe. It found that Europe-wide advertising and marketing was impossible. It found that patterns of distribution and retailing remained specific to each country, and that local knowledge of them was essential. It found that languages were essential, too, both for the packaging of products and for the people who would be selling them.

Pulling together the plans and experiences of a wide range of companies in Europe, we find that the "Colchester-Buchan" diagram on page 229 gives an impression of what businesses are likely to be "Eurohomogenous" and what are likely to remain "national-distinctive". Broadly speaking the combination of high added-value with either a company or a rich individual as customer means that a product can be branded and distributed across Europe without an urgent need for local skills, local investment and local adaptation of the product. On the other hand, the cheaper the product and the closer you get to the consumer, the more investment you must make in local understanding, local product variation and local distribution.

Thus an Italian salesman with little English could hope to sell a

Lamborghini with the steering-wheel on the wrong side to a company director in Slough. The expensive merger and acquisition team of Crédit Suisse First Boston can jet all over Europe without its bankers changing their ties or greatly adapting their style. But Unilever or Indesit will both be very careful to perfect their local distribution and marketing, and their national variations in washing powders and washing machines. The computer company or machine-tool manufacturer will have a product-led, pan-European sales strategy. Sainsbury or Abbey National will be very wary about assuming that the British approach to retailing or retail banking will work in France.

A health warning: this chart may raise many businessmen's blood pressure. It applies to products not companies. It is schematic, and the authors cannot justify the position of the dividing line, nor even claim that a sudden dividing line exists. Exceptions spring readily to mind: megabrands like Coca-Cola make a point of transcending national cultures. Some very expensive service companies – lawyers or securities firms – will make a particular point of not transcending national cultures. The chart does *not* imply that a company whose products are below and to the left of the line should have no pan-European business strategy, merely that it ought to remember ingrained national differences when devising its strategy and in assessing its own strengths.

Project 1992 is an act of progressive and now-unstoppable deregulation: hard though its detractors may find this to believe, it is eroding barriers to business. All deregulation instils in businessmen an intense urge to "do something" – to invade before being invaded, to buy another firm before someone else buys it, or buys you. The lesson after London's "Big Bang" was that it tended to be right to buy the biggest and best in a newly accessible market – if you could afford it, get it and manage it; or to buy thriftily and with clear aims. Focus emerged as the crucial ingredient for success: the buyer must rigorously decide what business he wants to be in and what he needs abroad to develop it. Our diagram could give him a modest steer here. The mistake of many in the "Big Bang" was to buy something largish and roughly right – something the buyer would never have bought but for the excitement of the times. The same wisdom-with-hindsight may apply in the late 1990s in Europe.

Coming Clean

What sort of European Community is Europe relaunched towards? The evolution of the EC has long been dubbed a "journey towards an

The "Colchester-Buchan" diagram

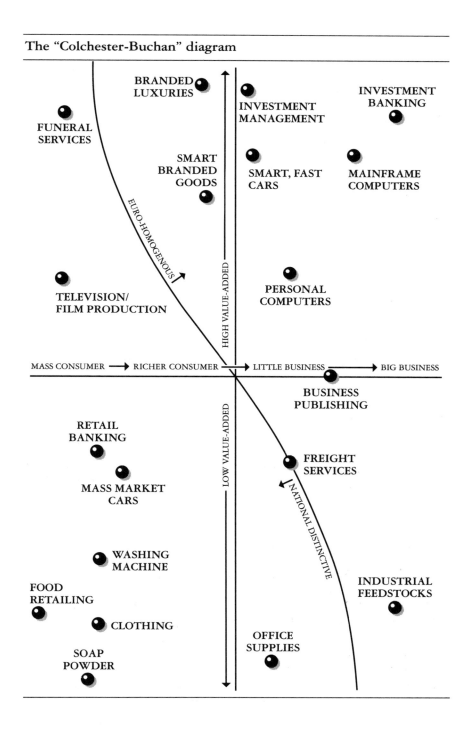

BRANDED
LUXURIES

INVESTMENT
MANAGEMENT

INVESTMENT
BANKING

FUNERAL
SERVICES

SMART
BRANDED
GOODS

SMART, FAST
CARS

MAINFRAME
COMPUTERS

EURO-HOMOGENOUS

TELEVISION/
FILM PRODUCTION

PERSONAL
COMPUTERS

HIGH VALUE-ADDED

MASS CONSUMER → RICHER CONSUMER   LITTLE BUSINESS   → BIG BUSINESS

BUSINESS
PUBLISHING

RETAIL
BANKING

LOW VALUE-ADDED

FREIGHT
SERVICES

MASS MARKET
CARS

NATIONAL DISTINCTIVE

WASHING
MACHINE

INDUSTRIAL
FEEDSTOCKS

FOOD
RETAILING

CLOTHING

OFFICE
SUPPLIES

SOAP
POWDER

unknown destination". The Single European Act repeated in its preamble 1983's solemn declaration of Stuttgart that the EC's members were intent upon "transforming relations as a whole among their states into a European union". But no definition of Union has ever been spelt out. There was convenience in this vagueness: it allowed the shaping of the EC to be a process rather than a project. Different people could cling to different beliefs about what the project was.

This vagueness is an invitation to duplicity – sometimes called "Europe by stealth". Europhiles can use a ceaseless process of logic ("given that the Commission now has control of x, it is surely logical that it should also control y, which greatly effects x") to lever the Community towards a federal Europe, without actually saying so. British Europhobes tend to use arguments about the ideology of the Community ("too much undemocratic, bureaucratic meddling from Brussels") without admitting that they would find a democratic, unbureaucratic Brussels just as awful.

Yet as time goes by, the range of choices about the "unknown destination" shrinks steadily. We can start by eliminating what the Community already isn't. Mrs Thatcher said in her Bruges speech that "willing and active cooperation between sovereign states is the best way to build a successful European Community". This book has made it exhaustingly clear that the move to majority voting in the building of the great market, coupled with the move to a mutual recognition of rules, cemented the "supranational" nature of the EC. It acquired the power to demand, when need be, the "not-so-willing cooperation of something-less-than-sovereign states". So Mrs Thatcher's description of Europe-building no longer holds. Europe already has a degree of central government, of which Jacques Delors provocatively said in the late summer of 1988: "in ten years time 80 per cent of economic, and perhaps social and tax, legislation will be of community origin."

One can draw lines above the EC as well. National sovereignty in the absolute sense of the word is retained: if a member cries "shan't" and walks out, the EC possesses no military force to bring the miscreant to book. The foreign policy coordination of the Twelve, while active and useful, remains firmly non-supranational. Decisions on it require consensus. The members' armed forces remain completely independent, though most are party to the NATO alliance. Governments remain free, in the absolute sense, to manage or mismanage their macroeconomic policy and currencies as they wish. They retain their own police forces, and Brussels has no central policing powers at all.

230

But some of those upper limits are being blurred *de facto*, if not *de jure*. The exchange rate mechanism of the EMS already effectively constrains members in their monetary policies for, short of quitting, they need the agreement of the other members to adjust their exchange rates. The combination of the 1992 banking "passport", and the promised lifting of all exchange controls is going to make this constraint tougher. If the Schengen agreement between France, West Germany and the Benelux countries to lift all border controls is honoured, the police in France, say, will have to honour demands by the Germans that someone be arrested in France. Equally France will have to accept that German police can pursue criminals some way into France and arrest them. So police-sovereignty will be compromised, too.

However one defines sovereignty – and books can be written on the subject – the practical measure of it must be the amount of say that a country has in determining its own future. In a world of world-straddling nuclear weapons, financial dealing and environmental pollution, sovereignty is diluted, though less so for the very powerful and potentially self-contained nation, such as America, or for the deeply withdrawn and self-denying one, such as Albania or Burma.

Sir Leon Brittan, the senior British commissioner in Brussels notes that sovereignty is "not like a family heirloom, which you take out and dust down every now and then, to make sure that it is still in your possession and intact". This holds particularly true for the small to medium-size states that make up the European Community. Their sovereignty – their freedom of manoeuvre – is much diminished by their contract of association with each other and is constantly being shrunk further as the EC develops. Those to whom the Community feels like a tightening strait-jacket must answer the question: could they do as well or better, acting on their own, in raising and protecting the living standards of their citizens?

The momentum now building up towards EMU shows where the line between today's EC and European federalism is most clearly under threat. Nigel Lawson insisted early in 1989, when the Delors blueprint for EMU was published, that "It is clear that EMU implies nothing less than European government – albeit a federal one – and political union: the United States of Europe." His basis for saying this was that national central banks would be replaced by an American-style Fed, and that the Delors report called for binding European controls on individual members' budget deficits. Whether such controls would make the Community a United States is a moot point: they would certainly shift it powerfully in that direction.

The willingness of eleven of the twelve members to discuss such treaty amendments suggests that, far from speaking plainly of a nationalism that other Europeans feel but camouflage, the British government is out of touch with the readiness of most continental Western Europeans to move towards some form of political union, in which national parliaments will be subservient to an increasingly powerful government at the centre.

The great test of this readiness will be the intergovernmental conference on EMU which will start at the end of 1990. This will be a rerun of the Luxembourg conference with which the relaunch of the EC began. The same techniques will doubtless be on display – there will be attempts to use the EMU treaty-changes to boost the powers of the European Parliament and, who knows, further to extend the scope of European political cooperation. But it will be rerun with a difference. Britain will not be seducible, this time, by something it badly wants, as the lure of the great market seduced it in Luxembourg. And, despite the agreement to talk about EMU, explosive differences lurk on the matter between the West Germans and the French and Italians.

The Germans will be determined that any replacement for their Bundesbank must have the same non-inflationary independence. They insist that there must be central control of national budget-deficits by the EC Council of finance ministers: they fear that spendthrift members will otherwise borrow excessively, reassuring their investors with the solidity of the EC currency and the "name" of the Community. So the Germans want to strengthen the European Parliament to get that budgetary vetting under democratic control. It is far from clear that other continental members will buy all this German perfectionism. Part of their motive, after all, is to wrest the monetary rigour out of German hands and spread responsibility for monetary policy more widely.

The vigour of Europe's relaunch has taken both authors of this book by surprise. The surprises could continue. But there are grounds for suspecting that other arguments could hinder the EMU conference from reaching its momentous conclusion. Our chapter on EFTA (Chapter 16) described how EFTA countries could well decide that anything short of membership is not worth the candle and thus, by applying for membership, revive the "widening versus deepening" debate. Europeans still do not feel European in the way that Americans feel American. They still feel Dutch, French, Scottish, Bavarian. The Germans will soon have every reason to feel still more German. Is this inherent nationalism really consistent with an American-style federalism?

In short, there is much scope for argument before Britain finds itself wondering whether to exercise its veto over a treaty amendment that would hand a great deal of new power to the Community's centre. But if it were to come to such a point, Europe's journey towards an unknown destination would be at an end. The destination would clearly be a federal one. And Britain would be deciding whether to accept a place in confederal Europe, to try to block its emergence, or to bow out and return to the ranks of EFTA.

Europe's Common House

New forces have emerged of late to push the EC towards federalism. The Community has, through its relaunch, through America's slow withdrawal, through the unravelling of Eastern Europe, become an odd sort of power in the world. Once tolerated sniffily at the world's summits – and then only economic ones – the status of the EC abroad has changed fast over the past two years. The Soviet Union and Comecon countries have recognised it, opened embassies to it, and tumbled over one another to sign up varied cooperative pacts with it. The Group of Seven rich nations charged the European Commission in the summer of 1989 with coordinating Western assistance in Eastern Europe – a plainly political job. And James Baker, the American secretary of state, wants new "institutional and consultative links" with the EC in forging the new Europe.

What makes a superpower? Economic strength is the foundation, as Britain learnt, America worriedly senses and Russia must regret. The EC's economy now matches America's for size. It is no longer fanciful to talk of the Community as one economic power: the twelve members have turned themselves into more than a free-trade area. They are letting their systems, values and standards infect each other and thereby creating political interdependence and "ever closer union".

It was European outsiders, in EFTA, who first sensed the force of this change. In 1989 they began to rethink their own political independence because of the new EC's looming presence in their lives. They want to win more say in EC matters that affect them, and will now negotiate this as a block, directly with Brussels. Meanwhile the conference on revisions to the Rome Treaty to turn Europe into an economic and monetary union will – even if this fails to deliver a European currency – undoubtedly leave the EC speaking more like a single power in the world's economic forums.

Yet the EC does not have a foreign policy in the same way that it has an environmental one, or a trade one, or an agricultural one. The members agreed in the Single European Act to "endeavour jointly to formulate and implement a European foreign policy" and that this policy should embrace non-military matters of security. But the Commission's external brief is broadly restricted to trade. The rest of the EC's foreign policy depends upon direct cooperation between the twelve foreign ministries – European political cooperation. A secretariat coordinates this. A rolling troika of the foreign ministries of the previous, present and next presidents of the EC speak for the Community abroad. The Commission is, thanks to the Single European Act, "associated" with this process and preserves a constant presence in the troika. But the approach relies upon consensus of all members and thus reflects only the lowest common denominator of their resolve on any issue. It it is quite good at issuing statements, not so good at taking actions.

Such consensus-building was adequate to the tasks of Europe's postwar order. The Warsaw pact was then the main threat. America and NATO countered it. The Europeans could manage their individual post-colonial crises and become prosperous in their Common Market under the American umbrella. But it is going to be impossible to persist with this East-West order now that communism is collapsing. One reason for this is that the two Germanies will not and cannot be made to choose between reunification and the convenience, for the rest of the West, of gradually winding down the balance of military power across the Yalta lines. Visions of "one country, two alliances" are an invitation to German neutralism, of Germany on the loose again.

So one aim of Europe's next "architecture" must be to bind a united Germany into the West – which means to the European Community; but also to preserve and reshape the alliance between America and Western Europe to protect the values both share, against whoever threatens them from wherever. The other aim must be to provide a structure in which the liberated countries of Eastern Europe can feel their way towards democracy and market economy. Association agreements must be struck with them and developed, promising them trading access to the great market, easing flows of finance to them, and holding out the prospect of eventual membership of the EC.

The Americans will not want to dominate this process, and are not alienated by the prospect of not doing so. They sent an eloquent signal when, in July 1989, they asked the European Community to organise the West's assistance to the reforming countries of Eastern Europe. They sent another in December through James Baker. They now see the EC and the US as matching parts of a recast and reoriented NATO. But the Community's capacity to make foreign policy will need to be strengthened to fill this role and its role as a component of the new NATO will have to be established clearly.

The implication of such reasoning and assertions is obvious: here is yet another powerful nudge in the direction of a federal Europe. An independent foreign policy is one of the prouder symbols of sovereignty. Those who resist it will be forgetting that the alternative could be a slow slide back to nineteenth-century nationalism, with Germany again the potential bogeyman. Nationalism was relatively easy to contain within Yalta-Europe. The Common Market, created originally to prevent intra-European war breaking out again, did not have a hugely demanding job doing this in its first thirty years. No longer: the great European flux of 1989 is the challenge that the European Community was created to meet.

Now Make It Democratic

Majority decision-taking, mutual recognition of many laws, a Commission with strong powers of law-making initiative, momentum towards economic and monetary union, a mounting need for a common foreign and security policy: this adds up to a lot of government. It prompts the obvious question: is Europe's government under adequately democratic control? No question is more riddled with potential insincerity than this one. Eurocrats ask it in search of more legitimate power, whether they truly need that power or not. Members of the European Parliament do the same. National parliamentarians ask it not because they wish to make the central power more legitimate, but because they wish to stress the legitimacy of power at the national level. Government ministers ask it for the same reason, uncomfortably aware that their direct influence through the Council of Ministers in Brussels adds, oddly, to their independence from national parliaments at home.

Chapter 4 went quite fully into the evolving power of Europe's institutions. It is clear to us that the question of the accountability (the word is dreadful, but now ubiquitous) of these institutions will loom ever larger over the coming decade. In our view three principles should be borne in mind when deciding what to do about it.

● For the foreseeable future, people in Europe will think about themselves as nationals first, and Europeans second. Europeans do not see themselves as European in the way that Americans feel American. Language still divides them powerfully. There is no European equivalent of the networked TV soap-opera that defines American life for all Americans. As Europeans get wealthier they will attach more, not less, importance to their national and regional specialness: that trend towards national apartness is visible in America today. So any drive towards democratic accountability must go with the grain of national feeling not against it. The EC should for the moment consist of nations that have bowed to some central lawmaking, rather than people.

● That leads straight to a rigorous interpretation of "subsidiarity" – the rubbery piece of Eurojargon that is often intoned and seldom heeded. Only do things from the centre that are usefully done from the centre. And only impose things from the centre that *must* be imposed from the centre. A European programme for language-teaching can usefully be offered from Brussels, but need not be imposed: ditto expensive cooperation in space research. Rules on subsidies must be imposed from the centre: ditto essential safety rules on traded goods. Speed limits and workers' hours can be left to nations. The British army used to have a dictum: "If it moves, salute it. If it's fixed, paint it." The Brussels version should be: "If it can cross frontiers, draft a directive. If it can't, hands off."

● Because of both of the foregoing, it would be misguided to seek the next improvement in democratic accountability mainly by boosting the powers of the European Parliament. This would assume "Europeanness" to be the norm. It would assume European laws to be the norm, and national laws to be the concession. What is called the "democratic deficit" is best closed by making sure that the law-making forum of the member governments – the Council of Ministers – operates more openly and is more responsive to the wishes of national parliaments. It is thus in the Council and in the national parliaments themselves that the next steps towards accountability should be taken.

The Council, which has the ultimate power over European law-making, currently operates as a twelve-sided bargaining-shop, with the give and take a poorly kept secret. That was necessary when law was being passed by unanimity: nothing would ever have been decided otherwise. The same question of practicality made it impossible for ministers to be too constrained by their national parliaments. They had to be able to return home saying "sorry chaps, that was the best deal we could negotiate." But majority voting – or the unexplored prospect of it – now sets the tone in the Council. And if EMU ever involves central control of budget deficits, it will have to spread there too; otherwise national budgets will be permanently deadlocked. The extension of weighted majority voting (big countries have more votes than small ones) means that the need for the Council to be a bargaining shop is reduced. So let national parliaments send their ministers, or their stand-ins, to Brussels and let them see how they argue and how they vote, and who wins. Just as the American Senate was set up to discover the majority opinion of the state governments, so the Council should openly elicit the majority opinion of the EC's member governments.

The way that national parliaments select and influence their European councillors must remain up to them. The West German *länder* (federal states) already insist on forming part of the German delegation to the Council, so that they can keep an eye on the activities of government ministers there. The Danish parliament requires ministers to consult it before Council meetings and set out their intended negotiating positions. The British parliament is bad at vetting the European law that its ministers are negotiating in Brussels. Partly, this faithfully reflects the British parliament's weak grip on its government ministers. Partly, it is because Westminster is woefully set up to examine draft European law: it can't quite bring itself to face up to the problem. Much more dialogue with the British members of the European parliament would help.

As for the European Parliament, its job is to represent the people of Europe as a whole and to debate Brussels law more on party/ideological and less on national lines. It has recently had its ability to amend European law greatly boosted (see chapter 4) by the Single European Act. This new "cooperation procedure" between it and Commission and Council is working well and should be extended across EC lawmaking. But for the moment this directly-elected parliament will remain Europe's secondary legislature, awaiting the day when the Community of European people truly eclipses the Community of European nations.

The European Community was launched by a political conviction that Europe should not fight another nationalist war. After a heady first twelve years, its momentum flagged. It was relaunched, not by dramatic street demonstrations and historic surrenders of power, but by unleashing a pent-up desire for an open market. This bureaucratic coup triggered changes in the EC's constitution, which in turn refreshed its appetite for political union. Is a federal Europe imminent? No: if that means the United States of Europe, where a president can say with a straight face "My fellow Europeans" and not sound phoney. Yes: if that means that twelve countries have attained such sophistication and share so many basic values that they gainfully submit themselves to common laws and some democratic means of making them.

APPENDIX I

Cockfield's Blueprint for the Single Market

The June 1985 White Paper contained, or promised, no less than 297 legislative proposals. The actual number (for the moment) is 279, because 18 of the measures were dropped along the way, as the Commission decided against making certain proposals or consolidated others. (For example, public procurement, a very big chunk of the European economy, was in the end covered by only four directives in the 1992 plan.) The overall number of proposals will probably still seesaw up and down if the Commission comes up with after-thoughts to the White Paper (like its anti-tax fraud plans to accompany the all-important capital liberalisation) or fails to deliver on some of its White Paper pledges (such as the opening-up of defence procurement). Breath-taking though the White Paper was in its scope, by no means all of its measures were new; some like the proposal for a European Company Statute went back to the early 1970s, but had never been acted on. What follows is a brief guide to the most significant proposals in the White Paper.

Removing the Physical Barriers

Control of Goods
● Introduction of a single customs check at intra-EC borders (in effect since January 3rd 1989). This means that truck drivers need only stop at the customs post of the state they are entering to complete the necessary paperwork, not of the country they are leaving. Only intended as an interim measure, until intra-EC border checks are removed entirely.
● The Single Administrative Document (SAD), introduced on January 1st 1988, is a standardised customs form which, despite the eight copies that have to be sent off to various people, has considerably simplified the shipping of goods around the Community.

Animal and Plant Health Controls

The general aim is that, after 1992, checks on meat and livestock consignments will be carried out at the place of dispatch within the country of export, though the importing state will be able to make spot checks.

● This will require states having a high degree of trust in each other's controls. In order to foster the necessary mutual trust, the Commission has come up with a raft of proposals to eradicate/control such diseases as swine fever, foot and mouth, brucellosis and tuberculosis.

● Other directives are designed to promote intra-EC trade in meat, eggs and milk. For instance, frozen meat must reach, and retain, an internal temperature of minus 12 degrees centigrade under a directive in effect since January 1st 1989; the production of EC-traded eggs is to conform to EC-wide standards by the end of 1991; under a directive in force since January 1st 1989 heat-treated milk must satisfy certain conditions before it can be sold to another EC state.

● Trade in, and transport of, pedigree cattle, pigs and sheep, or their semen or embryos is to be regulated by a series of directives.

● Much of the plant legislation is directed at controlling pesticides, or making sure that pesticide controls do not themselves become a restraint on EC trade. For instance, a directive now in effect sets maximum levels for pesticide residues in cereals, fruit and vegetables; no bushel of grain or peck of apples can therefore be kept out of another EC state if it has less pesticide residue than the EC maximum.

Control of Goods carried by Individuals

● A variety of directives, approved or proposed, have as their aim the progressive raising of tax-free and duty-free allowances for travellers until such allowances supposedly disappear along with internal EC border checks by the end of 1992. In addition, there are a number of tax exemptions for the temporary import of private or rented cars.

● A proposed directive would require all firearms dealers to be registered, and to supply detailed information of any firearms shipments to the EC state into which the firearms were being imported. People travelling from one member state to another with firearms would need to carry an authorisation with them.

● Other problems related to the abolition of internal EC frontier controls – such as immigration, crime and drug control – have been left outside the White Paper's scope and for individual member states to resolve.

Removing Technical Barriers

Free Movement of Goods

● A 1983 directive requires member states to tell Brussels of any technical standards they plan to adopt, and a directive in force since January 1st 1989 extends the scope of this to all industrial and food products. Whenever the Commission submits a standards proposal covering a particular sector, the member states may not adopt rules of their own within twelve months of the Commission submission.

● Machinery. A directive, passed in 1989 and coming into effect on January 1st 1992, will set minimum safety standards for roughly half of all machines made or used in the Community.

● Simple welded pressure vessels must conform to basic EC safety standards from January 1st 1990.

● Personal equipment or clothing, worn or held for protection against industrial safety and health hazards, is the subject of another proposed directive.

● Toys, for the enjoyment of children under fourteen years, must conform to new safety standards from January 1st 1990, with a wide range of exceptions ranging from Christmas decorations, to fireworks, darts and bicycles.

● For cars, the Community has been striving for EC-type approval since the early 1970s, but has not yet agreed on standards for windscreens, tyres and weights and dimensions. New standards on exhaust emissions were agreed in 1988–89.

● For tractors, the same sort of EC-type approval came into effect on December 31st 1988, and rollover protection bars for narrow gauge tractors were required from June 26th 1989.

● Food. A raft of directives, approved or proposed, cover additives, preservatives, flavouring, wrapping, and labelling. The labelling directive, coming into force on June 20th 1992 is important because of the new approach permitting the free circulation of differing foodstuffs provided those differences are clearly marked for the consumer. Another key directive, coming into effect on June 20th 1992, will set common procedures for food inspection.

● Pharmaceuticals. Since July 1st 1987 national authorities have had to consult an EC committee before permitting or banning the marketing of a wide range of high-technology drugs. In addition, new rules governing proprietary medicinal products, vaccines, toxins, serums, allergens, medicinal products derived from human blood and radiopharmaceuticals will all come into effect on January 1st 1992.

● Chemicals. Rules on the classification, packaging and labelling of dangerous preparations come into force on June 7th 1991, while common restrictions have been agreed on such things as asbestos, polychlorinated biphenals (PCBs) and detergents.

● Construction products. From June 27th 1991 new rules will come into effect to promote the safety, hygiene, durability of construction products.

● Noise. Tower cranes, household appliances, lawnmowers and hydraulic diggers have all had their noise level regulated in specific directives.

● Fire safety in hotels is the subject of a (non-binding) EC recommendation.

● Pricing of non-food items. From June 7th 1990 the selling price and unit price of a good must be clearly identifiable on products sold around the EC.

● Testing. To try to avoid duplication of tests in twelve different markets, EC states have agreed on principles of good laboratory practice, and on ways of checking whether or not their laboratories conform with these principles.

Public Procurement
● Loopholes have been closed in 1970s-era directives requiring public bodies openly to invite tenders for their works and supply contracts.

● The transport, energy, water and telecommunications sectors, hitherto excluded from requirements for competitive cross-frontier bidding, would be covered by EC public procurement rules under a proposed directive being negotiated.

● Complaining companies would have some right of redress against public authorities, including possible court injunctions and damages, under another proposed directive.

Free Movement of Labour
● The right of an EC citizen to reside in another EC state, independent of whether or not he or she has or is seeking work, would be established under a proposed directive.

● Member states have agreed, from January 4th 1991, to recognise each other's higher-education diplomas.

● Pharmacists have had their qualifications mutually recognised since October 1st 1987.

● General medical practitioners can work throughout the Community provided their training follows certain guidelines laid down in a 1986 directive.

● Nurses will have their qualifications mutually recognised under a directive passed in 1989.

● Self-employed commercial agents have been subject to EC rules since January 1st 1990.

Financial Services

● Banking. The Second Banking Coordination Directive, approved in late 1989, establishes " a single passport" for banks and credit institutions. By virtue of being authorised in their home EC state, they may establish branches and/or supply services in all other EC states. Ensuring that banks respect prudential rules on capital and solvency will be the responsibility of home-country regulators, though host-state authorities retain control over the way that credit institutions actually conduct their business.

● Insurance. From December 30th 1989 insurers need only a licence in their home country to sell non-life policies to large companies in other EC states.

● Life insurance would be saleable across national frontiers to consumers actively seeking it, under a directive being negotiated.

● Plans to allow the sale of insurance, life and non-life, to the man-in-the-street (so-called mass risks) were due to be announced by the Commission in 1990.

● Unit trusts or mutual funds. The freedom to set up Undertakings for Collective Investments in Transferable Securities (UCITS) in any EC state and to sell their products anywhere else in the EC, on the basis of home-country control, was established on October 1st 1989.

● The information required in share prospectuses will be harmonised from April 17th 1991.

● Insider trading will be regulated by a directive passed in 1989.

● Investment services. A single passport for the establishment of stockbrokers and investment consultants around the Community, and the free provision of their services on the basis of home-country control, has been proposed.

Transport

● Airlines. Restrictions on fares and market access, plus capacity-sharing arrangements on routes, were relaxed under a 1987 Council decision, and EC governments look set to inject further competition into

this highly regulated sector during 1990.
● The airline sector's longstanding exemption from EC anti-trust rules were partially removed by a 1987 EC regulation.
● Road haulage. A 1988 regulation commits member states to phase out by January 1st 1993 the system of bilaterally-negotiated quotas; these authorised individual cross-frontier journeys by hauliers and led frequently to trucks making unladen return trips.
● Cabotage. Still under negotiation is a proposal that would allow trucks from one EC state to act like cabs-for-hire in another member state, and to pick up and set down goods in EC states other than their home base. A similar proposal would provide the same cabotage freedom to non-resident bus operators.
● Water transport. Proposals to allow cabotage among canal barges and ships along inland waterways and coastal routes are also on the table.

New Technologies and Services
● Television. From October 3rd 1991 member states cannot restrict receipt and retransmission on their territory of TV broadcasts from other EC states which conform to certain standards on local European content, advertising and protection of minors.
● Mobile phones. A variety of directives and recommendations are designed to promote the linking up of (hitherto largely incompatible) cellular digital communications systems.

Capital Movements
● By July 1st 1990 eight EC states are committed to lifting all exchange controls, while Spain and Ireland have until 1992, and Portugal and Greece until 1994–95, to follow suit. Of the major EC states, France beat the deadline by six months, making it legal from January 1st 1990 for Frenchmen, for instance, to have bank accounts abroad or foreign-currency accounts at home.

Company Law
● Joint ventures. From July 1st 1989 companies from different member states have been able to set up European Economic Interest Groupings, a flexible form of joint venture whose main advantage is that the capital requirement is minimal and whose main disadvantage is that it must be small (employing less than 500 people).
● "European" companies. In 1989 the Commission revived, and revised, its old proposal to create a European Company Statute (ECS) under

which companies could incorporate themselves independently of the national company law of any member state. The major, and perhaps sole, attraction of the statute is that it might enable companies to deduct losses incurred by their subsidiaries in other member states from the profit taxable in the EC state where they are headquartered. The main disadvantage, in the view of some states such as Britain, is that companies availing themselves of the ECS would have to choose between one of three forms of participation in management by their workers.

Intellectual and Industrial Property
● A Community Trademark has been proposed to allow the acquisition of intellectual property rights Community-wide and governed by EC law.
● Semiconductor design is given protection under a 1987 directive.

Company Taxation
● The Commission is still pushing three directives, dating back to the late 1960s and mid-1970s. They are designed to: defer the taxation of the assets of a company swallowed up in a cross-border merger; to ease the double taxation of dividends paid by subsidiaries in one member state to a parent company in another member state; and to set out arbitration procedures between EC states in double taxation disputes.

Removing Fiscal Barriers

Value-Added Tax
● The Council has agreed, and the Commission has grudgingly accepted, that VAT will for an undefined interim period still be taken off exports and re-imposed on imports, even after internal EC border checks disappear after 1992. To prevent VAT fraud, member states have agreed on a complex process of matching up documentation between exporter and importer to ensure that goods have not gone astray without proper payment of VAT.
● To avoid trade distortions, the Commission initially proposed bringing rates within 14 to 20 per cent for goods bearing the standard rate of VAT, and within 4 to 9 per cent for certain necessities such as food and energy. It has since conceded that some zero rates of VAT might be retained, while the higher band might be replaced by a single minimum rate of 15 per cent. There is no agreement on this yet.

Excise Duties
● The Commission has abandoned its initial plan for single Community-wide excise rates for alcohol, tobacco and fuel, and proposed instead a series of target rates at which member states should aim.

For a more thorough analysis of the White Paper, consult two excellent works – the *1992 Handbook*, by Mark Brealey and Conor Quigley, published by Graham & Trotman in the UK, and *Countdown 1992*, published four times a year by the EC Committee of the American Chamber of Commerce in Brussels.

APPENDIX II

*The Commissioners and their Portfolios**

Jacques Delors *France*
President
Secretariat General
Monetary Affairs
Spokesman's Service
Forward Studies Unit
Joint Interpreting and
    Conference Service
Security Office

Karel Van Miert *Belgium*
Transport
Credit and Investment
Consumer Protection

**Henning
Christophersen** *Denmark*
Economic and Financial
    Affairs
Coordination of Structural
    Instruments
Statistical Office

Martin Bangemann *Germany*
Internal Market and
    Industrial Affairs
Relations with European
    Parliament

Peter Schmidhuber *Germany*
Budget
Financial Control

Vasso Papandreou *Greece*
Employment, Industrial
    Relations and Social Affairs
Human Resources, Education
    and Training

Manuel Marin *Spain*
Fisheries
Cooperation and Development

Abel Matutes *Spain*
Mediterranean Policy
Relations with Latin America
    and Asia
North-South Relations

Christiane Scrivener *France*
Taxation and Customs Union
Questions related to Fiscal
    and Social Levies

Ray MacSharry *Ireland*
Agriculture
Rural Development

Filippo Maria Pandolfi   *Italy*
Telecommunications,
   Information and Innovation
   Industries
Science, Research and
   Development
Joint Research Centre

Carlo Ripa di Meana   *Italy*
Environment and Nuclear
   Safety
Civil Protection

Jean Dondelinger   *Luxembourg*
Audio-visual and Cultural
   Affairs
Information and Communication
   Policy
Citizens' Europe
Office for Official Publications

Frans Andriessen   *Netherlands*
External Relations and Trade
   Policy
Cooperation with other
   European Countries

**Antonio Cardoso E
Cunha**   *Portugal*
Staff, Administration and
   Translation
Energy and EURATOM
   Supply Agency
Policy on Small and Medium
   Sized Firms
Crafts, Commerce, Tourism,
   Social Economy

Sir Leon Brittan *United Kingdom*
Competition Policy
Financial Institutions

Bruce Millan   *United Kingdom*
Regional Policy

* Allocated on December 16th
1988, and, barring unforeseen
circumstances, held until the end
of 1992.

INDEX